17.50

D0015555

DE

TALES OF A
NEW AMERICA

TALES OF A NEW AMERICA

ROBERT B. REICH

𝕿imes
BOOKS

Library of Congress Cataloging-in-Publication Data
Reich, Robert B.
Tales of a new America.
Bibliography: p.
Includes index.
1. United States—Politics and government—1981–
2. United States—Economic policy—1981–
3. United States—Foreign relations—1981–
4. Public welfare—United States.
I. Title.
JK271.R39   1987   973.927   86-23139
ISBN 0-8129-1624-7

Designed by Ann Gold

Manufactured in the United States of America

9 8 7 6 5 4 3 2

First Edition

FOR ADAM

CONTENTS

INTRODUCTION

I write this at a time when many Americans are confused about what America stands for. Many of the courageous souls who still call themselves "liberals" find that they are without bearings. The ideals that had guided them since the 1930s and through the postwar decades seem less clear, and the premises of public debate in recent years, strangely disorienting. Many who call themselves "conservatives," although more confident in their assertions than at any time since the start of the New Deal, are bedeviled by the possibility that their self-assurance may be vicarious—attributable to the ebullience of the man now occupying the White House rather than to the discovery of any fundamental moral truths. On the horizon is a presidential election that may determine which set of concerns endures longer.

You may ask: Is it really necessary to probe the public consciousness and examine the reigning public philosophy? Are not most of us guided by a gritty pragmatism that eschews any overarching approach to our society's problems?

Between the transient moods elicited by political advertising or lofty rhetoric and the detailed policy prescriptions manufactured by the inhabitants of Washington think tanks and universities spreads the conceptual terrain in which public problems are defined and public ideals are forged. This is a realm of parable and metaphor, the source of our collective vision. To dismiss this realm as "ideological"—meaningless because irrational and unempirical—is to miss the point that value, not fact, is the currency of the realm. It is to neglect the importance of values for motivating a society. It is to preempt or cheapen all discussion about whether we are motivated in the right direction.

The current confusion reflects turmoil and change in this realm. Our collective vision is slowly shifting in response to a radically different world. Hence the importance of examining what the prevailing vision has been, and what it might be.

Since this is a realm of values and purposes, a journey into it must follow a route marked by interpretations and illustrations rather than formal proofs. In this book I have drawn from several disciplines, selected from a wide range of examples, and connected ideas and phenomena not normally juxtaposed. But I am relying on you, the reader, to be an active explorer as well. You will need to ask yourself: How do these illustrations resonate with my experience? Are these interpretations plausible and meaningful to me? Do they help me better understand my own values, or lead me to question them?

In undertaking this journey, I have relied on the help and insights of many people. The enterprise has come as close to collective entrepreneurialism (a term with which the reader will become acquainted) as is possible without relinquishing single authorship. Only in an academic environment as marvelously disrespectful of traditional academic boundaries, and as supportive of interesting but risky intellectual ventures, as the Kennedy School at Harvard, would I have found a group of people willing to take on the topic and encourage me forward. I am particularly grateful to Michael Barzelay, whose interest in the relation between ideas, politics, and economics continues to kindle my own; to Ronald Heifetz, whose insights into group psychology and cultural avoidance have influenced my thinking about political mythology; and to Bill Hogan, whose hard-nosed approach to public policy has forced me to connect these larger concepts to practical policy questions. I have benefited from Steven Kelman's understanding of American political institutions, and Mark Moore's continuing interest in the capacity of myths and visions to mobilize public action. Howard Frant and Rob Muller, graduate students here, donated their time and perspectives. I am especially indebted, as before, to Jack Donahue, whose tenacity forced me to rethink and rewrite, and whose insights added immeasurably to whatever strength the book now possesses. Several colleagues and students at the Harvard Law School, where I have been teaching about the relationships between law, politics, and industrial structure, have also aided in the venture. I am particularly grateful to Phil Heymann for sharing with me his insights into law and political ideology and for his continuing interest in probing these dark corners.

In addition, I am grateful to a number of people who took an early interest in this project, and offered valuable advice and counsel along the way. Larry Smith and Hendrik Hertzberg got me started; Jack Beatty and Bill Whitworth encouraged me to write an essay for *The Atlantic* that foreshadowed several of the themes in this book; Paul Erickson, Mark Koerner, Robert Bell, and David Kastan provided background on American myth, literature, and politics. The manuscript benefited from readings by Robert Ball, Sidney Blumenthal, Samuel Beer, Nancy Bekavac, Lincoln Caplin, George Gilder, Ray Dalton, Jim Dillon, Doug Dworkin, David Ellwood, John Isaacson, Robert Kuttner, Marc Lackritz, Nancy Altman Lupu, Herman Leonard, George Lodge, Shelley Metzenbaum, Richard Neustadt, Michael O'Hare, Rafe Sagalyn, Paul Starr, Phil Steele, Richard Stewart, and Jim Verdier. Jon Segal, as before, brought to bear his unique blend of enthusiasm and moral support. Above all, I owe thanks to my intellectual partner, friend, and wife, Clare Dalton, whose insights into critical theory and feminism have enriched my perspectives on economics and politics, and whose grace under fire has been an inspiration.

—ROBERT B. REICH
Cambridge, Massachusetts
October 1986

PROLOGUE

THE AMERICAN STORY

CHAPTER 1

FOUR MORALITY TALES

1

You've heard the story a hundred times, with different names, different details. George was a good man, the son of immigrants who had made their way to Marysville. They came with no money, with nothing but grim determination and hard-won freedom. Dad worked all his life in the mill; he was union, hard, and proud. George was quick by nature, dogged by necessity. He studied hard at school, and after school worked long and well at anything that would bring in a few dollars. George was good at sports, but he had little time for games. He had few close friends, and yet he was fair and decent with everyone, and quietly kind to anybody in real trouble. He never picked a fight in his life. But in eighth grade, when the town bully Albert Wade was slapping around the smallest kid in the class, George stepped between them without saying a word. He let Wade throw the first punch, then put him away with one straight left, turned around, and walked away.

George finished high school in 1943, and joined the army the day he graduated. Four months later he was in Europe. On the sixth day of the Normandy invasion his squad was on patrol, passing through a French orchard when a German machine-gun nest opened up from behind a stone wall, picking off the squad one by one. George broke from cover and, dodging from tree to tree, raced toward the Nazis as bullets chewed the bark and ground around him. He took out the nest with a grenade and his rifle, and he saved his buddies, but he never wore the medals they gave him and he never talked about it much. After the war he came back to Marysville and married Kate, his childhood sweetheart. He raised three kids, and he started a little construction business, which his hard work and integrity gradually made into a big construction business. By and by, George made a lot of money. But his family continued to live modestly, and he gave generously to the local boys' club and an orphanage he founded. He was generous with his time, too, and headed the community chest. Still he kept pretty much to himself until Albert Wade inherited his father's bank, the only bank in town. Wade risked his depositors' money on shaky loans to his cronies, bought and bullied his way into power with Marysville's political leaders. When he was elected mayor the election smelled bad to everyone, but only George openly accused Wade of corruption. For six months Wade's bank refused every mortgage on houses built by George's company, and George risked everything in the showdown. But in that tense town meeting, one of the city councilmen Wade had paid off could no longer hide his shame under George's steady gaze and simple question from the back of the room. He spilled how Wade had rigged the election. Albert Wade went from city hall to county jail, and George went back to his family, his work, and his quiet service to Marysville.

George's story is an American morality tale. It is a national parable, retold time and again in many different versions, about how we should live our lives in this country. George is the American Everyman. He's Gary Cooper in *High Noon*. He's Jimmy Stewart in *It's a Wonderful Life*. He's the American private eye, the frontier hero, the kid who makes good. He's George Washington and Abe Lincoln. He appears in countless political speeches, in newspaper stories, on the evening news, in American ballads, and sermons.

Everyone has a favorite variation, but the basic theme is the same and speaks to the essence of our national self-image: Ours is a nation of humble, immigrant origins, built out of nothing

4

and into greatness through hard work; generous to those in need, those who cannot make it on their own; a loner among nations, suspicious of foreign entanglements, but willing to stand up against tyranny; and forever vigilant against corruption and special privilege.

The American morality tale defines our understanding of who we are, and of what we want for ourselves and one another. It is the tacit subtext of our daily conversations about American life. It permeates *both* American conservatism and American liberalism. And—the essential point—it is a fundamentally noble, essentially life-affirming story. Much is made of the American political distinctiveness of a Constitution inspired by theory rather than by tradition. But there is a subtler yet equally profound *cultural* distinctiveness as well, a national sense of identity rooted not in history but in self-told mythology. Political scientist Carl Friedrich captured the distinction in 1935: "To be an American is an ideal, while to be a Frenchman is a fact."[1]

This basic mythology, however integral to the American identity, is so vague as to admit of many interpretations, to present itself in multiple manifestations over time. At different times in our history, different aspects of the parable have come to the fore while others receded. Some variants of the myth are more faithful to its essence than others; some variants are more supple accommodations to current American reality than others. Our history is punctuated with wrenching national contests between competing versions of the ideal; both world wars, for example, forced us to decide whether we must love peace more or justice more. Indeed, these episodes of editing our common mythology, as painful as they may be, are themselves affirmations of the American distinctiveness. This book is premised on the observation that another such episode seems to be at hand.

2

The most important aspect of political discourse is not the appraisal of alternative solutions to our problems, but the definition of the problems themselves. This simple truth is easy to miss because what we *see* when we look at politics is a series of particular problems and possible remedies: How to contain Soviet aggression? Improve American competitiveness? Eliminate poverty and hunger? Manage the size and curb the intrusiveness of government? Editorial pages overflow with worries and suggestions. Political candidates brandish new ideas. Economists diligently tally the costs and benefits of the various proposals. Congressional committees hold hearings. Television documentaries present experts pontificating from behind desks. Disagreeing specialists abuse each other for the edification and entertainment of the populace at large. Public opinion, as measured in the latest poll, swings to and fro. This is what we take for public discourse.

But in the background—disguised, unarticulated—are the myth-based morality tales that determine when we declare a fact to be a problem, how policy choices are characterized, how the debate is framed. These are the unchallenged subtexts of political discourse. We debate specifics, and on almost every issue we instinctively define a spectrum ranging from "left" to "right" and align ourselves along it. But our varying readings of the American morality tale condition how this spectrum is drawn. And the basic contours of our mythology organize the way we think about issues; they bound the field of argument.[2]

Public problems don't exist "out there." They are not discrete facts or pieces of data awaiting discovery. They are consequences of our shared values. Without a set of common moral assumptions we would have no way of identifying or categorizing problems and their possible solutions. Some questions are rarely asked. What is at the root of our quarrel with the Soviets? Does it make sense to speak of American economic competitiveness? Is a citizen's poverty his own misfortune, his own due, or a social problem? What precisely do we mean by government intervention, or the market? These questions do not enter public discourse because so much of the ground from which they spring is taken for granted. To ask them directly is often to end a conversation, because there is nothing left to say; on such basic questions we have collectively, albeit tacitly, reached either essential agreement or stalemate. And yet it is that which we leave unsaid in our debates, not the words that fill the air and the pages, that says the most about us.

As good American pragmatists, wary of grand themes, we prefer the ellipses of metaphor. To the extent that we reflect upon these deeper premises at all, we do so through the stories we tell one another about our lives together—stories like that of George. These tales embody our public philosophy. They constitute a set of orienting ideas less rigid and encompassing than an ideology but also less ephemeral than the "public mood." The stories interpret and explain reality and teach what is expected of us in light of that reality.[3] They situate us, allowing us to understand where we are in an otherwise incomprehensible sea of facts and events. In so doing, these stories give meaning and coherence to what would otherwise seem random phenomena: a new Russian missile, a shuttered factory, a starving child. Our morality tales inform our sense of what our society is about, what it is *for*.

Every culture has its own parables.[4] Conveying lessons about the how and why of life through metaphor may be a basic human trait, a universal characteristic of our intermittently rational, deeply emotional, meaning-seeking species. Cultural parables come in a multitude of forms. In modern America, the vehicles of public myth include the biographies of famous citizens, popular fiction and music, movies, feature stories on the evening news, and gossip. They may also take more explicitly hortatory forms in judicial opinions, political speeches, and sermons. In whatever form, they are transmitted constantly, and all around us—in our schoolrooms, dining rooms, poolrooms, and newsrooms. They shape our collective judgments. They anchor our political understandings. The specific details of the stories we tell need not have any particular connection to fact, an insight that some political orators grasp instinctively. What gives them force is their capacity to make sense of, and bring coherence to, common experience. The lessons ring true, even if the illustration is fanciful.

There is a danger in this, of course. It is not that the public can be readily led into believing lies or embracing destructive values. Cultural parables are deeply rooted and resistant to manipulation by controlling elites. Myths cannot be made to order. Propaganda—the attempt to dictate mythology—is a pitiful device; there is evidence that the critical sensibilities of those who must endure it grow exquisitely acute. (Soviet citizens are accustomed to making inferences from the most subtle of clues.)[5] The danger is more insidious. A mythology is a culture's device for interpreting its reality and acting on it. But what if the reality changes and the mythology does not?

Even when a culture's parables lose their vitality—their compelling connection with the broader reality in which the culture finds itself—they may continue to inform and entrance. This can go on for a time. The culture can continue to act as though its myths were sound guides to behavior. If the culture is powerful enough relative to other powers in its environment, if its members' ambitions lean more to conservation than to greater development, the penalties for following outmoded myths may at first be small. We can continue, without great cost, to embrace the conviction that the world is flat only until we develop the competence to sail to the edge. It is at that point—when we restrain our potential out of fear of falling off, or greet any stranger as a devil from beyond the edge—that the stories we tell ourselves can metamorphose from myth to damaging delusion.

3

George's story embodies four basic American morality tales, our core cultural parables. They are rooted in the central experiences of American history: the flight from older cultures, the rejection of central authority and aristocratic privilege, the lure of the unspoiled frontier, the struggle for harmony and justice.

1. THE MOB AT THE GATES. The first mythic story is about tyranny and barbarism that lurk "out there." It depicts America as a beacon light of virtue in a world of darkness, a small island of freedom and democracy in a perilous sea. We are uniquely blessed, the proper model for other peoples' aspirations, the hope of the world's poor and oppressed. The parable gives voice to a corre-

sponding fear: we must beware, lest the forces of darkness overwhelm us. Our liberties are fragile; our openness renders us vulnerable to exploitation or infection from beyond.

Hence our endless efforts to isolate ourselves from the rest of the globe, to contain evil forces beyond our borders, and to convey our lessons with missionary zeal to benighted outsiders. George fought the "good war" against the Nazis; Daniel Boone, a somewhat less savory campaign against Indians; Davy Crockett, Mexicans. The American amalgam of fear and aggressiveness toward "them out there" appears in countless fantasies of space explorers who triumph over alien creatures from beyond. It is found in Whig histories of the United States, and in the anti-immigration harangues of the late nineteenth and early twentieth centuries. We heeded George Washington's warning to maintain our independence from the monarchical powers of Europe, and then proceeded for more than a century to conquer, purchase, or otherwise control vast territories to our west and south.

In this century Woodrow Wilson grimly rallied Americans to "defeat once and for all . . . the sinister forces" that rendered peace impossible;[6] Franklin Roosevelt warned of "rotten apple" nations that spread their rot to others; Dean Acheson adopted the same metaphor to describe the Communist threat to Greece and Turkey immediately after Hitler's war; to Eisenhower, South Vietnam was the first in a series of dominoes that might fall to communism; to John F. Kennedy it was "the finger in the dike," holding back the Soviet surge. The underlying lesson: We must maintain vigilance, lest dark forces overrun us.

2. THE TRIUMPHANT INDIVIDUAL. This is the story of the little guy who works hard, takes risks, believes in himself, and eventually earns wealth, fame, and honor. It's the parable of the self-made man (or, more recently, woman) who bucks the odds, spurns the naysayers, and shows what can be done with enough drive and guts. He's a loner and a maverick, true to himself, plain speaking, self-reliant, uncompromising in his ideals. He gets the job done.

Determination and integrity earned George his triumph. Benjamin Franklin employed a carefully conceived system of self-control (Franklin's *Autobiography* is but the first of a long line of American manuals on how to become rich through self-denial and diligence). The theme recurs in the tale of Abe Lincoln, log splitter from Illinois who goes to the White House; in the hundred or so novellas of Horatio Alger, whose heroes all rise promptly and predictably from rags to riches (not only through pluck; luck plays a part too); and in the manifold stories of American detectives and cowboys—mavericks all—who reluctantly get involved in a dangerous quest and end up with the girl, the money, and the glory.[7] It appears in the American morality tales of the underdog who eventually makes it, showing up the bosses and bullies who tried to put him down; think of *Rocky* or *Iacocca*. Regardless of the precise form, the moral is the same: With enough guts and gumption, anyone can make it on their own in America.

3. THE BENEVOLENT COMMUNITY. The third parable is about the American community. It is the story of neighbors and friends rolling up their sleeves and pitching in to help one another, of self-sacrifice, community pride, and patriotism. It is about Americans' essential generosity and compassion toward those in need.

The story is rooted in America's religious traditions, and its earliest formulations are found in sermons like John Winthrop's "A Model of Christian Charity," delivered on board ship in Salem Harbor just before the Puritans landed in 1630. He described the enterprise on which they were embarking in the terms of Matthew's version of the Sermon on the Mount: The new settlers would be "as a City on a Hill" whose members would "delight in each other" and be "of the same body." America began as a nation of religious communities, centered in the church and pledged to piety and charity—Shakers, Amish, Mennonite, New England Congregationalist. Biblical language and symbols continued to propel American social movements committed to enlarging membership in the benevolent community—the drive for emancipation of the slaves, women's suffrage, civil rights. "I have a dream that every valley shall be exalted, every hill and mountain shall be made low," said Martin Luther King.

The story extends beyond religion to embrace social solidarity and civic virtue. It summons images of New England villagers who meet to debate their future; of frontier settlers who help build one another's barns and gather for quilting bees; of neighbors who volunteer as fire fighters and librarians, whose generosity erects the local hospital and propels high school achievers to college; of small towns that send their boys off to fight wars for the good of all. The story celebrates America's tradition of civic improvement, philanthropy, and local boosterism.

It also tells of national effort on behalf of those in need. The theme permeated Roosevelt's New Deal, Truman's Fair Deal, Johnson's Great Society: America is a single, national community, bound by a common ideal of equal opportunity, and generosity toward the less fortunate. E Pluribus Unum.

Our popular culture has echoed these sentiments. Three hundred years after John Winthrop's sermon they could be found in Robert Sherwood's plays, the novels of John Steinbeck and William Saroyan, Aaron Copland's music and Frank Capra's films. The last scene in *It's a Wonderful Life* conveys the lesson: Jimmy Stewart learns that he can count on his neighbors' generosity and goodness, just as they had always counted on him. They are bound together in common cause. The principle: We must nurture and preserve genuine community.

4. THE ROT AT THE TOP. The fourth parable is about the malevolence of powerful elites, be they wealthy aristocrats, rapacious business leaders, or imperious government officials. The American parable differs subtly but profoundly from a superficially similar European mythology: The struggle is only occasionally and incidentally a matter of money or class. There are no workers pitted against capitalists at the heart of this American story. It is, rather, a tale of corruption, decadence, and irresponsibility among the powerful, of conspiracy against the broader public.

This morality tale has repeatedly provoked innovation and reform. Experience with the arbitrary authority of the English Crown produced in the Founding Fathers an acute sensitivity to the possibilities of abuse of power. The result was a government premised on the Enlightenment idea that power must be constrained and limited through checks and balances, and be kept firmly tied to the consent of the governed. A century later America responded to mounting concentrations of private economic power through antitrust laws, designed to diffuse such power, and later by government support for other groups—labor unions, farmers, and retailers—capable of exercising countervailing power.[8] The nation dealt with concentrations of governmental power through civil service rules that limited favoritism, and through electoral reforms and limitations on campaign contributions, to render politicians more accountable to the public. Government power also was held in check by periodic efforts to extend power to the states and cities, to open government decision making to greater public observation and scrutiny, to reduce the power of senior legislators, and to limit the ability of the president to take action without congressional approval. Since the beginning, in sum, Americans have been suspicious of elites and anxious to circumscribe their power.

At their worst, suspicions about the Rot at the Top have expressed themselves in conspiracy theories. America has harbored a long and infamous line of rabble-rousers, from the pre–Civil War Know-Nothings and Anti-Masonic movements, through the populist agitators of the late nineteenth century, the Ku Klux Klan, Senator Joseph McCarthy, and Lyndon LaRouche. They have fomented against bankers, Catholics, big corporations, blacks, Jews, foreigners, either or both major political parties, and other unnamed "interests." In this version of the story, the Rot at the Top is in a great conspiracy with the Mob at the Gates to keep down the common man and allow evil forces to overrun us.[9]

Our popular culture revels in tales of corruption in high places. At the turn of the century, muckrakers like Upton Sinclair and Ida Tarbell uncovered sordid tales of corporate malfeasance; their modern heirs (revealing CIA depredations, White House scandals, and corporate transgressions) are called investigative reporters. The theme recurs in real or invented stories of honest undercover agents—Sam Spade, Serpico, Jack Nicholson in *Chinatown*—who trace the rot back to the most powerful members of the community. It's embodied by the great bullies of American fiction: Judge Thatcher of *Huckleberry Finn*, Broderick Crawford as the Huey Long-like character in *All the King's Men*, Lionel Barrymore's demonic Mr. Potter in *It's a Wonderful Life*. And in the tales of humble folk, like the Joad family of *The Grapes of Wrath*, who struggle valiantly against avaricious bankers and landowners. The moral is clear: Power corrupts, privilege perverts.

4

These are stories of aspiration. They summon us to duty and destiny. Importantly, the American ideal can never really be fulfilled. The goals it mandates are at once too vast and too vague for objective achievement. To pursue them is its own accomplishment. The striving gives meaning to our collective life; the aspiration bestows on us a national identity. In this respect, America may be unique; probably no other culture so clearly defines itself by its morality tales. As a nation of immigrants without a deep common history, we are bound together by a common hope.

Sometimes the four tales take the form of self-congratulation: Celebrate our triumph over savages and evil abroad! Rejoice in the opportunity open to each of us to gain fame and fortune! Admire our generosity and compassion! See how we have overcome vested privilege! But the same stories can be cast as rebukes, exposing the great gulf separating what we are from what we want to become, or how far we have fallen from an ideal we once achieved. The world is succumbing to tyranny, barbarism, and devastation, while we stand idly by! Hard work and merit are sabotaged by convention, chicanery, and prejudice! We are selfish, narcissistic, racist, indifferent—look at the poor and hungry in our midst! Our democracy is a sham, and everything important is controlled by a venal cabal at the top!

Pride in what we have accomplished, shame in what we have not—these are the ways we recount the four mythic tales and incorporate them into our daily lives. We hear them on the evening news and read them in the press. We reiterate them over lunch when gossip turns to affairs of the day ("Did you hear about—?" "It just shows you—"). Our jokes, tellingly, often refer to these fables and our failures to manifest their mandates. No other culture so celebrates its Mark Twains and Will Rogers, its satirists and debunkers.[10]

The pride or shame that come from seeking to live out these four parables also shape our politics. The great reform movements of American history—the Jacksonian war on the Bank of the United States in the 1830s, the abolitionist crusades of the mid-nineteenth century, the Populist-Progressive agitation of the 1880s and 1890s, the New Deal of the 1930s, the War on Poverty and Vietnam protests of the 1960s, even the Reagan "Revolution"—can all be viewed as periods in which the gap between aspiration and perceived reality grew too painfully wide for many to endure. The dissonance was too loud; the hypocrisy too transparent. If we were to continue to tell one another the same stories, it was necessary to take dramatic action.[11]

Political rhetoric in America is essentially prophetic rather than pragmatic. Challengers tell tales of shame and betrayal, incumbents speak with pride and promise. Both refer not to the mundane present but to a nation "to be," which has yet to fulfill its national destiny. The tone is often messianic, evangelical. The four parables appear as stories of salvation and redemption: America is to be a promised land of "New Frontiers" and "Great Societies." It will triumph over evil. It will light the world. We will all be blessed with freedom and wealth, make manifest our compassion, and celebrate the triumph of the common man. Such, as we all know perfectly well, is our destiny.

5

The four basic parables have endured throughout American history. But in each era they have been combined and conveyed in slightly different ways, emphasizing a distinct message. Variants develop, come to dominate, and eventually evolve. The evolution can be endorsed and possibly accelerated, but never dictated, by political leaders. The art of political rhetoric has been to reconfigure these stories in a manner that affirms and amplifies the changes already occurring in the way Americans tell these tales to one another. The best political tales, like any parables, are those which most elegantly and simply interpret what's happening to the average person, which render coherent the citizens' experiences of fear and shame, pride and hope.

In the early part of this century, for example, Progressive leaders merged the parables of Rot at the Top and the Triumphant Individual. The lesson was that Big Business—the trusts—blocked worthy citizens from their rightful places in society. Corruption in high places was thwarting personal initiative, stifling upward mobility for the little man. Woodrow Wilson put the matter bluntly in a speech during the 1912 presidential campaign, promising to wage "a crusade against the powers that have governed us . . . that have limited our development . . . that have determined our lives . . . that have set us in a straightjacket to do as they please." In his view, the struggle against the trusts would be nothing less than "a second struggle for emancipation."[12] (For Wilson, the Mob at the Gates—the large, bellicose, prewar European states—represented a similar challenge to democratic freedoms, and required a not unrelated dispersion of power.)

By the 1930s, the parables had shifted. Now the key thematic link was between Rot at the Top and the Benevolent Community. Now the lesson was that the mutual prosperity of common people was under attack by leaders of big business and finance. In the 1936 presidential campaign, Franklin D. Roosevelt warned against the "economic royalists" who had impressed the whole of society into "royal service." "The hours men and women worked, the wages they received, the conditions of their labor . . . these had passed beyond the control of the people, and were imposed by this new industrial dictatorship," he warned in one speech. "The royalists of the economic order have conceded that political freedom was the business of the government, but they have maintained that economic slavery was nobody's business." What was at stake, he concluded, was the "survival of democracy."[13]

The shift from the Progressives' emphasis on the Triumphant

Individual to the New Deal's Benevolent Community was more than an oratorical device. It represented a change in Americans' understanding of social life. The Great Depression had provided a national lesson in social solidarity; nearly every American family felt the effects of poverty and insecurity. The Benevolent Community became intimately relevant as relatives and neighbors sought to help one another, as government became the insurer of last resort, and then as Americans turned together to winning Hitler's war. Roosevelt explicitly described the purpose of the New Deal as "extending to our national life the old principle of the local community." "We are determined," he said, "to make every American citizen the subject of his country's interest and concern."[14]

In the 1980s, Ronald Reagan drew on the same parables, but they were substantially reconfigured. Repudiating Roosevelt's national community, Reagan redefined the Benevolent Community as small, traditional neighborhoods in which people voluntarily helped one another, free from government interference. The Rot at the Top referred to Washington insiders, arrogant government bureaucrats, and liberal intellectuals who wanted to grab power and stifle creativity. The Triumphant Individual was the business entrepreneur who started work in an attic or garage and ended up spawning an entire industry. And the Mob at the Gates comprised a wide assortment—illegal immigrants, drug traffickers, Third World debtors and revolutionaries, terrorists, greedy trading partners, and, above all, Communist aggressors—who threatened our way of life. But America would prevail. "America is back and standing tall," Reagan said in 1984. "We've begun to restore the great American values—the dignity of work, the warmth of family, the strength of neighborhood, and the nourishment of human freedom."[15]

6

All four of our morality tales refer to a *collective* identity. They affirm a *common* destiny. Thus a fundamental theme in the American mythology is membership—inclusion and, necessarily, exclusion. In American political life, as in our sporting events and lawsuits, the pronouns "us" and "them" contain the essential information. They signal the boundaries beyond which loyalties and commitments do not extend. We trust that others like "us" will fulfill mutual obligations that yield joint benefits. But for "them" we have only pity or disdain.

In the story of the Mob at the Gates, "they" are dangerous outsiders. Their specific identity, and the quality of their menace, has varied throughout our history. "They" have been, at one time or another, American Indians, French, English, Mexicans, Southerners, European immigrants, Germans, Japanese, Chinese, and Russians, to name a few. That members of these groups have on occasion done us injury is true but not essential; that the pigment of their skin is different from that of most Americans is often, but not necessarily, the case. What unites them is that, at some point, "we" have defined ourselves as definitively not like them, and our thorough repudiation of what they represent has buttressed our sense of what we stand for.

Similarly, as Triumphant Individuals we are characterized partly by contrast with who we are not. In this story, "they" are featherbedders, menial workers, and time servers. They are the men in gray flannel suits who dither and grovel in the offices of large organizations, workers who mindlessly follow routine, petty bureaucrats, and all the other slackers who fail to pull their own weight. That even entrepreneurial garages go dark unless the bureaucrats at the local utility keep the electricity coming may seem to suggest a more complicated story of how we get things accomplished in America, but the stirring distinction between the change master and the time server endures.

A comparable dividing line runs through our conception of the Benevolent Community. On one side of the line the governing principle is solidarity; on the other side it is altruism, even paternalism. "We" are solid citizens who ask no more than our due, who offer or accept help only in cases of unanticipated and uncontrollable calamity. "They" are *the poor*, dependent by nature and perhaps by choice. We assume, mistakenly, that they are mostly black or brown. Our sense of mercy requires that we

17

limit their suffering; our sense of justice requires that we accompany our charity with proper discipline.

Finally, in the tale of Rot at the Top, "they" are business tycoons, wealthy aristocrats, Washington insiders, or any others who seem to exercise unaccountable power or enjoy unearned privilege. "We" are the common people, too often robbed of true authority, unfairly dispossessed of our proper rewards, innocent victims of the venality and incompetence of self-serving elites.

Dividing the world into "us" and "them," of course, is a universal and perhaps inevitable human trait. But when the dividing line is accepted without question by all sides of the political debate, it renders our convictions about credit and blame, about the sources and solutions to our problems, sturdily resistant to evidence. This is dangerous when it undercuts the possibility of mutual responsibility and reciprocal gain. As we attribute to "them"—dangerous outsiders, lazy workers, the poor and the deviant, the scheming elites—the problems that bedevil us, we simultaneously limit our repertoire of responses to two broad categories: First, we can discipline them. By being tough and assertive, we can compel them to repent, lay down the law on acceptable behavior, and punish them when they transgress. Alternatively, we can conciliate them. Through generosity, understanding, and toleration we can socialize them, bring out the best in them, and seduce them into changing their ways, into becoming more like us.

It is in large part this pervasive mythic division between the "us" and the "them" that explains the American propensity to squeeze the most collectively diverse and individually complex public choices into a linear array of options anchored, on the one end, by toughness and on the other, by conciliation. These are our contested principles, in issues ranging from foreign policy to welfare. Our public discourse, thus constrained, is often comfortably straightforward but perilously incomplete.

Our morality tales are increasingly at odds with the new challenges we confront. The prevailing versions have little relevance to the relationships that frame our lives—with other peoples of the earth, within our firms, toward our poor, toward our

leaders. The prevailing versions do not speak of mutual obligation. They neither celebrate joint gain nor forebode reciprocal
loss. Our morality tales, too long unexamined, are losing their
power to inform our present. Once again we must revise and
reaffirm our declaration of identity.

CHAPTER 2

THE PREVAILING VERSIONS

1

The terms "liberal" and "conservative" (along with their more recent "neo" variants) denote two fundamental orientations toward public issues. They anchor American political discourse. Each orientation harbors internal contradictions and inconsistencies; neither comprises a logical structure of opinions founded on first principles. And many who think of themselves as one or the other often find that on certain specific issues their sympathies lie in the other camp. Nevertheless, Americans tend to define their stances across a remarkable range of issues by reference to conservatism or liberalism.[1]

These two orientations are not comparable to the conflicting ideologies that animate politics in other cultures. They are best understood, rather, as different interpretations of the same four morality roles—the Mob at the Gates, the Triumphant Individual, the Benevolent Community, the Rot at the Top. Both are inspired by roughly the same values; both project similar ideals of the perfect society. Both feature a division of the world into "us" and "them." The conservative version sees "them" as unruly and exploitative, yielding only to discipline. The liberal version sees "them" as misguided and needy, deserving of and open to accommodation and charity. In recent years the conservative version has been more compelling to a majority of Americans.[2] It is important to understand why.

Many liberals have refused to credit the currently reigning conservatism with a philosophy at all. They prefer to see it as a thinly veiled scheme to further enrich the wealthy. Some conservatives doubtless embrace their positions out of pure self-interest. But such cynicism is rare. The majority of conservatives, I venture, are attracted by the ideas themselves; the stories make sense.

Other liberals have conceded conservatism's new claim on the public's sentiments but see it as a sign of the temporary reversion toward private interest and away from public activism that periodically overcomes a reform-weary citizenry.[3] This view, however, fails to account for the reformist zeal of the new movement and its aggressive use of public power to transform the American system. The new conservatism is no simple rejection of "big government," for it is content to subordinate a significant part of the economy to the military, and aims at expanding the powers of the police, teachers, and other designated public disciplinarians.

Still other liberals have sought to attribute the change in public attitudes to the congenial personality of Ronald Reagan, rather than to any philosophical shift. History will note that the president was an artful orator and a master of parable. He brilliantly acted the part of America's cowboy hero—the tall and rugged town marshal, who kept the peace with integrity, optimism, and self-deprecating humor.[4] But this explanation overlooks the groundswell of support for conservatism that arose before Reagan arrived in Washington. The new conservatism was a wider phenomenon than Reaganism. The ideological chest-thumping of the Reagan administration, for example, obscured Jimmy Carter's quieter but profound conservatism. Reagan's success lay not in changing the nation's view of how the world works—he had been saying the same things for years, after all, without sparking much of a response—but in giving clear voice to themes the public had finally shown itself ready to embrace.

The new conservativism is attractive because it manages to

make sense out of a great deal of our troubling collective experience since, roughly, the assassination of John F. Kennedy. It refashions resonant new versions of America's core myths. It extracts from these reinterpretations a set of plausible lessons. The first such lesson describes a world "out there" grown more ruthless and sternly warns that as individuals and as a nation we must struggle for survival against the Mob at the Gates. Another speaks of Triumphant Individual entrepreneurs who must be liberated and spoiled workers whose wage demands could ruin our economy. A third talks of dependency and excess in our Benevolent Community and charges us to require responsibility of the objects of our benevolence. The last warns of slackness and corruption in our political system that inflict on us an unaccountable flood of wasteful public spending.

All four lessons convey much the same moral: We are in danger of losing our way. We must impose discipline and responsibility on "them"—malign outsiders, free-riding workers, welfare cheats, bureaucrats and politicians—in order that we may fulfill our grand destiny. The parable presents an intricate blend of dissenting Protestant theology and social Darwinism—of salvation, redemption, and triumphant survival. The overarching lesson is dramatically clear, and it applies to a range of public issues. Its power lies in its simplicity and scope, and its evocation of unarticulated fears and hopes.

2

Consider, first, the new conservative position on foreign policy. For years liberals had sought to appease the Soviets, placate the less-developed nations of the Third World, and coddle our allies. As a result, the story goes, we became an easy mark. The Mob at the Gates took advantage of us. Our defenses were down; the Soviets surged ahead of us in armaments. Emboldened by our passivity, they viciously subjugated Afghanistan, cracked down in Poland, and expanded their influence in southern Africa, Southeast Asia, and Central America. Simultaneously, the United States was being taken for a ride by Third World nations that demanded our aid but persistently sided with our adversaries and voted against us at the United Nations. Other Third World nations have threatened default on loans from our banks. We have been overrun by illegal immigrants who defy our borders, take away our jobs, and live off our social services. Drug traffickers in Asia and Latin America, undeterred by cynical governments, pump poisons into our cities. Iranian thugs humiliated us; terrorists kill and maim at will. Even our allies have refused to cooperate with us in limiting East-West trade.

The problem, thus posed, admits of only one approach. We must impose discipline. We must regain our credibility, and the way to do that is to get tough with this Mob at the Gates. We should dramatically increase our military defenses, get the Soviets (and their Cuban allies) out of Central America and Africa, give aid to Third World nations only when they play on our side, and crack down on international terrorists without undue squeamishness about who gets in the way. We should get tough on illegal immigration and drug smuggling. We should tighten up on East-West trade, so that the Soviets cannot easily take advantage of our technology. We should "play hardball" with our allies on trade and defense. We should threaten to retaliate against Japan if its markets are not fully open to our products. And we should impose austerity on Third World debtors, ensuring that they repay their debts and end their profligate ways.

Liberal indulgence toward the Soviet Union is thought to have threatened our very survival. According to foreign-policy hardliners, we cannot conciliate the Soviets, nor should we try to. The danger of nuclear war will recede only when the Soviet Union transforms itself from a totalitarian state into a freer and more democratic one. Liberal accommodation has only fortified Soviet totalitarianism. By this view, pressures for change are growing within a Soviet Union collapsing from economic and moral decay. We should promote this internal disintegration by "a combination of active resistance to Soviet expansion and political-military blackmail and the denial of economic and other forms of aid."[5] To hasten that process we will have to be tougher than they are.

3

The conservative story covers economic policy as well. For years, the tale goes, America's Triumphant Individuals—its entrepreneurs—have been held back by slack and sloth elsewhere in the economy.

The liberal solution to the tendency of the economy to succumb cyclically to recession and underemployment was for the government to spend freely enough to restore demand. But this approach, inspired by the British economist John Maynard Keynes, ultimately proved its own undoing, according to the conservative story. Government went on spending beyond its means, even during times of buoyant growth. Undue government solicitousness also bred expectations that Washington would always step in to snap the economy out of slumps and slowdowns. The result was a breakdown of social discipline. Conservative economists condemned the laxity: "The standard brand of liberalism . . . was still undisciplined, still devoid of guidelines or limits."[6] The government went on a spending binge through the late 1960s and the 1970s, while workers went on a corresponding wage binge. Succeeding presidents tried to keep the rate of unemployment too low, relative to what the economy could manage without fueling inflation. By the late 1970s prices were out of control. Such irresponsibility undermined the integrity of the entire economic system.

The lesson of this story, too, is clear. We must restore discipline to the economy. We had to "break the back" of inflation in the early 1980s through tactical unemployment, to remind workers of their vulnerability to joblessness should wage demands get too high, and we must stand ever ready to do so again. Future economic policy must "take the control of inflation as its first priority" and relegate unemployment to a lower concern.[7] To control inflation is to impose discipline on the system, particularly on the inflationary wage demands of workers.

Another strand of this conservative parable emphasizes the imperative to discipline the insatiable public sector. If we fail to constrain the federal budget, by constitutional amendment if necessary, productive entrepreneurs will be starved of resources. Businessmen are motivated by money; paring their financial rewards through taxation saps their will. Conservative thinking holds: "The key to growth is quite simple: creative men with money. The cause of stagnation is similarly clear: depriving creative individuals of financial power."[8] Public spending, of course, simply reflects the set of common endeavors that cannot be coordinated by the market. In the conservative view, however, this set is small, and claims for government action are presumptively illegitimate. While conservatives frequently oppose public spending in the abstract with more vigor than program by program, the mythic theme is clear: We must discipline "them," those illegitimate claimants on resources, so our nation's inventors and investors can be freed to create new wealth.

4

The modern conservative's position on social welfare and other underpinnings of the Benevolent Community is consistent with the rest. First, according to this tale, the welfare system is riddled with waste and fraud. Second, when welfare *has* gone to those it was intended for, its effects have often been perverse. It has encouraged poor teenage girls to have babies and deterred them from marriage and work, trapping children in a lifelong culture of dependency and irresponsibility. At the same time, criminal suspects have come to enjoy so many rights that our police are incapable of keeping order, so drugs and crime infest our cities. We have forbidden teachers to control their classrooms and have been more concerned about equality and self-expression than about competence in basic skills, with the result that our schools are failing to educate—a failure particularly damaging to the poor in inner cities. The three forms of laxness have reinforced one another: The easiest path for inner-city youths has been to drop out of school, and then for the girls to have babies and live off welfare, and for the boys to live off girlfriends on welfare and the proceeds of crime.

This overall tale is backed by a plethora of studies purporting

to show the inefficacy or the downright malignancy of welfare—
and of the related permissive approach to education, law enforcement, and child rearing. One conservative sociologist examined
the data on poverty and welfare, particularly those covering the
period since the Great Society, and discovered that despite the
striking growth in welfare spending during this interval the plight
of poor blacks did not improve. His conclusion: We failed to deal
with poverty because we created all the wrong incentives—to get
into poverty rather than to get out. We undercut discipline and
responsibility.[9] Some educators have come to much the same
conclusion about American education. "Permissive progressiv-
ism," with its emphasis on self-expression rather than self-control, perverted our schools.[10] The same story echoes in the work
of criminologists, who attribute the dramatic increase in crime
between 1960 and 1980 to a permissive approach to child rearing
that stressed self-expression instead of self-control.[11]

The only solution, in the minds of many of these conservative
thinkers, is to reverse course. Although not every one of them
would agree with all aspects of the prescription, the general lesson
is the same: We should eliminate welfare except to victims of
sudden and unexpected hardships. We should allow our teachers
to punish and expel. We should empower our police officers and
judges to mete out swift and certain punishment. And we should
teach our children self-control. In short, we should restore social
discipline.

5

The conservative tale about the Rot at the Top is too well known
to require detailed elaboration. Ronald Reagan himself became
the most vocal exponent of the tale. "Government is not the
solution to our problems," he proclaimed on more than one occasion. "Government is the problem." The story tells of excessive
red tape, intermeddling bureaucrats and policy professionals, and
ballooning government expenditures—unrestrained, out of control. And the moral of this tale is essentially the same as the
others: We must exert discipline over the taxers and spenders,

the bureaucrats and meddlers, who otherwise would go on consuming ever more of our resources and compromising our precious freedoms.

What is so compelling about all these arguments—drawn from foreign policy, economics, sociology, and politics—is that they are mutually reinforcing. They tell one interwoven story. No conservative thinker, and certainly no politician, subscribes to the full complement of these views. (Ronald Reagan gave voice to many of these themes without putting them into effect. His budgets were not marked by excessive discipline.) But the details of these arguments are less important than the central set of parables that informs them. Liberal permissiveness has rendered us vulnerable to exploitation. Without discipline, there has been no accountability. Without accountability, decadence has crept in, irresponsibility has become endemic, the system has lost its moral fiber, and we have let ourselves become victims.

This coherence gives the story enormous appeal. It rings true with elements of almost anyone's personal experience. It offers a comprehensible and comprehensive explanation for what has happened to postwar America. Bundling such disparate issues together into a single tale of decadence, slackness, and assertiveness gives comfort. The comprehensive explanation suggests a way of coming to terms with the source of the decay and eventually reversing it. It is only a matter of recognizing the prevailing pattern and applying the moral. In its simplicity, consistency, and plausibility, the new conservative public philosophy provides a near-perfect mythology.

There is a final feature that helps to explain the emotional appeal of modern conservatism, and to distinguish it starkly from its philosophical forbears. Traditional conservatism was dour. It spoke of austerity and self-discipline. It emanated the gray gloom of Herbert Hoover and William Howard Taft. It dwelled on the shameful side of the morality tales. As such, people regarded traditional conservatism the way they regard a bitter medicine or a strict diet—good for you, perhaps, especially after you have gone on a binge, but fundamentally unpleasant nonetheless.

This new brand is markedly different. It preaches austerity

and discipline, to be sure, but with the crucial revision that the discipline is not for "us" but for "them." The conservatism of the late 1970s and 1980s was astonishingly successful at convincing many Americans that vast changes in national priorities could be achieved to the benefit of nearly all and the detriment of only a small number of demonstrably undeserving claimants. For the rest of us, the message was cheerfully optimistic—the proud side of the morality tales. We could achieve whatever we want to achieve, be whatever we want to be, or in the vernacular of the day, "go for it." There were no limits on our strivings, no constraints on our impulses.

The two parts of the message are not inconsistent. To discipline "them," it is necessary that we be strong. We must be ready to exercise our will and impose our vision with self-confidence, pride, and enthusiasm. It is always easier to be righteous when you know that you are right. As Teddy Roosevelt (Ronald Reagan's favorite president) represented in word and deed, ebullience and aggression are nicely complementary. The 1984 Republican platform proclaimed the imperative to discipline the Soviets, crack down on welfare cheats, and stringently control public spending, while the convention hall echoed to the strains of "Happy Days Are Here Again."

The new conservatism, in sum, has brilliantly blended two rather distinct messages: On the one side, authority, control, and discipline for "them"; on the other, liberation, optimism, and exuberance for "us." It thus endeared itself to millions of Americans uncomfortable with the disturbing suspicion—a suspicion that Jimmy Carter's more traditionally dour conservatism had unforgivably failed to dispel—that the world had changed, and that coming to terms with it might end up requiring us to fundamentally revise the stories we told one another about it. "No need," said Reagan, and we cheered.

6

The liberal response to this new conservative version of our national morality tales has been notoriously unconvincing. This has not been because liberal thinkers have suddenly lost their capacity for analysis, imagination, or insight. Even in recent years they have shown no end of cleverness in devising new programmatic solutions to specific public problems. Those who bemoan the liberals' dearth of new ideas have not been paying attention. Policy prescriptions are not the problem. The failure has lain deeper, with a liberal public philosophy that no longer embodies a coherent story that rings true for most Americans.

The prevailing liberal story draws upon the same morality tales as does conservatism but interprets them in the radically different terms of altruism and conciliation. The liberal gloss on the American mythology is perfectly familiar: First, the Mob at the Gates must be treated with understanding and tolerance. Poorer nations deserve our aid. We should work in concert with our allies, while appreciating that their needs and priorities may be different from our own. And we should patiently pursue a structure of peaceful coexistence with the Soviets, through trade, cultural exchanges, and arms control. Second, individuals rarely triumph when they can't get work; economic policy should ensure full employment, so that every citizen can find a market for his labor. Inflation can be restrained by an income and price policy that, unlike the conservative remedy, does not depend on unemployment to keep down prices. Third, the nation, as Benevolent Community, must come to the aid of the needy. Similarly, the more fortunate among us should contribute more to common purposes; taxes should be progressive. Finally, it is scheming economic elites who comprise the Rot at the Top; they must be restrained by a strong and compassionate government empowered by and dedicated to the common people.

The liberal public philosophy has its own coherence. Only through generosity and conciliation can we maintain domestic tranquility and global peace. Only through peace can we ensure prosperity. Only through prosperity can we afford to be charitable and conciliatory. The logic is internally consistent. And this philosophy surely conveys a moral vision no less valid than that of modern conservatism.

But the central parable of generosity and tolerance has seemed to many Americans disconcertingly naïve in a world they perceive as colder and crueler. Popular wisdom now teaches that détente promotes Soviet aggression, and Third World aid generates corruption and profligacy. "Full-employment" budgets invite workers to demand higher wages, thus fueling inflation. The welfare system does not reduce poverty, it perpetuates it. Government is too big, too meddlesome, too wasteful. The new conservatives did not invent these connections; they had only to point them out. Charity and conciliation are doubtless worthy goals for our personal lives, but such sentiments cannot sustain a nation in the world as it is. Altruism seems a feeble foundation for a public philosophy.

7

Yet in fact altruism per se never figured prominently in the liberal public philosophy that dominated American political discourse from the start of the New Deal to the end of World War II. It was the precept of solidarity, a sentiment crucially distinct from altruism, born not of specific legislation or programs but of concrete, common experiences—the Depression and World War II—that profoundly affected almost all Americans. The goals of reviving the economy and winning the war, and the sacrifices implied in achieving them, were well understood and widely endorsed. The public was motivated less by altruism than by its direct and palpable stake in the outcome of what were ineluctably *social* challenges.

The New Deal was concerned primarily with social insurance rather than with the redistribution of wealth. The Social Security Act of 1935, for example, was based on the principle of private insurance; one's benefits were to depend, for the most part, on one's contributions. Roosevelt was quite explicit about his distaste for welfare: "Continued dependence upon relief," he warned in his 1935 State of the Union address, "induces a spiritual and moral disintegration fundamentally destructive to the national fiber. To dole out relief . . . is to administer a narcotic, a subtle destroyer of the human spirit."[12] The problem, and the responsibility, were broadly felt. More than a third of the nation was "ill-housed, ill-clad, and ill-nourished." This was not some separate and distinct group in need; it was "us." The solution, quite obviously, could not be a redistribution of income from us to them, nor even from a more wealthy them to us. The problem demanded a national effort to improve the way the system worked. FDR called upon "this great army of our people, dedicated to a disciplined attack upon our common problems."[13]

Responding to the Mob at the Gates required a similar collaboration, not just among Americans but also between America and its allies. We were all in it together, fighting the fascists and then, immediately after the war, forging a system to rebuild the world economy and maintain the peace. Conservatives had sought to isolate America from an irredeemably wicked world. The liberals who came of age during the Depression and the war sought to remake the world. They created new institutions to bind nations together: a system of fixed exchange rates; an International Monetary Fund and a World Bank to improve international liquidity and spur development; a General Agreement on Tariffs and Trade to promote world commerce; the United Nations and the World Court to mediate disputes among nations, and regional pacts like the North Atlantic Treaty Organization to isolate incorrigible outlaw states who defied the American-led campaign for global harmony.

By the middle point of the century, American liberalism was triumphant. It had triumphed over economic disaster, it had won the war, it was magnificently winning the peace. Conservatism was seen to have pushed us into the Depression, balked at joining the good fight against fascism, and then recoiled from subsequent global responsibilities. It was relegated to the status of a fringe philosophy, a largely ignored alternative version of the American story.[14] The liberal interpretation of our basic myths was clear and compelling: We needed to work together to forge a new world. It celebrated the common man. It was optimistic about the future and commonsensical about the present. It spoke to "us," and we heard it.

8

The liberalism of the 1960s was different. In the stunning economic boom engineered by postwar liberal policies, many Americans experienced for the first time the exhilaration of rapidly rising incomes. Cars, highways, and suburban homes brought unprecedented mobility, privacy, and independence. "Solidarity" became a more abstract sentiment, with no obvious relevance to most Americans' everyday lives. In a richer America, the guiding principle of social solidarity was slowly and subtly transmuted into altruism. The stories Americans told one another had less to do with reciprocal obligation and mutual benefit than with the painful necessity of helping "them."

The 1960 report of the President's Commission on National Goals[15] had made no mention of poverty among blacks nor, for that matter, of poverty itself. This was not because material want was extinct in America or somehow wholly invisible. It was rather that a greater or lesser degree of deprivation still seemed quite unremarkable, a fundamental aspect of the human condition that America had to an unprecedented and rather astonishing extent managed to limit. When poverty had so recently been the rule, it only gradually came to be seen as a troubling exception. But before that decade was halfway through, commentators were talking about the "other" America,[16] and Lyndon Johnson was calling for a crusade against "the one huge wrong of the American nation." The war on poverty was to be "a moral challenge that goes to the very root of our civilization."[17]

That challenge was rooted in the sense that John F. Kennedy's death left America with an unfinished moral agenda. No well-organized interests had pressed for a national campaign against poverty; no grass-roots movement had mandated it. The war on poverty emerged largely from liberal opinion leaders—from academics, journalists, and editors—who saw it as a national responsibility, and from Johnson, who saw it as a personal mission. It also had a second, highly significant set of origins: For reasons that were entirely plausible, but also in part a matter of historical accident, the war on poverty was intimately linked to the civil rights movement. Even though the majority of the poor were white, as they always had been and would continue to be, America's discovery of the poor as a group coincided with and became merged with its belated effort to extend political rights to black Americans. Johnson laid out the logic for this connection: "You do not take a person who, for years, has been hobbled by chains and liberate him, bring him up to the starting line of a race and then say, 'You are free to compete with the others,' and still justly believe that you have been completely fair."[18]

This commingling of the two national failings, racial discrimination and poverty, made eminent sense at the time. But it accentuated the distinction between "us" and "them," and cemented the perception that social programs were mandated not by a sense of solidarity, but by altruism tinged with guilt. Most Americans did not feel poor. But here was a distinct group with different colored skin and a different culture, who lived in poverty largely because we had discriminated against them for generations. It was not a matter of reciprocal responsibility and mutual benefit, but of removing an injustice. "Their cause must be our cause too," Johnson declared. "Because it is not just Negroes, but really it is all of us who must overcome the crippling legacy of bigotry and injustice."[19] His words were stirring but incompletely convincing. Many Americans felt that in fact it *was*, to a great extent, "just Negroes" who required the assistance of the rest of us. Thus the Great Society rested from the start on the shaky foundation of ethical duty rather than mutual responsibility and reciprocal benefit.

Yet at the time this foundation seemed sufficiently firm. The special conditions of what would prove an odd and passing moment of American history allowed "us" to be generous to "them" with little identifiable sacrifice. The extraordinary growth of the American economy during the 1960s made it possible for the nation to wage a war on poverty, and then another on North Vietnam, while enjoying a broad rise in living standards. Keynesianism, the then-dominant economic doctrine, held that such public spending, far from impoverishing the middle class, would serve to keep the vast economic machine going at full throttle.

Lyndon Johnson talked reassuringly of the "fiscal dividend" awarded by economic growth. "Today, for the first time in our history, we have the power to strike away the barriers to full participation in our society. Having the power, we have the duty."[20]

Other aspects of Great Society liberalism appeared to be similarly painless. Extending civil rights to blacks cost the majority of Americans relatively little. Segregation in southern schools, luncheonettes, and hotels could be banished at small cost to those of us who lived elsewhere. At the same time, we could afford to be benevolent in our dealings abroad. The United States was preeminent in the world economy by default, with no serious trade competition from overseas. So the nation could afford to indulge its allies and the Third World; boosting foreign purchasing power could only result in more American export sales— where else would they spend the money?—and would help prevent communism to boot. Our political leadership of the Western world was unquestioned, so we could magnanimously yield to our allies on smaller matters. And the government had learned how to "fine-tune" its fiscal and monetary policies sufficiently well, it was thought, that workers could get generous wages and pension benefits, and managers could promise automatic cost-of-living increases. In all these respects, the liberal public philosophy of the 1960s and early 1970s entailed a peculiarly cut-rate form of charity. We could give "them" whatever they needed or wanted, and it didn't seem to hurt "us" a bit.

This easy altruism was reinforced by prevailing pluralist ideas about American democracy. By the 1960s pluralism had come to serve both as a description of the American political system and as a prescription for its continued health. American politics was powered by the maneuvers of shifting and overlapping interest groups, whose leaders bargained with one another over the nature and purpose of public action. The result was assumed to be a reasonably stable, responsively democratic political system. To many Americans, these features helped explain why democracy had continued to survive so well in the United States, in contrast to its easy susceptibility to mass movements in other nations.[21]

In this pluralist view, the "public interest" was nothing more (or less) than an accommodation among group leaders, with no substantive content apart from the benefits those leaders lined up for their constituents. Groups asserted their claims, and the jostling and horse trading got underway; what emerged was enshrined as the national will. Policies that could placate a greater number of interest groups were by definition the most conducive to the public good. Pluralism contained no principled limits on what compromises should be reached or how far government should go to accommodate the various groups that made up the public.

These two intellectual currents—Keynesianism and pluralism—were easily combined. Just as Keynesianism legitimized the idea of activist government as a way to stabilize the economy, pluralism legitimized it as a way to stabilize politics. Both currents were ultimately propelled by the comforting notion that some people could be helped without imposing undue costs on others. Full employment in the economic sphere, coupled with the ongoing accommodation of interest groups in the political sphere, would ensure that everybody got his, by and by. Public issues were subtly transformed into group claims, all of which could eventually be satisfied. The logic of public action could be left vague. There was no finely honed and rigorous liberal public philosophy—no story about where we were going or who we were—because there seemed to be no need for one.

9

Postwar liberalism was doomed to excess. Its fullest flowering, in the 1960s and early 1970s, occurred in an anomalous moment of history during which the United States was particularly unconstrained, its economy buoyant, its power unequaled. This was a sheltered and rich environment, a cultural hothouse unlike anything America had experienced before or is likely ever to experience again. Any public philosophy so germinated would be enfeebled once it left the hothouse. Liberalism was no exception. As the economy began to slow in the 1970s and American preeminence came under challenge, it was no longer possible for some groups to benefit without the burden manifestly falling on others. But because liberal pluralism lacked any definition of the public good apart from the sum of group claims and any coherent principles for screening and balancing such demands, conflicts grew harsher, and claims more insistent.

By the late 1970s liberalism and, inevitably, the Democratic party appeared less the embodiment of a vision of solidarity and more a tangle of narrow appeals from labor unions, teachers, farmers, gays, Hispanics, blacks, Jews, the handicapped, the elderly, women—proudly separate, vocally self-aware and self-interested subgroups. Of course these demands were no more parochial than those from traditional Republican claimants—bankers, oil companies, insurance firms, doctors, and corporate bureaucrats, among others. But that is precisely the point. The traditional Democratic constituencies had previously represented "us," the common people. The voices of unionized workers and farmers, of mechanics and common laborers, had been our voices. In the liberal parable, the bankers, industrialists, and special interests had been cast as "them," admittedly useful but corruption-prone elites requiring constant surveillance lest they enrich themselves and exploit the common man.

Decades before, the Progressive historian Vernon L. Parrington had drawn the distinction:

> From the first we have been divided into two main parties. Names and battle cries and strategies have changed repeatedly, but the broad party division has remained. On one side has been the party of the current aristocracy—of church, of gentry, of merchant, of slave holder, of manufacturer—and on the other the party of the commonality—of farmer, villager, small tradesman, mechanic, proletariat. The one has persistently sought to check and limit the popular power, to keep control of the government in the hands of the few in order to serve special interests, whereas the other has sought to augment the popular power, to make government more responsive to the will of the majority, to further the democratic rather than the republican ideal—let one discover this and new light is shed on our cultural tendencies.[22]

The decay of the community of the common man, the splintering of the Democratic party, made this distinction untenable. Each of the modern Democratic constituents appeared to be just another one of "them," with no more legitimate claim on the nation than any other. Although they might garnish their demands with references to the common good, these obeisances were understood as mere formalities—appropriate attire for public occasions. None spoke of the social obligations attendant upon the receipt of public benefits. All seemed simply and cynically intent upon getting as much as they could.

By the late 1970s, accordingly, the liberal public philosophy conveyed no central principle to organize and rank political claims. There was no story to explain the new reality in which we found ourselves. Liberalism offered nothing but a feeble and unconvincing call to charity and conciliation, routinely discounted as window dressing. The central function of politics was to accommodate claims, rather than to forge ties of reciprocal responsibility. The best government was the one that gratified the greatest number of groups and enraged the fewest. "Responsiveness" became a cardinal public virtue.

Claims were routinely asserted as rights. Welfare recipients, criminal defendants, students, recent immigrants, blacks, and the elderly, among others, declared themselves entitled to specified benefits. Such demands—made in both formal legal proceedings and informal public argument—served to further dramatize that the claimants were different from everyone else. They were members of unique groups with special needs, which the majority must acknowledge and accommodate. Quite apart from whether the majority acceded to these claims (and this depended largely on which group demanded what), the mere act of claiming was itself divisive, further separating "them" from the rest of us, and thereby undermining the ideal of social solidarity. The language of entitlement suggested that the claimants owed nothing to the majority in return; because claimants had a presumptive right to what they were demanding, obligations all flowed in one direction, to "them" from the rest of us.

Liberal politicians, as a result, had no compass for determining what they stood for. There were no governing principles on which they could draw. They typically fell back on the only available sources of guidance: the claims put forward by leaders of the various groups that comprised the liberal constituency, and the results of polls which revealed in greater detail what the members of these groups wanted for themselves. The speeches and position papers of liberal politicians dutifully appealed to group sentiments; party platforms predictably promised something for every group in attendance.

This is not to suggest that conservative politics was any less influenced by the concerns of its constituents or that conservative groups were more restrained in asserting claims on the public. But at the least, by the end of the 1970s, there was coming to be a coherent conservative viewpoint that allowed such claims to be sifted and ranked. Even more importantly, conservative politicians were able to provide the public with a plausible story about why the nation would be better off—why "we" would benefit—from a policy of accommodating the claims of conservative constituencies. There was no such integrating philosophy on the other side. Fractious subgroups, each promoting its own agenda, were all that liberalism had to show to the citizenry.

10

The philosophical watershed, where conciliating "them" gave way to disciplining "them," came with the administration of Jimmy Carter, the Democratic president who carried into policy many of the central precepts of the new conservative public philosophy. Carter understood the public's growing disdain for government. He had campaigned as an outsider, against Washington, and what he termed "the complicated, confusing, overlapping, and wasteful government bureaucracy." For Carter, the Rot at the Top was located along the Potomac.[23] Similarly, the proliferation of asserted rights was perverting the Benevolent Community: Carter decried "fraud, waste, and abuse" in the burgeoning welfare system and sought its overhaul. (Carter's abortive reform effort adopted the model of the negative income tax, first proposed by conservative economists in the Nixon administration.) Carter's conservative tendencies became particularly open in the latter years of his administration. He appointed Paul Volcker chairman of the Federal Reserve Board and supported the Fed's decision, in October 1979, to limit the nation's money supply in order to combat inflation, even though interest rates and unemployment would quite predictably rise as a result. And it was Carter, and his national security adviser, Zbigniew Brzezinski, who ended détente with the Soviets. The Mob at the Gates had become a more palpable threat. In the wake of the Soviet invasion of Afghanistan Carter embargoed grain sales to the USSR. When the Soviets deployed SS-20 missiles in Eastern Europe, Carter moved to install comparable American weapons in Western Europe.

This renunciation of liberal conciliation was not a random shift in political fashion, nor was it inspired by delusion. The Soviets *were* acting more aggressive. Inflation *was* soaring, and unionized workers indeed *were* collecting pay gains outpacing productivity. Something *was* seriously amiss in the welfare system. Government regulations *were* growing costly and cumbersome. Jimmy Carter was a man of generally liberal instincts; so were the majority of his countrymen. But they adopted the conservative public philosophy because it seemed to offer insight into what was happening and what to do about it. The world was already divided into "us" and "them"—the Soviets and other foreigners, greedy workers, meddling bureaucrats, and the clamorous poor. The choice was to be either charitable and conciliatory toward them or assertive and tough. The first alternative was demonstrably not working. It was time to try the second. America's metaphors shifted: We had to stop soft-pedaling and play hardball, better to be hard-nosed and hardheaded than soft-hearted and wishy-washy, time to take a hard line rather than be a soft touch. Absent any respectable alternative—without any new vision of social solidarity to replace that which liberalism had abandoned—the public's perception began to be shaped by the conservative parable.

CHAPTER 3

THE NEW CONTEXT

1

Cultural myths are no more "truth" than an architect's sketches are buildings. Their function is to explain events and guide decisions. Thus while it is pointless to challenge myths as unrealistic, it is entirely valid to say that a culture's mythology serves it well only to the extent it retains its connection to the reality the culture faces. Myths must evolve as the context evolves. Stories that stay rigid as realities change become ever less useful cultural tools.

The new conservative story conveys an important set of insights. Permissiveness—that is, liberalism's overwhelming preference for smoothing over rather than facing conflict—contributed to an environment in which unaccountability flourished, both at home and abroad. In abdicating public authority, America issued an invitation to irresponsibility. But the skeins of cause and effect behind the breakdown of Great Society liberalism are far more tangled than the conservative story suggests. The mythology that inspired liberalism in its salad days of the 1960s can indeed be faulted for failing to address the harsh realities of the 1970s and 1980s. The world *has* changed. But the change has not been along a single dimension, from benign to hostile, mandating an equally simple shift from conciliation to toughness. A subtler, more sweeping transformation has been taking place that touches on most areas of public concern—the Soviet threat and the Third World, the national economy, the poor within America, the role of government. The stresses Americans began experiencing in the 1970s are intimately connected with an evolution of the global economy and society.

2

Some of the symptoms are painfully familiar—the two oil shocks of the 1970s, the flood of Japanese automobiles and consumer electronics into America, the loss of American jobs in basic manufacturing, the unrest that periodically erupts into violence in obscure places around the globe. Other aspects of the transformation are less well understood. Two central trends stand out.

The first is that America's economic position in the world is becoming less distinctive. The rest of the world is catching up, and America's preeminence by default is over. Beginning in the late 1960s, and continuing to the present day, the cost of sending things or information around the globe has fallen dramatically. This is due, principally, to rapid advances in technologies of transporting and communicating, to such innovations as container ships, satellites, and computers. Until recent times most goods were produced close to where they were to be consumed; the main exceptions were certain minerals, agricultural goods, and economically unimportant exotica. This pattern has been breaking down at an increasing pace. Consumers of cars, refrigerators, television programs, insurance policies, and even money, often live in different nations or on different continents from the producers. The producers, in turn, often depend on far-distant sources for components, designs, or information. It is now often cheaper to ship raw steel across an ocean than across the United States. Slight differences in interest rates may induce a New York corporation to raise money in Tokyo or in Bonn instead of on Wall Street. Across an unprecedented range of goods and services, quality and cost matter more than location: Whoever can do it best and cheapest, anywhere in the world, sells to whoever is

41

willing to pay the best price, anywhere in the world. The elegant curves of supply and demand that so charm economists are meeting up in the oddest of places.

Similarly, the tastes and preferences of people around the globe are gradually converging. If modern communications technology has failed to endow humanity with a shared moral sense, it has at least managed to induce shared appetites. On the streets of Lima or Fez, for example, it is not unusual to hear British rock music emanating from compact recorders designed in Japan and assembled in South Korea, while the listeners wear Levi's.

By the late 1960s, the industrial nations that had been devastated by World War II were once again full participants in the world economy. But this commercial transformation has not been solely, or even most importantly, a matter of trade among the United States, Japan, and Western Europe. Our economic fate is increasingly shaped by developments in the Third World, especially in Latin America and Southeast Asia.

The second central trend is demographic. The planet's population balance has been tipping ever more precipitously in the direction of the poorer nations. In 1950 two thirds of mankind lived in the Third World; by 2020, the proportion is expected to be five sixths. To put the matter in some perspective, consider that for all eternity up to 1932, when modern American liberalism came of age, the world's population had expanded to approximately 2 billion people. This is less than the *increase* in the Third World's population between 1932 and 1985.

These nations are wildly heterogeneous and share no other feature but relative poverty. For centuries or millennia, many African, Asian, and Latin American cultures have been characterized by fatalism. Most people harbored little hope of improving their material situation, and this has been a rational accommodation to hard reality. But as money, technology, goods, and services flow with ever greater ease around the globe, more of the world's poor billions have come to know that a more comfortable life exists. Nothing undermines centuries of resignation as readily as a television commercial.

Nor are their ambitions fanciful. An ever larger number of

these people have not just the will but the full capacity to participate in the world economy; many have already joined in. Large-scale production of basic goods continues to migrate to the Third World. As recently as the mid-1960s the inhabitants of Taiwan, Hong Kong, South Korea, Mexico, and Brazil primarily made basic products—like clothing, shoes, toys, simple electronic assemblies—that called for cheap labor but little in the way of sophisticated capital equipment; indeed, Japanese industry had been largely limited to such basic goods a few years previously. By the mid-1970s several of these countries had followed Japan's lead into steel and other basic capital-intensive processing industries. Japan, meanwhile, had become an exporter of steel-making equipment as well as basic steels, and had moved its industrial base into products like automobiles, color televisions, small appliances, consumer electronics, and ships—all products requiring technical sophistication as well as considerable investment in plant and equipment. By 1985 Taiwan, South Korea, and several other nations had themselves become major producers of these complex products. At the same time, poorer countries like the Philippines, Sri Lanka, and India were taking over the production of clothing, footwear, toys, and simple electronic assemblies. This second wave of industrializing nations was inexorably pushing into more advanced technologies as well. By the mid-1980s China was the world's sixth-ranking industrial nation; Brazil and India almost tied with Canada for ninth place.[1]

As these newcomers to modern global capitalism jostle for room, established industries in advanced nations have been squeezed. Factories have closed. Workers have faced the loss of traditional jobs, and have had difficulty shifting into new ones. The growth trend of these economies has flattened markedly, amid calls for tariffs and quotas against foreign goods. The United States has not been immune to such demands.[2] To be sure, a basic goal of American foreign policy during the postwar era was precisely to modernize the economies of poorer nations, lest they succumb to communism. It may seem inconsistent and certainly ungracious for us now to blame these nations for our economic problems. But few could foresee that the pace of change would be so quick and that America's economic preeminence would be so suddenly at risk. When John F. Kennedy entered the White House, America accounted for 35 percent of the world's economic output; by 1980, its share had fallen to 22 percent. In 1960, almost 22 percent of the world's exports were shipped from the United States; in 1980, the figure was 11 percent.[3]

The anxieties this evolution has provoked in America are naturally most familiar to us, but the effects in other nations of this accelerating integration have been far from tranquil. Rapid change has sparked upheaval in much of the Third World. Violent shifts in oil prices have played havoc with many developing economies. Some have sunk deeply into debt; others are confounded by inflation. Sudden industrialization also has contributed to urban poverty and corruption. The material benefits of enhanced world trade have been accompanied by a humiliating sense of relative deprivation. The enticements of commercial capitalism have aroused appetites faster than incomes, while undermining traditional cultures. The consequent social unrest has encouraged extremist left- and right-wing regimes and, on occasion, fundamentalist uprisings. The dilemma parallels that of the United States as manufacturing plants shut down: How can this immensely promising process of integration be encouraged without undercutting the cultural foundations on which continued progress depends, without spurring into devastating action the forces of reaction and retreat? *This* is the new context confronting America, and the rest of the world as well.

3

The rest of this book will explore in detail how our reigning cultural mythology is disturbingly at odds with this context, assess the costs of this disjuncture, and speculate on how our parables might evolve to incorporate a new set of cultural challenges. First, it will reexamine the parable of the Mob at the Gates. The liberal ideal of magnanimous accommodation is an out-of-date and dangerously unbalanced guide to our dealings with the other peoples of the earth. The conservative story rightly

perceives the Soviets' readiness to exploit Third World instability. But as will be evident, the conservative parable is also
perilously incomplete. Third World tensions are manifestations
of the economic and social transformation of the globe. Their
connection to the East-West rivalry is in most cases derivative
and wholly secondary. Our national interests are undeniably affected by the ability and willingness of Latin American nations
to pay off their debts; by the speed with which American and
European workers shift out of basic mass production; by how
global corporations allocate functions to different sets of workers
around the world; by the oil cartel's manipulation of petroleum
prices; by the flow of deadly drugs into the United States, and of
deadly weapons to all manner of semi-sovereign groups; by South
Korea's and Taiwan's advances into high technology, by China's
convulsive drive toward modernization, and by violent contests
between dictators and revolutionaries in the world's tropics. But
it requires lengthy training and a concerted effort of imagination
to divine Soviet machinations behind all these events. Even where
the Soviets attempt to intervene, there are many other, more
powerful forces at work in most of these areas. To treat such
occurrences as occasions for secondhand warfare between the
United States and the Soviet Union leads to tragically myopic
prescriptions. Yet the conservative mythology holds no other role
for the impoverished majority of mankind than as a pawn in the
East-West struggle.

Subsequent chapters probe the parable of the Triumphant
Individual. Surely conservative economists are correct in arguing
that our economy must avoid the systemic fraud of inflation and
ensure adequate incentives to save and to incur financial risk.
Our inventors and managers undeniably merit encouragement as
well as respect. Post–New Deal liberal tax rates and spending
policies doubtless did undermine economic discipline, and unrestrained wage demands helped fuel inflation. But our economy
has suffered less from either capital shortages or inflationary wage
pressure than from a decay in our capacity to collaborate.

For nearly two decades before 1970 the average working
American had produced around 3 percent more goods and services

by the end of each year than at the start. Then in the 1970s the annual increase in the rate of productivity fell dramatically. Not even the economic recovery that began in 1983 returned productivity to its former level of growth.[4] It is difficult, although certainly not unknown, for an individual to become wealthier without producing more. It is impossible for a society to do so. Almost no growth of productivity in America has meant almost no increase in the real incomes of Americans. From the end of World War II until 1973, American families enjoyed steadily rising incomes. This trend stopped. In 1986, even after years of rousing growth in the gross national product, average family incomes were a bit lower than they had been a dozen years before.[5]

The drop in productivity growth has been rooted in our difficulties adapting our economy as opportunities and constraints have changed. By the 1980s, 70 percent of the goods that Americans made were potentially exposed to foreign competition; our economic policies and habits of thought, formed in an era of autonomy, were unprepared for this transformation. Some of our companies simply moved along with the current, setting up their low-skilled operations in poorer areas of the globe, while relying on the Japanese for their high technologies. Others preferred to dress up their balance sheets by resorting to creative accounting, and through cosmetic mergers and acquisitions. Others made common cause with workers in demanding government protection from foreign competition. Still others sought refuge in defense contracting. Meanwhile, what we considered to be a "normal" rate of involuntary unemployment crept upward, from 4 percent in the 1960s to around 7 percent. This higher figure hinted at a pervasive mismatch between what many Americans can do and what they need to do to be part of the newly competitive world economy. It signaled a failure of adaptation.

As a nation's economic structure becomes more a matter of choice and strategy, economic growth has come to depend less on the gross level of investment, more on how investment is channeled into adaptation. Mass production of physical things—increasingly the province of low-wage competitors—has become far less important to America than the manipulation of ideas, embedded within bundles of goods and services that are continuously evolving. In advanced nations, wealth flows from the collective abilities of groups of people to piece things together in new ways, to conceive of new possibilities, and to make continual improvements in what has come before. A culture is *economically* successful to the extent it encourages such broad-based innovativeness. The lure of substantial wealth and the threat of severe poverty doubtless serve to inspire great feats of personal daring and ambition, as the conservative tale of the Triumphant Individual suggests. But the conservative parable casts entrepreneurialism as exceptional; a few Triumphant Individuals create safe, simple jobs for their less innovative neighbors. Yet in an era where such simple jobs are ever harder to retain, the capacity to innovate, adapt, and envisage the novel must be widely spread throughout the work force. The conservative story may be suited to a less sophisticated economy in which rare feats of individual audacity matter more than the continuous, collective habit of innovation. But it is out of sync with our own age.

The third fable we will examine concerns the Benevolent Community. Here again, the new conservative interpretation is in important senses a plausible response to reality: Poverty has persisted in America in defiance of liberal good intentions and large welfare budgets. Many of our impoverished communities suffer from social breakdown and the decay of civic and family responsibility.

But as I will seek to show, the conservative story fails utterly to take account of the larger setting in which American poverty has persisted. Poverty at the lowest rungs of the society is in large part a function of economic stagnation above. A rising tide lifts all boats, the saying goes; similarly, an ebb tide lowers all boats, and strands some. The entrenchment of poverty coincided with the collapse of growth in productivity and earnings, and the erosion of the manufacturing industries that had in the past offered access to the middle class. Women and baby boomers streamed into the workplace—some 19 million of them during the 1970s, and millions more since then. But many of these new entrants were driven by the need to prop up declining family incomes. Young workers, in particular, fell behind. Many could no longer afford to buy their own houses nor aspire to the standard of living enjoyed by their parents.

As upward mobility faltered, some Americans remained stuck at the bottom. America's poverty rate—the fraction of the population officially listed as controlling too little cash to tend to their minimal needs—stopped declining in 1973 and then slowly began edging up again. Conservatives are quite right when they charge that liberalism has failed to solve the poverty problem; they are quite wrong to say that liberalism caused the problem. As to the burgeoning social-welfare burden on the federal budget, it has surprisingly little to do with liberal efforts to aid the poor.[6] Most "welfare" has gone to the middle class, not to the poor, through programs like Medicare and Social Security. By 1980, the aggregate of these benefits was more than three times that for programs based on need. As a result, America's elderly were becoming more secure while large numbers of its children were sinking deeper into poverty.

The final chapters will consider the parable of the Rot at the Top. The conservative version sees corruption and unaccountability principally in the public sector. It deserves a degree of respectful attention. Few would argue that public programs are immune from incompetence or irresponsibility. Spending for defense, Social Security, and Medicare together comprise almost 60 percent of the federal budget, and are the fastest-growing categories of expenditure. Each could stand careful pruning, even more extreme reductions—though it is worth noting that none of these programs has been typically the object of conservative concern. Government regulators have also shown a disrespect, willful ignorance, or even hostility toward the private sector they are charged with overseeing.

But once again the reigning version of this American story is grossly incomplete. Posing the issue as a struggle between free enterprise and stifling government control, the conservative parable has obscured the central issue of how we organize and maintain that set of rules and constraints which we call the market. The conservative's idyllic "free market," unencumbered by government meddling, is a logical impossibility. The important question—left unaddressed by the conservative story and irrelevant to government's size—is whether these "rules of the game" ease and encourage economic change, or forestall it.

4

The conservative mythology is understandably comforting to an America confronted by a suddenly intractable world—mostly poor, mostly nonwhite—in which the United States is no longer preeminent. It summons us to defy the wholly natural erosion of an unnatural postwar economic and political supremacy, and to reject our new interdependence. It lets us blame our troubles on indulgence and naïve generosity, and promises renewal if only we forswear the flabby principles of altruism and conciliation. It charges us to bolster our power and exercise it boldly to reclaim our rightful hegemony.

But the conservative parable holds no place for the fundamental transformation of the world economy and society. It overlooks the key relationships between these changes and political instability around the globe, Soviet opportunism, the stagnation of the American economy, domestic poverty, and the relationship between American business and government. Its message of discipline and pugnacity, in other words, does not so much seek preeminence as presume it. This is an invigorating but reckless vision.

Modern liberalism, as we have seen, offers no real alternative. Rather than assert ourselves, the liberal story teaches that we should be charitable and conciliatory. But the objects of our conciliation remain the same as in the conservative story. "They" are the Soviets, the Japanese, Third Worlders, organized workers, and the poor.

The ongoing debate between liberals and conservatives in America assumes that the only pertinent issue is how much we should concede to "them." Yet in the new reality in which America finds itself, the real choice is not along the single dimension of conciliation versus assertion. The shrinking and rapidly evolving world we now inhabit offers unprecedented opportunity for mutual gain, but also ample incentive for the opportunism, exploitation, and betrayal that poison collaboration and derail progress. As coming chapters will seek to establish, our fundamental challenge is to define jointly promising endeavors and to forge durable ties of mutual obligation and responsibility. To a greater extent and for subtler reasons than either modern conservatism or modern liberalism appreciate, life on this planet has become less a set of contests in which one party can be victorious, and more an intricate set of relationships which either succeed or fail—we win or we lose together.

PART ONE

THE MOB
AT THE
GATES

CHAPTER 4

THE BOOMERANG PRINCIPLE

1

In the glory days of liberalism, the Mob at the Gates was a simple form of evil embodied in the likes of a Hitler or a Tojo. Today the hostile forces that inhabit the new American demonology are more complex: an aggressive Soviet Union, an equally aggressive Japan, European states that are unreliable allies and unfair competitors, Latin American debtors, communist insurgents throughout the world, Third World puppets of the Soviets, drug traffickers, terrorists, illegal immigrants. The world "out there" has grown more dangerous as it has got nearer.

Two centuries ago America was insulated by a broad expanse of sea to the east and by primitive civilizations to the west and south. George Washington could warn realistically about the dangers of aligning with any major power; Jefferson could give thanks that the nation was "separated by nature and a wide ocean from the exterminating havoc" of Europe.[1] Even in the first two decades following World War II the celebration of self-reliance could continue; America's increasing integration into the world was masked by its overwhelming dominance of it. Henry Luce spoke to the coming generation when, in 1941, he urged America to "exert upon the world the full impact of our influence, for such purposes as we see fit and by such means as we see fit."[2] The international organizations and agreements that we created at the end of the war—the United Nations, the General Agreement on Tariffs and Trade, and so on—were means by which to exercise this influence; these were no "entanglements," because we absolutely controlled them. We drew boundaries to delineate the nations of "the free world," who presumably had no other ambition than to become more like us, and set about "containing" Soviet influence in the benighted remainder of the globe.

It is a precept, governing the growth of families as well as nations: Nobody appears as invulnerable as one on whom others are totally dependent; nobody is as stunned by his subsequent dependency as one who once felt invulnerable. As the world evolved in the late 1960s and early 1970s, we clung to our older images. We could not subjugate Vietnam; Arab sheiks were threatening our energy supplies; the Japanese were thwarting our steel and automobile industries. There seemed to be only two possible responses to these new vulnerabilities, both drawn from our history. One was to withdraw—repudiating military responsibilities abroad, seeking "independence" from foreign suppliers of energy and anything else that mattered, and protecting our steel makers and other industries from cheap foreign competition. The other response was redoubled assertion: involving ourselves aggressively in every global conflict where we suspected a Soviet hand, guaranteeing supplies of critical raw materials by supporting friendly regimes who controlled valuable real estate abroad, and browbeating our trading partners into playing "fair." By and large, liberals and Democrats opted for withdrawal; conservatives and Republicans preferred assertion.[3]

Neither approach, however, is practicable today. A determined hermit may manage to isolate himself; a nation cannot. Our way of life is shaped and nurtured by a $50 trillion annual flow of global capital, a $2 trillion current of trade and investment in goods and services, a vast sea of information and technology, and a swirl of political forces emanating from every region on earth. There is no way to hide out without accepting a radically diminished national existence. Nor is it possible to unilaterally assert our will: We are now matched by several nations who are at least as productive as we are, at least as competitive in world markets, or at least as deadly. We are enmeshed in a global system that knows no neat boundaries. Our actions reverberate through this system and then, often disconcertingly, bounce back again.

In seeking either to intimidate or to wall ourselves off from the Mob at the Gates, we run the risk of frustrating global adjustment and thus, ironically, exacerbating the problems of Soviet adventurism, our economic stagnation, and domestic poverty. Let me label this dynamic the Boomerang Principle. As principles go, this one is pretty simple.[4] It takes effect whenever one actor in an interdependent system attempts to act unilaterally, in ignorance or defiance of the other actors. At first, typically, the actor meets with resistance; his initiative throws the rest of the system out of balance, and the system fights back. Either the other actors retaliate and the conflict escalates, or else they concede in unanticipated ways. Sometimes the system adjusts and endures; the initial actor may even gain from his assertion, though seldom precisely as he had intended. Often he loses. Sometimes the system collapses.

2

The Boomerang Principle applies to the complex and evolving world system in which America now finds itself. Perhaps the best illustration comes from following a single trajectory of national policy as it curves its way through the global political economy. Let us begin with the military buildup that commenced late in the Carter administration and continued with a vengeance under Ronald Reagan. Between 1981 and 1986, defense expenditures rose over 40 percent in real terms. Military spending, along with the 1981 tax cut, pulled the American economy out of recession. They also yielded an awkwardly large budget deficit, of course. But with money now moving so easily around the globe, America was able to finance its capital gap, and thus its arms buildup, by attracting money from abroad. All we needed to do was to keep our interest rates high enough to lure these funds.

Money faithfully follows the law of supply and demand: As foreigners bought more and more American securities, the price of the dollar climbed. Yet T-bills are not the only commodities priced in dollars; so are Chevrolets and Kansas wheat. The dollar's rise made American goods more expensive in world markets, and foreign goods cheaper to American consumers.

Tracing the path reveals further consequences of this "military Keynesianism," some of them welcome ones. The deficit-led American recovery helped to revive the rest of the world economy. With foreign goods so cheap, Americans obligingly went on a foreign-spending spree. In 1983 the increase in U.S. imports accounted for half the net growth in global trade. For Japan, much of Western Europe, and most of Latin America, exports to the United States made up the largest single component of their national earnings. Half of Brazil's $12 billion trade surplus that year was due to sales in the United States, as was virtually all of Mexico's export growth.[5] At the same time, the surge of bargains from overseas kept the lid on inflation at home; no American producer wanted to price himself completely out of the market.

3

Some of the consequences were less benign. So much money was pouring into the United States that the nation became a net debtor—owing more to the rest of the world than foreigners owed us—for the first time since 1917. A lot of this money could leave the country as quickly as it came in. As a result American banks became highly vulnerable to global financial trends. Electronic twitches on Telex machines could signal imminent bankruptcy.

There was a second, even more pressing problem. American manufacturers and farmers, already under siege by the rest of the world, saw their markets shrink radically at home and abroad. The excess of imports over exports swelled from $36 billion in 1980 to over $160 billion in 1986. American jobs in export industries were being lost. Some manufacturers moved abroad, where they could pay for parts, fuel, and labor in cheaper currencies.

Others withdrew from international trade, shifting into industries like food processing, insurance, and defense contracting where
foreign competition could not yet reach. Even giant companies
that had been world powerhouses of innovation and productivity—firms such as GE, Honeywell, General Motors, TRW, Westinghouse, and RCA—retreated into defense businesses, and began
distributing (under their own brand names) computers, subcom-
pact cars, and other advanced products made abroad.[6]

Other American firms sought shelter of a different sort. With
foreign goods priced so low, it was easy for companies to claim
intolerable injury and to charge foreigners with trading unfairly.
They took their cases to Washington. In 1979 sixty-two petitions
to restrict imports were filed with the U.S. International Trade
Commission; by 1984 the number had more than tripled.[7]
Hundreds of bills were introduced in Congress, designed to stem
the tide. The Reagan administration vowed to "get tough" with
our trading partners. Diplomatic arm twisting (and the threat of
unilateral protectionist legislation) extracted from other nations
"voluntary" agreements to hold back exports to the United States
of steel and automobiles, among other products. All this protectionist pressure had an effect. In 1980, 20 percent of the goods
produced in America were protected from foreign competition
by barriers other than outright tariffs. Just four years later, over
35 percent of our products were similarly sheltered.[8] The dollar
would eventually fall, but many of these impediments to commerce would remain.

4

Keep following the trajectory. Remember that it began with an
arms buildup, aimed at getting tough with the Soviets. But soon
trade tensions were mounting around the globe. Our Western
European allies applauded the American recovery, but they worried about the outflow of savings to the United States. How were
they to rebuild their older industries, they wondered, if their
capital was going to pay America's bills? To preserve their capital
and make themselves more attractive to international investors,

they were forced to raise their own interest rates as well. But this tactic made it more expensive for Europeans to borrow money, which in turn threatened to slow down their economies.

The Europeans—troubled by double-digit unemployment and eager to export—were also riled by American protectionism. The European Economic Community threatened to retaliate against American quotas on European steel and other products. Jacques Delors, the head of the Common Market Commission in 1985, summed up the state of transatlantic relations as "abysmal." Europe, he said, is the victim of an "increasingly aggressive and ideological American administration."[9] Canada, America's largest trading partner, was incensed when election-year pressures led to duties on certain timber products. Relations with Japan were not much better. In 1986—even as the dollar receded—the United States imported almost $60 billion more from Japan than Japan did from us. Congress thundered about retaliating by closing off more of the United States market to Japanese goods.

5

But it was in the Third World that the boomerang we are following took its sharpest turn. American protectionism hit less developed nations especially hard. Agreements that fixed the amount they could export to the United States by reference to some historical share of the American market, such as those negotiated for steel and textiles, stunted their industrial growth. And because Third World nations possess substantially less bargaining leverage with the United States than do European nations or Japan, they became prime targets for additional trade restrictions. In 1984 the Reagan administration sharply tightened the rules governing textile trade. The following year the administration imposed duties on billions of dollars' worth of previously duty-free Third World imports. The Commerce Department launched investigations of several Third World producers who were alleged to be subsidizing their exports. Quotas were imposed on sugar imports; this restriction alone would cost Latin American and Caribbean exporters some $180 million a year. Western Europe, facing severe unemployment and fearful that products originally destined for the American market now would be diverted to Europe, took similar steps to block imports from low-wage countries. By 1985 nearly one-fifth of the Third World's manufactured exports to industrialized nations were covered by quotas; nearly one third of their agricultural exports were meeting a similar fate.[10]

Follow the path further: Several of the largest Third World nations were deeply in debt. Most of these debtors were located in Latin America, virtually on our doorstep. They had borrowed enormous sums of money at floating interest rates during the heady 1970s, when their rapid growth and banks' eagerness to "recycle" Arab oil money made borrowing easy. But these loans had to be repaid in dollars, and the dollar was now more expensive than the borrowers had anticipated. At the same time, rising public and private debt in the United States, coupled with America's relative political stability, shouldered the Third World away from the world capital market. These nations, desperate to service existing loans and blocked from getting new money, were undercut by protectionism in their efforts to raise foreign exchange by exporting to America and Europe. By the middle of the 1980s these trends were converging to drive emerging nations back into poverty.

The United States chose to respond by relying on the "discipline of the market" as interpreted by international bankers. The Reagan administration left it to the International Monetary Fund, and to the large U.S. banks who held much of the Latin American debt, to work out austerity plans. Austerity was a nice way of saying lower living standards. The plans were intended to clamp down on these nations' consumption and investment to free resources for debt service. There was something vaguely unseemly about imposing austerity on them when their problems stemmed in part from our reluctance to pay for our arms buildup with higher taxes or lower domestic spending instead of borrowing the money abroad. But no American politician who valued his political career would whisper that the United States should endure austerity of anything like the degree Latin American politicians were expected to impose on their citizens.

The timing of these austerity plans would eventually be seen as unfortunate. Much of Latin America was just beginning to experiment with democracy. Beginning in 1980 generals had allowed power to pass to elected civilian presidents in Peru, Bolivia, Argentina, Honduras, Panama, Uruguay, and Brazil. These democratic forays were immensely valuable in themselves, of course, and no version of the American mythology would countenance a failure to applaud them. They were also critical to America's long-term security, for they held out the promise of gradual reform leading to a modicum of political stability and popularly based friendship with the United States. These newborn democracies were delicate. Antidemocratic forces were waiting in the wings (the military on the right, the communists on the left) to pick up the pieces if democracy should be seen to fail. And the economic squeeze the United States had unwittingly helped to precipitate by its budgetary policies, and had explicitly endorsed, was entirely capable of undermining support for the new Latin American regimes. High unemployment and collapsing living standards are not the most favorable accompaniments to democratic experimentation. The colonels and the comrades were both content to wait.

The United States, uncomfortable with the military right but in horror of the militant left, responded by increasing arms shipments to the anticommunist governments of the region, democratic or otherwise. There was no such increase in economic aid. In 1985, nearly two out of every three dollars of American aid to Latin America was in the form of military assistance. Between 1981 and 1985, military equipment was our fastest growing export to Latin America. This phenomenon did not greatly trouble those American manufacturers who had found commercial tranquility through specializing in weaponry, but it did distract these fragile nations from their primary mission. Peru, for example, which had been the first of the military-ruled nations to return to civilian rule in 1980, owed foreign banks over $13 billion and had to abide by their demands for austerity. Its democratically elected president, Fernando Belaúnde Terry, was a loyal ally of the United States, but leftists were gaining ground. Thus by 1982 Peru was spending $370 million a year on imports of arms; this was about half the sum it spent on educating its citizens that year, and substantially more than it spent on their health.[11]

The boomerang curves back toward where it began. Wending its way through the world economy, the financial disruption that began with the American defense buildup jeopardized our relations with our allies and the stability of Latin American democracies. The Soviets, of course, liked nothing better than a gradual dissolution of NATO and a disaffected Japan; they relished sharpened unrest in Latin America. To jeopardize these relationships in the name of toughness against the Soviets amounted to a peculiar strategy for national security.

6

Follow the boomerang back, finally, to its origin. The effects of economic stagnation in the Third World, and especially in Latin America, worked through the system until they reached the United States. In 1980 the Third World accounted for about 40 percent of American exports. But mounting protectionism in the United States cut these nations' earnings while the rising dollar and austerity campaigns sapped their purchasing power and slowed trade. Between 1981 and 1986, the drop in demand for American goods among indebted nations—even taking into account the growing arms trade—caused a larger deterioration in America's trade balance than did the influx of Japanese imports into the United States. The shrinking markets translated directly into shuttered factories, greater joblessness, blocked upward mobility, and greater American poverty.

Meanwhile, millions of Latin Americans poured into the United States. Some were fleeing political repression; others, destitution; still others, the social strains caused by rapid industrialization and fiscal austerity. The best guess was that more than a million Latin Americans slipped across the border each year. The consequences were mixed. America got the benefit of another generation of immigrants; each earlier wave had demonstrated the determination and ambition of those who chose to leave their homelands for America. But there were costs to pay, such as housing and educating these new immigrants. In 1982 federal, state, and local governments were spending more resettling immigrants from the Caribbean and Latin America than America was providing in foreign aid to the entire region.[12] Children born in the United States to illegal immigrants automatically become U.S. citizens, entitled to all the social benefits that any other citizen may receive. And beyond these direct costs, many American blue-collar and service workers were growing increasingly anxious that the new immigrants would take their jobs. There were calls to get tough on immigration—to reduce the number of aliens allowed in, to increase border surveillance, to end bilingual education, to penalize employers who hired illegal aliens.

The scourge of drug trafficking was not unrelated. As Latin American economies sank under the combined weight of indebtedness, fiscal austerity, and protectionism in the north, the production of illicit drugs became a major source of revenue. Bolivia's 1985 cocaine shipments to America brought an estimated $450 million into that small country, or almost 10 percent of its gross national product. This was roughly as much as Bolivia earned on its legal exports, and about twice the sum it devoted to the education and health of its citizenry. Since International Monetary Fund austerity began constraining legitimate enterprise, cocaine production has been one of the few thriving industries in Bolivia, and one of the few sources of good jobs. Thousands of Bolivian farmers raise coca plants; thousands more work in the factories that transform coca leaves into cocaine. Between 1982 and 1985 the population of the Cochabamba Valley, where most cocaine production is undertaken, doubled to 80,000 inhabitants. When at the end of 1985 Bolivian police and officials from the United States Drug Enforcement Administration raided Cochabamban farms and factories, they were met with armed resistance; when they finally succeeded in closing them, the Bolivian peso suddenly lost about 30 percent of its value. Bolivia then pleaded with American authorities for a $100 million bridge loan to forestall currency speculation in the face of falling drug revenues.[13]

7

This chapter has traced only one loop connecting our military, economic, and social policies and the wider world on which they work. These connections are complex and changeable. In 1986 the dollar fell precipitously, setting off another set of reactions as the American economy ceased pulling everyone else behind it. Oil prices also fell, setting in motion a broadly more benign reaction. (The members of the Organization of Petroleum Exporting Countries discovered the Boomerang Principle on their own; when they pushed up oil prices, they crippled the nations that were both their customers and the custodians of their new wealth. Oil prices eventually collapsed, OPEC's investments withered, and the rest of the world reduced its energy appetite and developed alternative sources.) But my one example should suffice to illustrate the general principle: Any bold, unilateral attempt at assertiveness, launched in defiance of the intricate system that absorbs the initiative, is quite likely to rebound in distressing ways.

We cannot withdraw in fear or distaste from the Mob at the Gates; our interests are too intimately bound up with theirs. Nor can we boldly assert our will; our control over the rest of the world is too contingent and tenuous. Rather, we must recognize their interests, appreciate their power, and seek out possibilities for mutual gain. This is neither Machiavellian manipulation, nor old-style accommodation, but it bears a resemblance to both. It is a good deal more likely that the world's transformation will work in our favor if other peoples find it in their interest to share our agenda, if the allocation of the costs and gains of change are generally seen as fair.

We can neither withdraw from, nor intimidate our way out of, the challenge to adapt. Nor can we delegate authority for dealing with this joint evolution to our military strategists, our bankers, or our besieged manufacturers and farmers. These nominees are ill suited to the role. Military strategists are worried about Soviet aggression, bankers about their loan portfolios, manufacturers and farmers about their profits. Each group holds responsibility for a limited domain of international relations and has every incentive to ignore the broader damage wrought by a narrowly tough stance.

The same effects set in motion by the recent military buildup, differing only in the particulars, could be expected from America's unilateral attempts to erect stronger bulwarks against cheap foreign goods, or support any and all anticommunist insurgents and anticommunist dictators around the globe, or subsidize exports, or build a giant barrier against hostile missiles, or even drastically reduce its budget deficit. To the extent that these steps were dramatic and vigorous, undertaken without careful consultation and coordination with other nations, and designed to benefit the United States at the direct expense of others, the Boomerang Principle is likely to apply. The world has evolved beyond the point at which either assertion or isolation is a tenable option for America.

CHAPTER 5

AMERICA'S TWO COMPETITORS

1

The United States is engaged in two global contests. The first is a political rivalry with the Soviet Union. The second is an economic rivalry with Japan. The first, which began shortly after the end of World War II, involves high technology and high finance and a delicate set of alliances. The second, which began about a dozen years ago, involves high technology and high finance and an intricate set of trading relationships.

Both contests are commonly cast as "races"—an arms race with the Soviets, a race for economic preeminence with Japan. But the metaphor is not quite apt, since neither contest can ever be definitively won. The arms race can be won only in ways that are implausible (we agree to become communists or they agree to become capitalists) or unthinkable (both sides are obliterated, but the loser is obliterated first or more thoroughly). The consequences of "victory" in the economic contest, if less cataclysmic, would also be unwelcome to both sides—neither we nor the Japanese would gain if one of us decided to forget about the cars and computers and retreated to the production of novelty salt-shakers and ashtrays, for then there would be less wealth to be traded. In these two contests, both contestants either lose or win together. In the one case, a joint victory means limiting the peril and expense associated with a deep and durable ideological quarrel; in the other, a joint victory means ever more efficient production and ever more rewarding exchange. But we tend to appreciate these facts only incompletely and intermittently, and the myth of the Mob at the Gates is much at fault.

The race with Japan, rather than being a race for trade dominance, *could* be a contest for adding value to a broadly expanding world productive system. In this type of race, the faster both contestants move ahead, the more likely it is that both will win, along with the other inhabitants of the globe. As each competitor seeks to add ever more value to what it sells worldwide, the planet's wealth is enhanced. New products meet people's wants at ever lower costs.

If America could choose, it would do well to choose this contest for adding value over either the arms race with the Soviets or the mercantilist race with Japan. So far we have been able to avoid making such a choice. Until recently, we were able to perform well in all contests simultaneously, because all depended on our technological prowess. The complex weapons systems of the arms race drew upon the same body of knowledge and skills as the complex technologies of the competitiveness rare. By increasing our technological capabilities in arms, we became more effective commercial competitors. But this is coming to be less the case. The arms race with the Soviets is exacerbating a mercantilist race with Japan, and simultaneously jeopardizing our ability to add value to the goods and services we sell worldwide. This in turn is undermining our defensive capacities. The result is another application of the Boomerang Principle.

2

Americans have always loved technology. Nobody commands more respect than the maker of a beautiful machine; nobody draws more envy than its possessor. In the two decades following World War II, Americans led the world in technology. We developed or radically improved precision gadgets such as semiconductors, microprocessors, lasers, sensing devices, and the software that tell the gadgets how to perform. High technologies became the building blocks both for advanced weapons systems *and* for commercial products.

Most advances in technology evolve from what has come before. The dramatic discovery or groundbreaking invention may win a prize and bring fame to its progenitor. But such break-throughs generally have less practical effect than the gradual accretion of improvements in existing technologies. Scientists, engineers, and tinkerers of all sorts mostly progress by applying their understanding of current technologies to new problems. They rearrange old solutions in new ways, make incremental improvements in previous ways of doing things, and try out new variations on old themes. Experience—the breadth and depth of familiarity with the technological endeavor—is what determines the technological fecundity of a culture. Our ingenuity in the postwar period, so crucial to our arms and our products, was the heritage of previous technological experience. So it is now, and will continue to be in the future. Thus a great deal hinges on what extent, and toward what ends, we develop and apply our scientific and technical resources.

America's postwar technological leadership was in part a product of commercial research and development, as our companies struggled to present consumers with ever more so-phisticated televisions, refrigerators, automobiles, and other ne-cessities of American life. But much of the experience that drove continued progress—the more important portion—originated in collective efforts to do wildly ambitious things, such as build an atom bomb, construct intercontinental ballistic missiles, and get men to the moon. Large projects like these would never be un-dertaken by individual companies; they are too risky and expen-sive. The knowledge they generate, moreover, inevitably leaks out to others who have not shared in the financing. Only gov-ernments have the farsightedness or the foolishness to take on such endeavors. Consider the National Defense Education Act, the space shuttle, and the billions of dollars the government has poured into semiconductors, jet engines, composite materials, computers, robots, and advanced manufacturing systems. In the late 1950s, for example, IBM developed magnetic core memories and the solid-state calculating machine—precursors to the modern computer—while under contract to the government. The government remained for some time the major purchaser of computers, the only commercial motive for continued development. When Fairchild and Texas Instruments invented the integrated circuit in the late 1950s, few commercial purchasers could afford the $120 price. But as the government bought millions of the chips for missile guidance systems and the moon project, the industry learned how to make them much more cheaply, and commercial applications blossomed.[1] In any other nation, this governmental function would be called "technology development," and openly understood as a legitimate activity. Here, such public initiatives undertaken with the goal of economic advance per se would be ideologically suspect. We have preferred to act as if we were trying to do something else; the chips and the robots come as a pleasant bonus.

For much of the postwar era, then, our technological prowess granted us a comfortable lead in both the military and economic contests. Improvements in the technologies of the arms race (and the closely related moon race) yielded experience that helped us add commercial value to what we sold to the rest of the world.

3

In 1986 more was spent on research and development in the United States than the combined research and development spending of Britain, France, West Germany, and Japan. Ironically, in an antigovernment era, the direction of high technology in America increasingly was being planned and executed by the public sector. That year the United States government funded almost 50 percent of all research undertaken by American companies, or about twice the proportion of private research funded by the Japanese government. The U.S. government paid for two thirds of all the basic research in the country. The voices that so readily decry any hint of central government planning were, in this case, conspicuously and lamentably silent.[2]

The great bulk of government-funded research was sponsored by the Department of Defense, particularly once the great military buildup got underway. The perceived Soviet threat provoked a call to action reminiscent of that which had launched the space program after *Sputnik*. In the late 1970s, only about half of federally sponsored research was defense-related; by 1986 it was 80 percent. Research and development had become the fastest growing major category in the defense budget.[3]

Beginning in the mid-1980s a dominant factor in American technology development, and potentially the largest research and development project in our history, was the Strategic Defense Initiative, or "Star Wars." This was the Reagan administration's plan for throwing up a shield around the United States composed of ground- and space-based weapons that would destroy any intercontinental ballistic missile heading our way. The amount initially budgeted for Star Wars research was not that high relative to the nation's total research budget—the entire effort was estimated to cost $26 billion over five years—but it covered the cutting edge. Measured by the numbers of scientists and engineers required, and by the technological challenges involved, Star Wars promised to be more significant than the Manhattan Project or the Apollo moon program.

The military effects of Star Wars were distant, contingent, and in the opinion of many experts highly debatable as the program got underway. But few knowledgeable observers disputed that its technological and economic effects would be profound. The technology used to create X-ray laser weapons could be adapted to super-microscopes or machines for unblocking arteries; the know-how garnered in designing particle accelerators could be applied to irradiating food products; sensors for tracking enemy rockets could be used for commercial optics and radar. Spinoffs and applications as yet unimaginable could create whole new generations of telecommunications and computer-related products that could underpin information-processing systems in the next century. Our European allies understood these implications. They were skeptical that Star Wars would work as advertised, that it could ever scour the skies clean of Soviet rockets, and they were anxious that the program would escalate the arms race. But they were seduced into joining the effort by the prospect of picking up expertise in the technologies involved, technologies that would be important to their future economic competitiveness.[4]

The Pentagon's high-technology policy was also being driven by a worry more immediate than the prospect of a Soviet attack— the fact that Japan was clearly outpacing us in technologies that would be critical to America's capacity to wage war in an era of advanced electronics. Lest this nation become dependent on Japan's high-tech mastery, the Pentagon hastened to protect its sources. The Department of Defense set in motion an all-out mercantilist campaign to maintain leadership in these militarily significant technologies. The areas that the Pentagon targeted for development were precisely those annointed "industries of the future" by Japan's Ministry of International Trade and Industry (MITI). Both MITI and the Defense Department launched parallel projects on very large scale integrated circuits, fiber optics, new materials like polymers and composite materials, super computers, and complex software. Japan was somewhat baffled as we denounced industrial targeting while enthusiastically engaging in it. But we insisted we were racing against the *other* guy; it was more or less a matter of coincidence that Japan shared the same track.

4

By the mid-1980s, however, the race courses had begun to diverge. The strands of technological development central to defense and industry no longer coincided so closely, and differences in final goals (MITI, concerned about commercial competitiveness; the Pentagon, concerned about industrial prowess only where relevant to weaponry) began leading to different results. America had a finite number of technical experts and laboratories, the supply of which grew only modestly in response to the surge in Pentagon dollars. Beyond that point, military research came at the expense of commercial research. Our fixation on technology to thwart the Soviets started to undermine our efforts to create commercial high-technology products that could compete successfully with the Japanese. The divergence was becoming clear in several ways:

First, the development and marketing of new commercial products is stimulated by domestic competition, which forces firms to improve their performance and aggressively seek foreign outlets. Although MITI allowed firms to cooperate on specific basic research projects, it rigidly enforced competition in the application of these technologies and the marketing of the products that resulted. The Pentagon was unconcerned about competition within American industry. Between 1981 and 1984— during the height of the most recent military buildup—America's top five arms contractors increased their share of total Pentagon contracts from 18 percent to 22 percent; the top twenty-five, from 44 percent to 52 percent.[5] In 1985 over 65 percent of the dollar volume of U.S. defense contracts was awarded without competitive bidding.[6] Most military projects called for such highly specialized items and services that the only contractors capable of supplying them were those that had worked on the same or related projects before. Even where competitive bidding occurred, the bids were often rendered meaningless by routine cost overruns. The Pentagon traditionally has been most comfortable with large, stable contractors insulated from the uncertainties of competition.

Second, creating new products successfully requires long lead times, during which firms can refine innovations, organize production, and make sure they have adequate capital, labor, and productive capacity to meet anticipated demand. Many MITI projects have spanned a decade or more. But by the 1980s most Pentagon programs were subject to relatively sudden changes in politics and in perceptions of national security needs. The precipitous rise in U.S. defense spending beginning in 1981 created bottlenecks in the production of some key subcomponents and capital goods, and shortages of engineers and scientists. In 1985 unfulfilled defense orders totaled over $100 billion—up 20 percent from 1984. And there was a shortage of an estimated 30,000 skilled machinists.[7] Under these constraints, commercial applications took second place.

Third, technological competitiveness requires that innova-

71

tions be transferable to commercial uses at relatively low cost. MITI has seen to it that new technologies are diffused rapidly into the economy and incorporated into commercial products. But the exquisitely sophisticated designs required by Star Wars and its related ventures—precision-guided warheads, advanced missile-tracking equipment, and sensing devices—would not be as transferable to commercial uses as were the relatively more primitive technologies, like the first integrated circuit, produced during the defense and aerospace programs of the late 1950s and 1960s. Indeed, it was because commercial technologies were diverging from military specifications that the Defense Department had opted to set up a parallel research and development system to ensure the availability of precisely the right customized gadgets. Rather than encourage American commercial development, defense spending on emerging high technologies was starting to have the opposite effect, diverting U.S. scientists and engineers away from commercial applications.

Fourth, new technologies generally become commercially important only when they become cheap to produce. Nearly every major advance of modern times lay economically dormant for a time after its development because it was too costly to find a wide market. The effort to bring down production costs can be as lengthy and difficult, and fully as important, as the initial development of a new technology. But the Pentagon is notably unconcerned about costs. It wants its high-technology devices to do what they are supposed to do, and damn the expense. Thus the innovation process is truncated; to the extent the military is involved, progress ceases before the cost-reducing stage is reached. Most big contractors with the Pentagon are paid on a "cost-plus" basis—with profits rising in pace with how much they spend producing a particular item. This formula does not inspire grand campaigns for production efficiency.

The Pentagon drew much unwelcome attention in the mid-1980s for its willingness to pay large sums for, among other items, an esoteric toilet. Such extravagance is not, as many charged at the time, the product of bureaucratic lethargy or indifference alone. It is due to something more insidious. The gadgets that the Pentagon commissioned had to be designed exactly for the complicated weapons systems in which they would fit; any small deviation, and the larger project might fail. There were no economies of scale in producing such devices. If specifications were sufficiently standardized for cheap, large-scale production, then anyone—including the Soviets, or people willing to sell to the Soviets—could make the components. Both parties to Pentagon contracts were eager to avoid that result—the Pentagon, because standard parts might imperil national security; contractors, because standardization and competition would most certainly imperil their balance sheets.

Consumers, on the other hand, prefer to buy things cheaply. Consumers do not like to be limited to a single supplier who is guaranteed a profit no matter how inefficient his production process. This is why we have capitalism. Firms making products in competitive markets must worry about their costs of production. The Japanese have mastered the art of embedding complex technologies in standardized products; American producers of complex technologies—many of them lured into somnolency by Pentagon contracts—have not.

Fifth, and finally, commercial success requires that producers be exposed to stiff international competition, so that they are forced (under penalty of extinction) to pay careful attention to what consumers around the world want, and constantly innovate in that direction. But the Pentagon increasingly has sheltered American companies from the risks of global competition. To avoid the possibility that we would become too dependent on foreign producers, the Pentagon buys American versions. ("Buy American" provisions, written into most procurement regulations, stipulate that American products be chosen so long as their prices are not more than 50 percent higher than foreign sources.) In recent years, whenever an American industry has been threatened by foreign competition—even if the industry (like footwear) is only tangentially involved in defense work—it has sounded the same alarm: Protect us, or the nation's defense will be imperiled.

Apart from occasional meddling by Congress or the press, the life of a Pentagon contractor is not a harried one. The Japanese pose no threat. There is little possibility that a competitor's innovations will render a product obsolete. Profits are guaranteed. Once sampled, such a life is almost irresistible, like a narcotic drug. By 1986 America's preeminent technology companies were exchanging the inconveniences of commerce for this more comfortable existence. Honeywell gave up on commercial computers and began concentrating on items like torpedoes and defense navigation devices. TRW was shifting out of bearings and tools, where foreign competition was stiff, and into defense electronics (in 1980 defense contracts provided 30 percent of its profits; by 1985, 50 percent). General Motors had acquired Hughes Aircraft, a major defense contractor, and was working on a wide variety of military contracts. Sixty percent of Westinghouse's profits came from defense electronics. And by acquiring RCA, GE had become America's sixth largest defense contractor, with 20 percent of its sales being to the military (in 1980, military sales had accounted for no more than 10 percent of either firm's income).[8] America's technology companies were busily withdrawing from the race with Japan.

5

There was also the matter of secrecy.

Experience in developing new technologies must be shared if it is to be put to use. Few scientists, engineers, or tinkerers have all the experience they need, firsthand. High technologies are sufficiently complex that those who seek to improve them must work with others close by, typically in teams. Even the teams must branch out to other teams, so that a wider network of ideas and insights can be exchanged informally, constantly. This ongoing form of exchange is what builds a Silicon Valley or a Route 128 around Boston. It generates social wealth.

What must be shared is not "information," in the sense of specific data or designs. It is more like gossip—a continuous discussion about ongoing activities. The value of sharing comes in the resulting accumulation of different approaches and results.

It comes in the development of common understandings about what technologies might "work" to solve what sorts of problems, and in wider insights into what current technologies can do and how they can be improved and adapted. Through such informal sharing of experiences, scientists and engineers learn from one another how they might do things differently next time. By contrast, mere "information," in the form of specific data or blueprints, is relatively useless for designing future generations of technology. It may solve an immediate technological problem, but it does not provide experience for solving the next one. It does not *teach*.

This distinction between sharing experience and providing information is an important one. It has been lost on the Pentagon. Defense officials worry incessantly that the Soviets will get information about our advanced technologies. But the Pentagon's increasing attempts to block access have only made it more difficult for American scientists and engineers to share experience with one another. Here again, the two racecourses have begun to diverge: In seeking to prevent Soviet access to our high-technology information, we have stifled our own high-technology learning.

By the mid-1980s the Pentagon was casting a veil of secrecy over a great deal of American research. Star Wars offered a pretext. Never before had America entrusted so much technological development to the Pentagon in so short a time, and in such a clandestine manner. A handful of Pentagon officials were preempting scientific resources and picking winners and losers of the technology race. Most decisions were made in secret. While there would be public debate about the wisdom of Star Wars as a defense strategy, there would be none among scientists, engineers, or politicians about the implications of these decisions for our economic future.

When the Japanese have targeted certain emerging technologies, decisions about which ones deserve advantageous treatment have been arrived at consensually, through ongoing conversations among trading companies, industry groups, and government analysts. But the Pentagon was never a model of decision making by consensus. The Pentagon's proposed budget for fiscal 1987 included $8.6 billion for research specified only by unintelligible code words. Thus about 5 percent of all the research to be undertaken in the United States, in both private and public sectors, would remain shrouded in mystery.[9]

Ever more research was classified as secret. A 1985 executive order made it relatively easy to classify documents without considering the public's need to know. Even unclassified research was being controlled. Under another ruling, the secretary of defense was authorized to stop disclosure of about a fifth of the unclassified technological research done under Pentagon contracts. In addition, the Pentagon and other government agencies were routinely insisting that they had the right to review university-based research before the results were published in scientific journals; they included prepublication-review clauses in their research contracts, classified as secret academic research already completed, and pulled scientific papers from academic conferences.[10]

The net result of this activity has been difficult to measure because so much of that which might be measured is, after all, secret. But few would contend that the Soviets have had any great difficulty obtaining whatever information they have sought about our latest weapons. Because so much of our high technology involves software and microelectronic circuitry, information can be smuggled out on minuscule tapes, intercepted through the airwaves, or simply transferred via satellite from a computer here to one there. The art of espionage has progressed far beyond suitcases filled with blueprints and exotic machinery.

While they probably have obtained the information they want, however, the Soviets have not obtained the experience on which it is based. This is a critical distinction. Shared experience cannot easily be purchased—not even in the open market through the merger or acquisition of a whole company (as some corporate raiders have discovered, too late). At most, the Soviets have been able to discover what we are building. This may have enabled them to gain an equal footing with us in some technologies for a short time, until we have made the next improvement.

The Soviets are the victims of their own success in this regard. Ironically, the more information they steal from us, the more difficult it becomes for their own scientists and engineers to garner valued experience, because the latest American designs preempt any invention on their part. The information supplies them with the answers, so there is no reason for them to learn how to find the answers (or, more subtly, the questions) for themselves. It is like trying to learn to solve puzzles with the answer book open in front of you, or learning directions from here to there as a passenger rather than a driver. The ready availability of help substitutes for direct experience, and thereby inhibits new learning. Without such experience, the Soviets have less capacity to make their own improvements on state-of-the-art technologies. Thus they are forever catching up. Had we set out consciously to ensure that the Soviets could never challenge our technological superiority, we could have come up with few better plans than to leak to them, steadily, our latest secrets.[11]

The irony is richer than that, however, because our secrecy has reduced our own capacity to gain collective experience, and thereby to innovate for the future. It is only through constant innovations over existing technologies that we can maintain our position in either race.

6

Thus the Boomerang Principle is at work. For our ability to maintain peace and deter aggression depends, fundamentally, on our overall prosperity, and that of others around the globe; the resources and commitments that national defense requires over the long term can be sustained only amid a growing and buoyant economy. Unlike the military and diplomatic contest that preoccupies our foreign policy, or the related mercantilist contest in products related to defense, the contest in commercial high technology can pay a dividend to the rest of the world in the form of better products at lower costs. It is also crucial to our long-term security. But in our preoccupation with the other races, this is the one race we (and consequently others) may lose.

CHAPTER 6

THE RISE OF THE JAPANESE-AMERICAN CORPORATION

1

The mythology that informs both popular opinion and congressional deliberation depicts America and Japan competing on a clearly delineated economic playing field. On the one side are Japanese corporations, aided by their government. On the other, American corporations, handicapped by theirs. The National Chamber of Commerce and other boosters of American business typically complain that the playing field is tilted, to Japan's advantage. The Mob at the Gates does not play the game fairly. To even things up, it is argued, their government must stop subsidizing and protect them. And ours must relax the antitrust laws, corporate taxes, and regulatory burdens that shackle American companies. In the mid-1980s American politicians of all stripes were threatening to close off the American market to Japanese goods unless Japan stopped "cheating." The Reagan administration, meanwhile, was busily dismantling the supposed impediments to American business.

This view is misleading in two central respects. First, as already suggested, America is by no means an exemplar of laissez faire. The United States government has been, if anything, rather more involved in technological development than has the Japanese government, although from the perspective of commercial competitiveness this involvement, by and large, has been perverse in recent years. Nor has the sin of protectionism been solely or even primarily a Japanese failing. The Japanese have deliberately limited imports of tobacco, beef, and baseball bats; cumbersome procedures have limited some other imports. But in several major areas of trade—automobiles, steel, textiles, services, and high technologies—American import barriers have been considerably higher than Japan's. Thus while the economic playing field is far from flat and open, this is not simply because "they" have been cheating.

The metaphor of America's corporate champions sallying forth to heroic (if rigged) battle is flawed in a more fundamental way, however. It rests on the presumption that the economic prospects of the United States are so tightly linked to the prospects of American-based firms as to amount to the same thing. Perhaps this premise was once tenable; it no longer is. By the mid-1980s, in the most competitive fields of endeavor, there were ever-fewer companies that could be considered uniquely "American" in resources, orientation, or loyalties. Trade competition across the Pacific was on the way to being dominated by one type of player. Sometimes it went by a Japanese name, sometimes by an American. It took several forms. Occasionally American firms linked up with their former rivals in joint ventures and purchase agreements. Or Japanese companies bought up American companies, or built new plants in the United States, employing American workers. Or American companies built plants in Japan, hiring Japanese. Regardless of form, the result was approximately the same—a transpacific entity, neither solely Japanese nor solely American, but something in between: a Japanese-American corporation.

If increasing global economic integration is both desirable and inevitable, one would think this is a welcome trend, and it is, to the extent that the rise of the Japanese-American corporation reduces the propensity of either America or Japan to seek advantage at the direct expense of the other (an effort that I have already suggested is likely to render both sides worse off). But the trend is less desirable if, as has been the case, it simultaneously reduces the willingness of Americans to develop our own skills and capacities.

The emerging Japanese-American corporation is problematic in this regard, for although it invests diligently in the skills of Japanese workers, it tends to shortchange American workers. As we shall observe, this is not because of any nefarious motive on the part of the Japanese; it is rather a function of the different ethical and economic premises they bring to corporate activity. The Japanese part of the Japanese-American corporation is dedicated to enhancing the wealth and influence of everyone associated with the firm; the American part, to enhancing the wealth of its shareholders (and top executives). The Japanese-American corporation will provide Americans with jobs, to be sure, but not with the training they need to keep pace with the new world economy. The image of trade competition as mostly a matter of rivalry *between* Japanese and American companies blinds us to this fundamental dilemma and the question it raises—who will attend to the long-term development of the American work force?

2

The case of Houdaille Industries offers an illustration.[1] This Florida-based manufacturer of computer-controlled machine tools set out in 1982 to block imports of competing Japanese tools. The company followed the prescribed route, guided by a prominent Washington law firm. It first petitioned the U.S. government for protection, accusing the Japanese machine toolmakers of dumping their wares here at prices below their production costs, with government subsidies making up the difference. That strategy failed for lack of evidence, despite the efforts of a Houdaille agent who prowled around Japanese machine tool factories with a video camera seeking signs of unfair government assistance. Next, Houdaille tried to persuade the Reagan administration to deny to American buyers of Japanese machine tools the 10 percent investment tax credit on equipment. After a bitter split in the administration over what to do, Japanese Prime Minister Yasuhiro Nakasone personally sought President Reagan's assurance that the company's request would be denied. Undaunted, Houdaille then made the rounds of the Defense Department and Congress, arguing that its own continued profitability was critical to national security.

When this last ploy failed, Houdaille abruptly changed course. In the spring of 1984 it announced that it would seek a joint venture with Japan's Okuma Machinery Works. Okuma would supply Houdaille with ready-made machine tools, which Houdaille would then market and distribute in the United States under its own trademark. "If we can't beat them," a company spokesman told *The New York Times*, "we'll joint venture with them." The new strategy might boost Houdaille's lagging profits, at least in the short term. It might even preserve some American jobs. But it brought to a halt one stream of domestic economic endeavor. American workers would no longer be developing this set of skills; competence in designing and making machine tools would be permanently surrendered.

By 1986 almost every American industry with a history of bitter conflict with Japan was showing sudden signs of born-again cooperation. Trade names were becoming irrelevant for distinguishing Japanese from American products. General Motors was buying diesel engines and subcompacts from Isuzu, and making cars in California jointly with Toyota; most of the robots and computerized machine tools it used to assemble its cars also came from Japan. Chrysler was getting many of its transaxles, engines, and subcompacts from Mitsubishi; Ford bought key parts from Mazda. Kodak's copiers were made by Canon; Kodak's 8-millimeter video cameras, by Matsushita, which was also supplying General Electric with televisions, disk players, and air conditioners. Honeywell's computers were manufactured by NEC, and the list goes on.[2]

Meanwhile, Japanese factories were beginning to dot the American landscape. Honda was making cars in Ohio; Mazda, in Michigan; Mitsubishi Motors, in Illinois; Nissan, trucks in Tennessee. (All told, Japanese automakers expected to build more than 1 million vehicles in the United States by 1990.) Hitachi was producing large-scale disk drives in Oklahoma and semiconductors in Dallas. Hundreds of Japanese high-tech companies were setting up shop in Oregon and California, assembling everything from personal computers to cellular mobile telephones. The locations of corporate headquarters said little about national orientation. IBM's top executives inhabited offices in Armonk, New York. But 10 percent of IBM's employees were Japanese, living in Japan, and a growing percentage of their officers and directors were non-American. And IBM was producing most of the computers exported out of Japan.[3]

Ownership was becoming blurred as well. In 1986 Ford owned one quarter of Mazda; Chrysler, almost one quarter of Mitsubishi. Kodak, 10 percent of Chinon. Nippon Kokan, Japan's second biggest steel maker, had a controlling interest in National Steel, and a 40 percent stake in Martin Marietta's California metals operations. As securities markets around the world became more closely integrated, private investors worldwide bought stocks based on profit expectations rather than nationality. Between 1980 and 1985, U.S. institutional investors increased their holdings of foreign stocks more than fivefold, from $3 billion to $16 billion.[4]

That Japan and the United States have been engaged in a heated contest over trade there can be no doubt. But by the close of the 1980s it was becoming ever more difficult to say which companies were representing which side. Company names, affixed to final products or displayed over factory gates and headquarters, or even engraved on stock certificates, revealed less and less about which nation's work force was actually doing what. Studies purporting to show relative market shares of Japanese and American companies in a given industry were equally beside the point. But of this there could be little question: no longer was the "American" corporation doing business across the Pacific the obvious custodian of America's long-term economic well-being.

3

The rise of the Japanese-American corporation could be explained, in part, by the new requirements of global competition.

In years past, large corporations in one nation often maintained subsidiaries in other nations. These subsidiaries were largely independent of their parent. They typically designed, manufactured and marketed their goods exclusively within their adopted country. They were like any other national company, except that a portion of their profits periodically were shipped back to their foreign parent. In the 1960s the Ford Motor Company had subsidiaries in Latin America, Australia, and all over Europe. In general, each produced a different line of cars; English Fords resembled American Fords in name only.

These subsidiaries prided themselves on being good corporate citizens of their adopted nations. They were run by citizens of the host country; they employed local workers; they sought to appeal to local tastes. Most people who consumed their products had little idea that these companies were answerable to foreign managers; when they were aware, they probably did not much care. There was no reason to.[5]

This changed when the trends we have already examined converged in the 1970s. First, the costs of sending goods and information around the globe dropped dramatically. This made it possible for the production of an item to be fragmented and parceled out to wherever each function could be undertaken most cheaply, and then routed to central locations for assembly. Second, the technologies of making things improved to such an extent that vast economies of scale became possible: The greater the number of identical units that could be produced at any particular location, the lower the cost of making each one. Third, the tastes of consumers around the world began to grow more alike.

Taken together, these trends meant that self-contained subsidiaries no longer made economic sense. For many industries, it was far more efficient to integrate the entire production process globally, with each subsidiary specializing in producing whichever part or service it could provide most easily. Many of the services associated with marketing and distributing would still, of necessity, be undertaken wherever the goods were to be sold. But even here there might be opportunities for global specialization and economies of scale, as in the provision of shipping containers, global warehousing, advertising, and insurance.

This phenomenon was not unique to the relationship between Japan and the United States, of course. Regardless of whose nameplates graced their exteriors, the trend was for automobiles, heavy equipment, computers, robots, esoteric electronic gadgets, not to mention the services associated with them (design, fabrication, sales, marketing, distribution, maintenance, and so on) to become multinational creations. By 1986 Ford was manufacturing a Mazda-designed car in Mexico, for sale around the world; AT&T was making its semiconductors in Spain, to be used in communications equipment assembled in Brazil for worldwide distribution. Consider the extent of this trend: As exports from America became a decreasing share of global trade, exports shipped by corporations *based* in America actually increased their share. Quite apart from the rise of the Japanese-American corporation, it was reasonable to suppose that by the close of the century neither General Motors cars nor IBM computers nor AT&T communications equipment would bear any special relationship to the United States. One would no longer be able to speak with pride, or concern, or any meaningful emotion at all, about "American" products.

4

In addition to this worldwide tendency, the special nature of the Japanese-American company has been shaped by certain unique concerns. Foremost has been Japan's desire to forestall U.S. trade barriers. If the Reagan administration succumbed so readily to protectionism, what about a future administration less ideologically committed to free trade?

How, then, to forestall American protectionism? By doing an end run around the borders. The strategy had two aspects. First, it was necessary to enter into supply contracts with American companies; second, to build new factories in the United States. In both respects, American workers would get jobs assembling Japanese components and then selling the finished goods to their fellow countrymen. Americans would become partners in Japanese enterprise. As a result, it was thought, the two nations would become a single, integrated, transpacific production system. There would be less demand for trade protection, because there would be less to protect.

By the mid-1980s the strategy was already bearing fruit. Corporations that were technically "American," but which had developed close relationships with Japanese suppliers and joint venturers, were steadfastly opposing tariffs and quotas on Japanese imports. Such devices would drive up the costs of their supplies. General Motors, IBM, GE, Kodak, and even Houdaille Industries could be counted on to support free trade. Also on the side of unrestricted trade were certain congressional districts in Ohio, Tennessee, North Carolina, California, and Oregon, where Japanese firms had set up manufacturing operations. Even the United Auto Workers were enthusiastic about the General Motors–Toyota joint venture in California, because it preserved American jobs.

The strategy had a second advantage for the Japanese. In supplying American companies with key components or entire products, to which the Americans thereafter affixed their trademarks and distributed as their own, the Japanese created a captive market for their wares. And they gained an inexpensive method of distributing them. This meant that the Japanese could negotiate large contracts, wholesale. The costs and vagaries of retailing could be avoided. Risks, accordingly, could be reduced.

From the viewpoint of the Japanese, these advantages were worth paying for. American corporations that have linked up with the Japanese have thus received attractive terms. American towns that have welcomed Japanese manufacturers have gained good corporate citizens. By the late 1980s the new Japanese-American corporation seemed to be serving both nations well. Or was it?

5

The Japanese strategy has benefited Japan in a third but more important way. It is here that Americans might appropriately be

concerned, because these benefits have not been entirely reciprocal.

Look closely at these new joint ventures and transnational
investments. There has been a pattern to them. Basic research
leading to initial product design continues to be carried out in
the United States. Then the specific design and production of the
most complex parts and sophisticated assemblies has occurred
in Japan. Back in America workers have put the final pieces together. And a different group of American workers has distributed, marketed, and sold the products to other Americans. In
other words, Americans have taken charge of the two ends of the
production process—the major research innovations and the final
assembly and sales. The Japanese have concentrated on the complex production in between, where large numbers of workers gain
technological and organizational competence.

Consider: Through the mid-1980s breakthroughs in chip design continued to occur in the United States. University-based
researchers and Pentagon contractors devised ways of cramming
ever more memory, logic, or speed into ever smaller spaces. But
the Japanese were better at producing the chips cheaply and reliably. So the Japanese licensed the designs and made them there.
American computer manufacturers (Honeywell, Sperry, Amdahl)
began linking up with Japanese semiconductor makers to get the
advanced chips they needed for their computers. At the same
time, American chip makers began setting up production facilities in Japan, to be managed and staffed by Japanese. The semiconductors that the Japanese started to fabricate in the United
States represented only the most standardized segment of that
market, for which all the jobs were relatively routine.[6]

It has been the same in automobiles. The new Japanese-
American auto company (regardless of whether its name is General Motors or Honda) has been making its engines, transaxles,
and complex electronic parts in Japan, along with most of the
robots and computer-controlled machines for putting the parts
together, and then assembling and selling the results in the United
States. The trend was particularly apparent in the production of
the smallest cars, which must be designed and manufactured

especially carefully in order to minimize costs and maximize comfort. As the Japanese have learned in producing everything from televisions to semiconductors, innovations in products and manufacturing processes often occur at the most compact end of a product line, where the engineering challenges are the greatest. For the same reason, development expenses often are highest at the compact end. But as part of a strategy for gaining experience in applying new technologies, the Japanese gladly bear these costs; the investment will pay off in a work force better able to innovate in the future.

It has been the same in telecommunications. The breakthroughs have continued to occur in the United States—particularly within universities and defense annexes. But the complex applications occurred in Japan. Regardless of whose nameplates appeared on the new private-branch exchanges, cellular telephones, and optic-fiber cables sold in America, a large proportion of their sophisticated innards were Japanese. It has been the same in consumer electronic products like videocassette recorders, compact disks, and audio disk players; the same for facsimile equipment, large-scale integrated circuits, and sensing devices. Even the steel mills that the Japanese have built or modernized in the United States got their advanced steel-making machinery from Japan.

6

Comparative advantage is among the most venerated of economic precepts. It boils down to the dictum that nations should stick to what they do best. To entrust the Japanese with turning our big discoveries into complicated components would by this view be eminently sensible. Japanese workers have been willing, on average, to work harder and for somewhat lower pay than their American counterparts. And Japanese production has been more efficient than the American, particularly with regard to the design, fabrication, and manufacture of complex equipment.[7] Americans have made money from transferring our Big Ideas to them.

They have made money by selling them back to us encased within terrific products and parts.

What is left out of this calculation is the value of *experience*. As has been noted, the accumulation of experience in designing and making new things is critical for improving upon them. The emerging Japanese-American corporation allocates to the Japanese the most important asset for the future—experience in making complex products cheaply and well. They learn how to organize themselves for production—integrating design, fabrication, and manufacturing; using computers to enhance their skills; developing new flexibility; creating new blends of advanced goods and services. They learn how to make the kinds of small, incremental improvements in production processes and products that can make all the difference in price, quality, and marketability. In short, they develop the collective capacity to transform raw ideas quickly into world-class products.

Such experience in *making* things is crucial for generating social wealth—in some ways more important even than the activities at either end of the production process, like invention or marketing and sales. Production experience tends to give large numbers of workers skills that have value in global markets. These skills can be applied generally, across all kinds of goods and services—not just the latest inventions. An entire nation benefits from having a large pool of workers who understand emerging technologies and can improve upon them.

By contrast, the activities at the two ends of the production process either involve relatively few workers, or else entail skills that have little value in trade. Only a comparatively few people gain experience inventing the new technologies to begin with. Basic inventions do not raise the overall level of skills in a society, nor do they generate broad experience. They do not lead to the kind of day-to-day improvements in a host of products and processes, across an entire economy, that can only come from a work force broadly engaged with the latest technologies. Basic inventions do of course yield improvements, but these are easily disseminated in blueprints, codes, and instructions—reaching Seoul almost as soon as they reach St. Louis. The jobs at the other end of the production process—routine assembly, marketing, and sales—may involve many workers, but most of these jobs do not teach skills that contribute much to a global economy. Many low-skilled assembly operations will be automated in years to come, or else done by workers in less developed nations at a fraction of the cost. Jobs in marketing and selling to one's fellow citizens are largely sheltered from international trade. (Knowledge about the tastes and needs of one's compatriots has worldwide value only to the extent that these compatriots are wealthy enough to purchase things from the rest of the world.)

The Japanese well understand this dynamic. That is why they place priority upon production experience rather than basic invention or final assembly and sales. Their overriding goal is to raise the competence of their work force in complex production. Complex products relying on advanced microelectronics, lightweight synthetic materials, sophisticated aerodynamics, or biomolecular manipulation are launchpads for gaining skill and experience in the world's newest technologies. Attaining immediate profits from these products (and related services) is less important to Japan than becoming a large and experienced world practitioner of the advanced methods that lie behind them.

7

There is a temptation to depict this as a plot through which the Japanese intend to emerge in a decade or so with the world's most skilled work force, and the highest potential standard of living. But there is nothing particularly sinister about all this. As has been suggested, this sort of race for adding value can be entirely benign—and would be, but for the skewed distribution of production skills that has been the particular consequence of the Japanese-American corporation. Production experience does not come in a fixed quantity, to be divided between Japanese and American workers. Both societies would be better off if both work forces learned how to devise higher-quality products at ever lower costs. For then each nation would have more to offer the other, with the result that both would enjoy even larger gains.

For us to blame the Japanese misplaces the responsibility. The problem lies not with *them*, but with *us*. American-based companies (or the American parts of Japanese-American corporations) could invest in more sophisticated production in the United States, developing in our work force the same base of technological competence and organizational experience that Japan is creating among Japanese workers. To do so would require broad sacrifices and commitments of the sort we are not accustomed to make or to demand of one another. I will discuss this point further in a later chapter.

Nor can the responsibility rest solely with American corporate executives. They have been performing exactly as they are meant to perform. We can safely assume that the vast majority of our executives are patriotic and care about the future of their country. Their primary responsibility, however, is to enhance the wealth of their shareholders—not to enhance the technological competence of the American work force. When these two goals conflict—because, for example, it is cheaper to buy advanced components ready-made from the Japanese than to build them here—our executives must opt for the shareholders. This is their legal duty. If they failed to do so, they could be sued, or taken over. These are the incentives we build into our capitalist system.

Telling our mythic tale of trade competition with Japan as if it depended on the relative prowess of Japanese and American corporations, with the help or hindrance of their respective governments, has distracted us from looking at the prowess of the American work force—and its capacity to add value to an increasingly international system of production. Once again, in focusing on a putative Mob at our Gates, we have neglected to address questions concerning reciprocal obligations and mutual benefits underlying our political economy. In this case, what is the responsibility of corporations doing business here—and of their various constituents—for investing in the future competence of Americans? How can American capitalism elicit this investment from them? Until we ask, we are unlikely to find satisfactory answers.

CHAPTER 7

LOCKING THE GATES

1

In the third century B.C., the Emperor Shih Huang Ti commenced the building of a wall along China's northwest border to seal off the Middle Kingdom from marauding nomads. Five hundred years later, Hadrian tried the same approach in England. A thousand years later the same solution was invoked by the lords of medieval Europe to keep out bandits and armies. In this century, the French built a fortified wall along their border with Germany. It is not a particularly new idea. The instinct to define and defend a safe bit of territory, secure against evil forces, runs deep in the species. High walls and tightly locked gates give palpable evidence of security. The bounded area, at least, is safe. So long as we stay within it, we feel invulnerable.

Most people who now inhabit the planet have been forced to give up this idea as a realistic goal. They are too often reminded of their dependence upon, and vulnerability to, others beyond their borders. Rather than raising their walls higher, they have had to take joint responsibility for managing sometimes difficult relationships across borders—helping to avoid joint losses, seeking joint gains. But in America, a land historically and geographically cut off from the rest, where we tell one another stories that celebrate self-reliance and warn of evils "out there," Americans cherish the dream of invulnerability.

When threatened, our instinct is to raise the walls higher and lock the gates tighter. When cocaine and other noxious chemicals began coursing into America, the primary response was to fortify our perimeters. Narcotics agents used paramilitary techniques to eradicate drug crops, interrupt supply routes, and seize contraband at the border. When inexpensive imports of steel, automobiles, televisions, and computer chips imperiled American jobs, demands arose for protection. Tariffs and quotas guarded the borders. When America's vulnerability to sudden rises in the price of foreign oil became apparent in the wake of the Arab oil embargo, the reflexive solution was "Project Independence"—a plan to free America from the need to import any oil at all. When what had been a stream of illegal immigrants turned into a flood by the late 1970s, a chorus of American voices demanded that we regain "control of our borders." Border patrol agents became more aggressive in capturing foreigners trying to enter illegally from Mexico; immigration officials, more ruthless in ferreting out aliens who had sneaked through or overstayed their visas. When we looked for a way to become less vulnerable to Soviet missiles in the mid-1980s, we came up with a variation on the same theme: The Reagan administration set out to build a wall in the sky.

2

The dream of invulnerability has led us to concentrate our efforts on warding off outside perils, often at the expense of tending to perils within. It is always easier to feel righteous than responsible. Consider cocaine. In the early 1980s the Reagan administration launched a major offensive against international drug trafficking. The effort involved the State Department, CIA, FBI, IRS, Drug Enforcement Administration, the Agency for International Development, and the military. Third World governments were cajoled or coerced into cooperating. The administration obtained legislation allowing military personnel and equipment to be used in the assault. Enforcers resorted to all the techniques of modern warfare—spies, informants, fancy electronics, armored vehicles, helicopters. It was a costly business: In 1985 the United States spent over $1.2 billion trying to stop illegal drugs from entering the country. The effort also cost the lives of several Andean peasants, drug runners, and narcotics agents in the field. It jeopardized American relations with Mexico and other Latin American nations whom we periodically accused of harboring drug traffickers.[1]

There is no question that drugs such as cocaine are dangerous. By defining our problem primarily as one of intercepting these substances before they get here, however, responsibility for controlling the poisoning was delegated to border patrols and foreign governments. The evil was declared external. The mythology of a Mob at the Gates led us to neglect the growing drug appetite of our citizens until it became overwhelmingly, painfully clear. By 1985, according to government estimates, one out of ten Americans had experimented with cocaine. Five million used it regularly. Twenty percent of all high school students had tried it at least once. Usage was not limited to central cities and marginal populations. It was endemic in the American middle class. All told, it was estimated that Americans were spending about $110 billion a year to buy illegal drugs. Sales were climbing over 10 percent a year.[2] With Americans willing and able to pay such sums to muddle their minds, no strategy to wreck the trade could be expected to succeed. Capitalism is a sturdy institution; enterprising drug traffickers are only slightly deterred by border patrols and helicopter gunships when so lucrative a market beckons. In 1985 twice as much cocaine found its way to America than five years previously.[3]

Drugs are at least half *our* problem. A fixation on the evil threatening our shores diverted our attention from this unsettling fact. As we pledged our resources to guarding the gates, we placed less emphasis on controlling our internal drug habit. While we were railing against foreigners, our own Department of Education's budget for drug-prevention and education programs was reduced from $14 million in 1981—an already paltry sum—to

$2.9 million in 1985; over the same period, federal funds for prevention and treatment of drug and alcohol abuse declined 20 percent. (In late 1986, when the problem suddenly became the object of frantic political activity, more money was appropriated for education and treatment, but the sum was still dwarfed by what we spent trying to guard the gates.)[4]

3

Consider a different sort of import, viewed as a menace by many American workers: cheap foreign goods. Americans employed making textiles, steel, and automobiles are understandably concerned that their jobs may vanish. Many already have. Defense officials worry about the nation's dependence on foreign sources of materials and technologies. Nearly everyone remains uncomfortable about our dependence on foreigners for oil. But here again, the indictment is delivered to *them*. Many of us vaguely consider foreigners at fault for shipping us all this stuff and not buying enough of our own exports. Japanese and Third World producers are said to be "stealing our jobs." They are "flooding our market" with their wares. We are being had, somehow. The apparent solution: Coerce them into holding back their wares to us and buying more of ours, and threaten them that if they won't, we will put up higher barriers and close our gates more tightly.

Our attention, accordingly, is focused on enforcement. Sometimes we catch them trying to circumvent our quotas by transshipping goods through a third country.[5] Sometimes we catch them "dumping" their goods in America at prices below their costs of production. American trade laws explicitly prohibit this and give the injured American producer an automatic remedy (in the form of fees added on to the price of the imported product).[6] This has become a popular avenue of redness for every distressed American industry. American semiconductor manufacturers, onetime champions of freer world trade, joined in during 1985, charging the Japanese with dumping their chips here. The terminology summons the image of a garbage truck pulling up to our shores, tilting its bed, and unloading on us. How dare they!

There remains, though, the disconcerting facts that Americans *want* to buy goods cheaply and can't make them as cheaply as can foreigners. If we did not have such an overwhelming desire for Japanese cars or South Korean steel or Taiwanese shirts, the problem would not exist. Inexpensive goods from abroad may cause some of us to lose our jobs or to feel nervously dependent on foreign producers. But such unpleasantness has not dampened our enthusiasm. Americans are delighted to buy "dumped" goods; we know them under the less pejorative term of "bargains." Nor is it particularly useful to rail at "them" for failing to buy more of our products, or to threaten them if they don't start to. There are few things more intransigent than an uninterested consumer. Not even a Japanese prime minister can motivate Japanese consumers to spend more and get less by buying American.

Our vulnerability to foreign traders is real, and not without costs. But even if it were physically or politically possible to block foreign-made goods from entering the country, the price would be appalling, for we would then have to make everything for ourselves. Robinson Crusoe's experiment in self-sufficiency entailed obvious inconvenience. Richard Nixon's "Project Independence," designed to free us from dependence on foreign oil supplies by 1980, came to nought: In 1980 the United States was importing roughly the same portion of the oil it consumed (37 percent) as it had in 1973. Independence simply was too expensive: There was no going back to the near self-sufficiency of the early postwar years.

To the extent that there is a problem, then, it exists at home. If foreigners can do something better and more cheaply, then we had best learn to do it as well, or learn to do something else that they cannot so easily rival. If they are willing to sacrifice profits now for the sake of larger profits in the future, then we had better make similar sacrifices if we hope to stay in the game. It is as simple, and as difficult, as that.

4

The problem of illegal immigration is analogous. In the mid-1980s the United States harbored an estimated 4 million illegals, and the number continued to grow at a rapid clip.[7] In the popular mind the fault lies with the immigrants and their countries of origin: Many of these nations are destitute, they have not created enough jobs to go around, they are repressive and unstable. So their citizens naturally want to leave there and come here. These people want to take advantage of our open and prosperous society. But, so the story goes, in coming here they exploit us. They take our jobs, use our social services, crowd into our cities, cause crime. The solution follows logically from the diagnosis of the problem: We must raise the walls as high as it takes to stem this human tide.

Of course as a nation of immigrants we could not object merely to the presence of foreigners. What has always been of concern is the *difference* between them and us—racially, ethnically, religiously. Thus the limits we have imposed on who can cross our borders and join our ranks has had a great deal to do with how much they have resembled us. In the eighteenth century there were racial restrictions on eligibility for naturalization. In the 1880s and 1890s we excluded the Chinese; in the first decade of this century, the Japanese. Then we instituted a national quota system based on what proportion of "us" were descended from the likes of "them."[8] In the 1970s and 1980s illegal aliens streamed into America from Mexico, the Caribbean Basin, and Latin America—speaking a different language from us, and holding to different customs. The obvious expedient, given our fear of the Mob at the Gates, was to make it tougher to get in illegally.

But again, what has been left out of the calculation—the internal factor—is perhaps the most important. Foreigners are attracted to America for many reasons, but the likelihood of a good job has always ranked high on the list, and still does. If no jobs were available, there would be little point to enduring the costs and anxieties of uprooting oneself and traveling to a strange land. The jobs awaiting illegal aliens are not, in general, prized by our own work force (picking perishable crops, sewing garments, assembling toys, caring for others' children), but they pay considerably more than their options at home. Much of the money these immigrants have earned is sent back home, to prop up their families' meager incomes. Of equal importance is the information conveyed about where such jobs can be had and how much they pay; brothers and sisters then join the northward march, to fill the available demand. In this, too, the present pattern resembles the past.

The reason that illegal aliens can find jobs in America so easily is that we are eager to buy their labor. Employers are happy to hire illegals because they cannot find citizens to do the work they need done, as cheaply or at all. And the American customers of these employers are happy to pay less for goods and services than they would had the employers been forced to hire American workers. If American employers were unwilling to hire illegal aliens, and American consumers unwilling to purchase their labors directly or indirectly, the flood across our borders would slow to a trickle.

Do we want foreigners to work for us, to do the jobs we are unwilling to pay each other enough to do? It is an awkward question, analogous to—indeed, in some ways a version of—the question of whether we want access to foreign goods made with cheap labor. It is fundamentally a decision about whether we wish to discipline *ourselves*, but the choice is muddied by casting the issue as one of controlling "them." Our inability to come to terms with this issue has repeatedly undercut attempts to reform the immigration laws. We have not settled on what we want the laws to do; we do not know what "reform" would look like.[9]

5

In seeking to ensure our national security, there is an even greater temptation to build the walls higher and lock the gates tighter, rather than to take joint responsibility with "them" for managing a relationship capable of yielding devastating losses on all sides. Before the Reagan administration launched its Strategic Defense Initiative, no real defense against intercontinental ballistic missiles was thought to be possible. No nation could dream of invulnerability; indeed, the policy of deterrence that kept an uneasy peace for decades was based on precisely this premise. So long as both superpowers were vulnerable to the other, neither would be tempted to start a war. Peace was enforced by the threat of—in the deadpan lingo of nuclear strategists—"mutual assured destruction." The principle was codified in a treaty signed by Richard Nixon and Leonid Brezhnev at the Moscow Summit of May 1972, the high-water mark of détente.[10] Both nations agreed to limit their antimissile defenses, conceding openly what everyone already knew: We were hostages to one another.

But the policy of deterrence, and the principle of mutual vulnerability on which it was founded, never sat well with Americans. The Russians could *get at us*, and all we could do was obliterate them in turn. The arrangement was painfully discordant with the American mythology. How could we ever find security in *vulnerability*? The Star Wars proposal resurrected the metaphor of a fortress. It reconnected security with the ideal of invulnerability. An impenetrable shield in space would put our fate back into our own hands. In mythic terms, defense (even if it would not work) was immensely more satisfying than deterrence (even if it would).

There was the danger that in substituting the comforting myth of invulnerability from the Mob at the Gates for the reality of mutual vulnerability and interdependence, we would lose interest in the more basic problem: how to ensure our mutual security at least cost, when each of us deeply distrusted the other. So long as we had no defense for their incoming missiles, and they had no defense for ours, the clearest and most pressing problem was how to reduce the risk that we would blow each other apart. Reciprocal responsibility was a necessity. Neither side could want to try a preemptive strike, for fear that it would elicit an immediate and devastating response. Because there was always the chance of miscalculation or simple error—a chance that presumably increased with the number and complexity of weapons—it was imperative that each side agree to limit and then reduce the number of missiles and nuclear warheads directed at the other, and stop testing new devices. Both American conservatives and liberals saw the wisdom of this goal; disputes centered on how we could be sure that they would fulfill their part of the bargain without gaining an advantage over us. (And from all accounts, they worried about us in the same terms).[11] But once the agenda turned toward creating a foolproof defensive shield in space, the problem of controlling nuclear arms seemed somehow less compelling. Before March 1983, when Ronald Reagan announced the Star Wars plan, significant pressure had been building for arms control. After the announcement, public interest in arms control appeared to wane. Our long-term security no longer seemed to depend on their willingness to agree to control armaments, or even to play the game by the rules. Through Star Wars, it seemed, we could escape from the grim reality of mutual vulnerability and dependence. We would no longer be their hostage. Reagan offered something superior to arms control—a method for making the United States impregnable.

In reality, we would remain vulnerable to the Soviets, and they to us. The two of us are locked in a deadly and yet delicate embrace. Whatever we do, they can do too; whatever action we take that increases their sense of vulnerability to us, they will respond in a way that increases our vulnerability to them. We are dependent on one another for our mutual safety. And yet it is more comforting to put up walls, to cling to a cherished myth. As with the other problems I have described, it seems easier to contain and control "them" than to take responsibility for dependencies that run in both directions.

The visceral appeal of the Star Wars proposal—to Reagan as much or even more than the rest of us—had nothing whatsoever to do with the cold logic of national defense. That it would very likely never work, that it would almost certainly be a hideously expensive approach to security, were quite irrelevant cavils. Star Wars was cast as a crusade—a national goal, like sending men to the moon—that Americans would find inherently attractive because it resonated with the stories we told ourselves about our life together and about the menace lurking beyond.

CHAPTER 8

REPRISE: THE ECOLOGY OF THE WORLD ECONOMY

A summary is in order. The preceding chapters have examined the myth of the Mob at the Gates and suggested how flawed a guide to reality it has become. The notion of a pristine nation, separate and apart from the rest of the world, which can either assert its will unilaterally upon the world or withdraw from it, has little relevance to the situation in which America finds itself. We cannot act alone. If we try to stimulate our economy while other nations opt for restraint, we summon a flood of imports and risk inflation and unemployment. If we raise our interest rates unilaterally to cover our investment gap, we ravage debtor nations, provoke worldwide interest rate increases, and invite a global recession. If we close our borders to foreign goods, we cripple our debtors' efforts to pay us back and invite retaliation from major trading partners, while we cut our own standard of living. If we develop dramatically new and more elaborate defensive systems, we can expect that the Soviets will do whatever they must to eliminate any strategic advantage we might otherwise gain. If we lend our support to any dictator or revolutionary distasteful to the Soviets, we come to represent little more to the majority of mankind than just the other one of "them."

We cannot keep things out. Our borders are permeable to anything for which Americans are willing to pay, as well as to

100

indisputably unwelcome cargoes: sulfur dioxide emanating from Mexican smelters, which causes acid rain in the Rocky Mountains; carbon dioxide and methane from all industrialized nations, which block the escape of heat from earth and threaten to alter the world's climate; airborne radiation from a far off nuclear-power plant gone awry.

Nor can we keep things in: Our borders cannot fully contain technology, whether as trade secrets or military intelligence. Regardless of how determined our efforts to embargo trade, our goods will often reach Libya or the Soviets or other proscribed destination. It is impossible to keep hold of profits earned within our borders but transferred elsewhere within multinational corporations seeking to avoid taxation.

It is becoming less clear who "we" are anyway. "American" corporations build factories abroad from which they ship goods to destinations around the globe. Foreign corporations establish operations here, employing American workers. "American" banks readily lend abroad; by 1985 the foreign exposure of our top ten banks was over 100 percent of their capital base. Many of us employ illegal aliens; most of us eagerly buy cheap and reliable foreign goods. We hold millions of dollars' worth of shares in foreign-based companies. And when foreign currencies begin rising against the dollar, we are just as likely as foreign speculators to turn our dollars into Japanese yen or German marks. Who is "us"? Who is "them"?

Faced with these awkward realities, there is a temptation to lash out—to be ever more assertive toward the rest of the world, or to build even higher walls around us. Nothing prompts a show of force as readily as a suggestion of frailty. Yet we are far from lacking in strength; perhaps we are too strong. Prizefighters are rarely masters of negotiation. We cast our relations with "them" as a series of tests of our "credibility," "determination," or "resolve"; we win or they win. But in truth many of our most troubling problems stem from our chronic failure to acknowledge the subtle interdependencies that bind us to the rest of the species.

The delicately balanced, complexly connected world system

makes it difficult for us to impose a loss on them without enduring pain ourselves, or to achieve a benefit without conferring benefits all around. Sheer assertion or sharp withdrawal redound to our detriment. Opportunistic ploys on one side invite the same on the other, until trust declines and dangers escalate. But a policy of passive acquiescence also invites exploitative maneuver. A clear-eyed view of our interests and options as they are conditioned by our ties to the rest of the world—which is not the same as the romance that our interests are simply the same as those of others—would render more fruitful our efforts to advance our goals.

There is evil abroad in the world, to be sure. But there is no mob. And there are no gates.

PART TWO

THE
TRIUMPHANT
INDIVIDUAL

CHAPTER 9

OF ENTREPRENEURS
AND DRONES

1

The myth of the Triumphant Individual colors the prevailing view of how our economy works. He is the entrepreneurial hero, whose daring and imagination fuel America's growth. He personifies freedom, unencumbered by yesterday's assumptions and arrangements. He creates the new and carries his culture forward. And there is definitely something to this. Our degree of entrepreneurial drive and the social legitimacy it enjoys have long distinguished America from other cultures. Generations of wide-eyed inventors and investors have kept us on the technological frontier. We are born mavericks and fixers. In a world of naysayers and traditionalists, the American personality has stood out—cheerfully optimistic, willing to run risks, ready to try anything. It was the American GI who could fix the jeep in Normandy while the French regiment only looked on.

But here too, as with the parable of the Mob at the Gates, we risk that a simple and satisfying mythology will blind us to the new challenge our culture faces. The global transformation that we have examined in earlier chapters requires of us a different and more subtle form of entrepreneurialism, which builds upon joint effort rather than individual conquest.

This chapter recounts the prevailing tale of entrepreneurial heroes and drone workers. Subsequent chapters suggest why that tale is out of touch with our needs and our times.

2

During the early decades of this century the novellas of Horatio Alger, Jr., ignited the American imagination. There were more than one hundred of them in all, selling a total of 20 million copies, with titles like *Bound to Rise, Luck and Pluck*, and *Sink or Swim*. They inspired a generation with a gloriously simple theme: In America it was possible to rise rapidly from rags to riches. Each story was essentially the same; Alger, like any successful entrepreneur, knew when he was on to a good thing. A fatherless, penniless boy—possessed of enormous determination, faith, and courage—sought his fortune. All manner of villains tried to tempt him into debauchery or separate him from his small savings. But our hero prevailed on the strength of character and divine providence, and by the end of the story was a wealthy and powerful man.

Americans at the turn of the century saw Horatio Alger stories personified all around them. Edward Harriman had begun as a $5-per-week office boy and came to head a mighty railroad empire; John D. Rockefeller had risen from a clerk in a commission merchant's house to become one of the world's richest men; Andrew Carnegie had started as a $1.20-a-week bobbin boy in a Pittsburgh cotton mill only to become the nation's foremost steel magnate. Two decades later, when boys were still reading the Alger tales, Henry Ford would make his fortune mass-producing the Model T, and become a national folk hero (and potential presidential candidate) in the process.

The Alger cosmology presented America with a noble ideal, a society in which imagination and effort summoned their just reward. The story endorsed large disparities in wealth, since riches were the reward for applying yourself, saving your money, and trading shrewdly. The key virtue was self-reliance; the admirable man was the self-made man; the goal was to be your own boss rather than to work for someone else. Andrew Carnegie articulated the prevailing view:

> Is any would-be businessman . . . content in forecasting his future, to figure himself as labouring all his life for a fixed salary? Not one, I am sure. In this you have the dividing line between business and non-business; the one is a master, and depends on profits, the other is a servant and depends on salary.[1]

As the century wore on, however, the popular image of the self-made entrepreneur grew increasingly anomalous within an economy of large publicly owned firms, conglomerates, labor unions, administrative agencies, and defense contractors. His solitary endeavors, propelled by pride, seemed self-indulgent to a society besieged by wars, depression, and inner-city enclaves of permanent poverty. His lack of formal education became a drawback in a system increasingly deferential to professional expertise. His ambition became an object of derision (what makes Sammy run?). His compulsiveness came to be seen as a menace to family life; his radical individualism, a subject of psychological colloquia. Having overvalued the entrepreneur in an earlier era, by the middle decades of the twentieth century we had come to undervalue him.

3

By the 1980s, however, the pendulum had swung again with a vengeance. The entrepreneurial hero was back to close out the century he began. Lido Iacocca, inspired by the words of his immigrant father ("you could be anything you want to be, if you wanted it bad enough and were willing to work for it"),[2] worked his way up to the presidency of the Ford Motor Company, from which he was abruptly fired by Henry Ford II, and then lived on to revive Chrysler from default, thumb his nose at Ford in a best-selling autobiography, remake the Statue of Liberty, and be mentioned as a possible presidential candidate. Peter Ueberroth, son of a traveling salesman, worked his way through college, single-handedly built a $300 million business, then organized the 1984 Olympics, became *Time* magazine's Man of the Year, and commissioner of baseball.[3] Steven Jobs built his own computer company from scratch and became a multimillionaire before his thirtieth birthday. There were many others: youngsters who gained dizzying sums trading in commodity futures or real estate; professors who struck it rich by selling their inventions or shares in their extracurricular ventures; youthful engineers who reaped great fortunes by quitting their companies and striking out on their own. The new heroes were "fighters, fanatics, men with a lust for contest, a gleam of creation, and a drive to justify their break from the mother company."[4] These were the stories that Americans were telling one another about success.

Contrasted with these uplifting tales were different sorts of stories about people engaged in stodgy, routine work within structured organizations. Some were blue-collar and unionized; others, the secretaries, clerks, and fast-food servers who filled the service sector of the economy; others, white-collar employees at the lower and middle ranks of businesses, who moved the same pieces of paper over and over. These jobs could be briskly summed up in the "help wanted" sections of the newspaper. These workers' routines were standard. They had little opportunity for discretion, little need for creativity. People who held these jobs were fungible; someone else could always be found to do the same work.

Earlier in the century the average American worker had been portrayed as a hero—the "backbone" of America, who kept the wheels of commerce turning. He was an artisan, a shopkeeper, a mechanic, or a farmer, whose diligence and common sense could be counted on. But his counterpart toward the end of the century had neither independence nor unique skill. In contrast to the business entrepreneur, the routine worker often appeared uninteresting and uninterested. He was no villain, but certainly no hero. Nobody with creative spark and entrepreneurial vision would settle for being a cog in a bureaucratic machine. In the new story, unionized workers, a small and shrinking but visible minority of the work force, often appeared to demand ever more wages and benefits for ever less work. Their nonunionized counterparts often seemed to do the minimum of what was expected of them. Middle managers were faceless bureaucrats mired in standard operating procedure. In the tales Americans began telling one another, routine workers were drones.

This shift in perception took place despite the fact that most Americans still held jobs that were far more routine than entrepreneurial. Many people aspired to become entrepreneurs, even if their ambitions were limited to selling cosmetics or diet aids door-to-door in the evenings. Many more accepted the idea that the entrepreneurial life was superior to their own, although they held out no realistic hope of changing their condition. Others simply resented their dronelike jobs, and were contemptuous of fellow workers whose own laziness and indifference reminded them of just how bored and disaffected they felt.[5]

The important point is that these two stories began to frame the way Americans perceived the operation of the productive system. Much of the political debate over economic policy tacitly or otherwise presupposed the existence of these two categories of activity: entrepreneurial and drone. In the popular mind, people were not fated for one or the other category; the distinction had nothing to do with class. Almost anyone could become an entrepreneur, with enough drive and daring. The economy needed both, of course—creative entrepreneurs to formulate the Big Ideas that would find their way into new products and production techniques, and drones to undertake the routine chores involved in realizing these ideas. But for the economy to grow and prosper, it was presumed necessary to reward people who opted to become entrepreneurs and discipline those who remained drones. Conservative economists sounded the theme: "All of us are dependent for our livelihood and progress not on a vast and predictable machine, but on the creativity and courage of the particular men who accept the risks which generate our riches."[6]

4

The question, then, appeared to be one of degree and form: how to reward the entrepreneurs, how to keep the drones in line. Two major lines of reasoning warned against taxing entrepreneurs—

directly or indirectly through regulation—to advance collective endeavors. The first rested on a theory of motivation. Entrepreneurs are driven by money; the more money they get to keep, the more energetic their efforts. And the public would benefit from all the new inventions and jobs created. The second justification rested on a theory of competence. The large profits that successful entrepreneurs generated signaled their superior skill and judgment in the use of money. They had demonstrated their insight and imagination. Thus successful entrepreneurs were ideally suited to decide how to use money for the greatest gain. Assigning anyone else—anyone who had not proven his personal knack for turning a profit—control over part of the entrepreneur's earnings could result only in a diminution of wealth.

It should be noted that both justifications were premised on the notion of *social* return. Profits that inured to the entrepreneur were considered proxies for public benefits, in the form of new inventions and jobs. An elegant economic theory supported this equation of profits with the common good. That these justifications often were articulated by the very same individuals who would be directly enriched by them should not detract from their persuasiveness. History is replete with far less sophisticated reasons for maintaining the wealth of the wealthy.

5

The other theme of the fable stressed the need to discipline those who were content to remain drones lest their importunings cripple entrepreneurial initiative. At most, wages should not exceed productivity. This was a logical requirement: If workers' wages increased faster than their capacity to create value, inflation would inevitably result. Similarly, it was stressed, resources should be concentrated in the hands of successful entrepreneurs because, beyond their superior competence, they were also more likely than drones to save rather than spend extra money. This view too had a certain logic to commend it: The rich tend to run out of ways of making themselves more comfortable sooner than they run out of money; for poorer souls, the reverse is true. Excessive wage increases during the 1970s were seen to have rendered the United States less competitive in world markets than it would have been had more of that money been invested in new plant, machinery, and invention. How could American firms with workers earning eighteen dollars an hour successfully compete with South Koreans at four dollars an hour, using the same equipment? They could not. Either American workers' wages would have to match foreign wages, or Americans would have to be better equipped. And it was entrepreneurs who must be induced to supply the equipment. In sum, the public would benefit in several respects if drone wages could be brought under control: inflation would be lower; investment would be higher and better targeted; American competitiveness would be improved.

The specific tactics for achieving this goal were not openly debated or broadly understood. But they were consistent with the predominant story, and they were generally effective. The key was tightening the money supply. This increased unemployment and dampened workers' ardor to press for higher pay. In conjunction with high budget deficits, tight money also raised the dollar, making more credible employers' threats to decamp to other countries where workers were paid in cheaper currencies if the demand of domestic drones got out of line. This approach, begun in the late 1970s, kept a tight lid on average pay and benefits throughout the early 1980s.

There was a further challenge, however. During the long period of steady growth in the 1950s and 1960s, drones had grown accustomed to staying put. If they were laid off their jobs during recessions, they received unemployment checks from the government that tided them over until the economy cycled up again and their jobs came back, as they always had. But now the perception spread that the same jobs would not be there on the other side of the recession, and companies took steps to cut their work forces, from hourly workers at the bottom, all the way up through white-collar drones at middle levels. This was universally considered unfortunate, but the reigning parable declared its necessity. The conservative disciplinarian had to be hard-nosed. In the tough new world of global commerce, companies could not afford the luxury of loyalty. Operating costs had to be cut, and one of the major operating costs was drone employment.

Throughout the 1980s American companies pursued a crusade of cost cutting. Unprofitable divisions were sold. Manufacturing was moved abroad, where labor was cheaper. The workplace was automated further, and many routine jobs were taken over by robots. White-collar bureaucrats were sent packing. The new tough attitude resonated in the butcher-shop metaphors of modern management: Companies had to "trim the fat" and "cut to the bone" in order to be "lean and mean."

Economic theory broadly endorsed these developments. If fewer workers could produce nearly the same output, then by shedding excess workers, the productivity of each of the remaining ones would increase. Those workers liberated from no-longer-economic activities would move on to other jobs where their labor could be applied more productively. As a result, the entire economy would grow. The model that still informs most economic theorizing holds that this is precisely how economies develop: Layoffs and losses pry workers and money loose from bad economic bets until they settle into the use where they yield the highest return. If circumstances change, the sequence of separation, search, and a new arrangement of resources sets in again. Drone workers are as fungible as money. Keeping them on the payroll out of loyalty is false charity; it makes no more sense than keeping money in a bad investment. Let them go and seek out the niche where they can do the most good, for themselves and the economy. So went the story.

Presumably everyone stood to gain from cutting excess employment to release drone workers for other pursuits. Consumers would pay less for the goods they bought. The workers who survived cutbacks would each be more productive. The entire economy would be more competitive, less shackled by slack and mismatches. While some workers might have difficulty finding new jobs right away, and might feel anxious and depressed about leaving their former surroundings, the overall gain would far exceed this passing pain. Without such ongoing transitions, it was argued, the economy would stagnate. We would all end up subsidizing one another to remain in jobs where we were no longer needed.

6

The liberal, conciliatory view of work in the economy accepted many of the same assumptions—that the world of work was divided between Triumphant Individual entrepreneurs and everyday workers—but came to different conclusions. Liberals took issue with the prevailing assertive conservatism on how much reward should go to entrepreneurs and how much discipline should be imposed on the rest.

The liberal quibble concerned degree. Successful entrepreneurs already earned so much that further riches would induce little extra effort. Moreover, while some entrepreneurs were doubtless energetic and creative, many were just lucky; wealth is no signal of superior competence, or a guide to the best stewards of the nation's future. Liberals also argued that entrepreneurs might be as creative in coming up with expensive new pleasures for themselves as in forging new investments for the economy; the rich may save more of their money than do the poor, or they may not. Even if they did reinvest their wealth, it was argued, the new investment might occur in another nation, or in speculative activities that generated few new inventions or jobs. Together, these arguments convinced many liberals that although economic growth depended upon entrepreneurs, their exertions need not yield such princely sums.[7]

The liberal ethos mandated compassion for everyday workers. Unemployment, it stressed, was a grueling experience for anyone. New jobs, at comparable wages, were seldom easy to come by for laid-off workers. When workers could not pay their bills, those who provided them with goods and services found that they could not pay their bills either. Thus towns and cities sank into depression. Property values declined, and the tax base shriveled as workers moved away in search of their economic niche. For these pilgrims in search of their most productive possibility, relocating to a new part of the country was emotionally and financially traumatic. As the community declined, the old homestead fetched a much lower price; houses in more buoyant areas of the nation were correspondingly more expensive. If both husband and wife needed to work to make ends meet, then the search for adequate jobs was doubly difficult.[8]

Liberals also worried about automation. If computers, robots, and the systems that linked the two could reduce even skilled tasks to preprogrammed rules, then eventually all drone jobs (blue-collar and white-collar) might be replaced by machines. And if that occurred, so the argument went, conservative economics would be pushed to its illogical limit: The nation would be capable of producing a great volume of goods and services at low cost, and the handful of workers who remained employed would be wildly productive. But few Americans would have the money to buy the things that were produced.[9] Even aside from these objections to the conservative parable of efficiently footloose resources, liberals condemned large differences in the wealth of entrepreneurs and drones as socially corrosive.

Together, these worries suggested to conciliatory liberals that we should be cautious in rewarding entrepreneurs and disciplining drones. Rather than use employment to deter wage demands that might lead to inflation, we should find a less painful way to curb inflation—perhaps through wage and price controls. Managers should be required to give their workers advance notice of any contemplated factory closing. They should compensate the workers whom they abandon and the communities they leave behind. Cheap foreign goods that threaten the jobs of American workers should be barred, or at least controlled through tariffs, quotas, and restraint agreements. "Dumping" should be prohibited. The government should mandate that a certain percentage of the value of goods sold in the United States derive from American workers. Limits should be imposed on the pace and extent of automation.

These sorts of proposals characterized the tepid liberal response to the resurgent conservative interpretation of the myth of the Triumphant Individual.[10] Liberalism essentially conceded the conservative explanation of *how* the economy worked, and disputed only the conservative judgments about how much in-equality was necessary and appropriate. Entrepreneurs may be of a different breed than drones, but even if more money would in fact induce in them greater effort and corresponding social benefit, we are a wealthy enough society to forego it in favor of a little better life for the drones. A measure more fairness is worth a measure less growth. Thus was the issue framed: In balancing entrepreneurs and drones, liberals tipped more toward the drones; conservatives, toward the entrepreneurs.

7

The liberal story was appealing to America, but it was an appeal of sympathy rather than inspiration. The plight of unemployed workers was disturbing to contemplate. Perhaps the pace of economic change did need to be restrained somewhat to reduce the pain. Americans were ready to be charitable.

But the conservative story held greater sway, and increasingly shaped the way Americans came to think about how the national economy was evolving, how it should adapt, and the role of individuals within it. The myth of the Triumphant Individual had always been about the hopes and dreams of America's never-say-die mavericks—pioneers, cowboys, explorers, immigrants, union organizers, rags-to-riches kids. Now, in the last decades of the twentieth century, the mantle fell to the business entrepreneur, the purest modern incarnation of the classic American hero. The conservative story defined progress. Entrepreneurs created the future. Drones, by contrast, represented the weight of the past.

CHAPTER 10

COLLECTIVE ENTREPRENEURIALISM

1

The orthodoxy that sees economic growth as a process by which entrepreneurs orchestrate the continuous rearrangement of fungible resources rests on the assumption that industries grow and expire in a predictable sequence. It goes something like this. Step one: An individual inventor—call him Henry—has a Big Idea. Henry comes up with a turbo-charged automatic vacuum cleaner that can suck up all the dirt and dust out of a room without anyone lifting a finger. Just leave the vacuum on a shelf for five minutes and—presto!—the room is spanking clean. Step two: Henry presents his Big Idea to a group of wealthy investors who are on the lookout for hot new prospects. They agree to back him in exchange for shares in the new venture. Step three: Henry and the investors hire Ralph, who sets up and manages the factory to make the turbo-charged vacuums, and Shirley, who peddles the product to retail stores. Step four: Thousands of turbo-charged vacuums are rolling off conveyor belts manned by hundreds of drone workers. Hundreds more workers distribute, sell, and service the new machines.

Step five: As production expands, the cost of producing each vacuum declines. This is because many costs—such as machinery, factory maintenance, and advertising—are incurred regardless of how many vacuums are made, so the more production the better. (Henry Ford notably capitalized on this fundamental concept in producing his Model T.) As the per-unit cost falls, the profit on each sale rises. The company starts to make a good deal of money. Step six: At this point Henry and his backers sell the Turbo-charged Automatic Vacuum Company to a big corporation—say, Westinghouse—for a very large sum. Henry returns to his attic to come up with another Big Idea, and his backers go on the prowl for another Henry. Ralph and Shirley become middle managers in Westinghouse's Consumer Appliance Division. Step seven: Now tens of thousands of turbo-charged vacuums are coming off the lines and the cost per unit has been pushed down to a pittance. The turbo-charged vacuum becomes the star of the Consumer Appliance Division, and Westinghouse earns a nice profit. Step eight: Westinghouse spends some of these profits acquiring another start-up enterprise, the Self-Destructing Picnic Plate Corporation. (Five seconds after it registers the disappearance of the last deviled egg, a microprocessor triggers a small explosive charge; nothing but water vapor and environmentally benign ash emerge from the fireball—saves messy cleanup.)

Step nine: Many American households now own a turbo-charged vacuum cleaner, and a competitor is about to introduce a new line of comparable machines. In response, Westinghouse drops the price of its model and embarks on a cost-cutting campaign. Ralph and Shirley, along with hundreds of workers, are laid off. Step ten: Profits have declined so far on the turbo-charged vacuum that Westinghouse decides to terminate the line. The factory and equipment that produced it are put to other uses or sold for scrap; the remaining workers, terminated. But Westinghouse does not regard the excursion as a failure. To the contrary, the turbo-charged vacuum cleaner netted a great deal of money for the firm. And anyway, the self-destructing picnic plate is just hitting its stride.

2

This sequence or something like it has been repeated in American industry often enough to be seen as the rule. And the rule has gone from being a description of what is to a prescription for what must be. Invention is distinct from production. Entrepreneurial efforts focus on Big Ideas—fundamentally new products or new ways of making things. The most successful of these Big Ideas will have a predictable life cycle, extending from an unprofitable period at the start, to a rewarding harvest season of expanding sales and mass production, and then to an eventual maturity and decline as the market becomes saturated and as other Big Ideas render the product obsolete.[1]

This suggests that a business firm, if it is to remain consistently profitable, should have a portfolio of Big Ideas at different stages of their life cycle. The typical large firm does not generate Big Ideas internally, but buys start-ups that seem likely to yield high profits when their Big Ideas reach full-blown mass production. Corporate headquarters uses the profits from its herd of winners to buy further promising start-ups. And it quickly withdraws from businesses that have reached the end of the line. Thus the ideal firm balances out rising and declining Big Ideas by diversifying its portfolio.[2] In the mid-1980s the widely diversified firm—buying Big Ideas embodied in start-up firms and selling off the carcasses of Old Ideas—was more or less the rule.

3

From the standpoint of the lone genius like Henry, or even of the corporation like Westinghouse, this pattern makes economic sense. But from the standpoint of a national economy and the vast majority of people who depend upon it for their work and, ultimately, their standard of living, the pattern is more problematic. The only way that people like Ralph and Shirley and all the drone workers under their care can be assured of jobs and steadily rising real incomes is if entrepreneurial geniuses like Henry continue to conjure up successful Big Ideas quickly enough to replace the declines at the other end. In America, this recipe worked for a while.

But as I have sought to show, high-wage economies can no longer depend on standardized mass production. Big Ideas like Henry's can be shipped in blueprints or electronic symbols anywhere on the globe. Workers in South Korea, Taiwan, or Mexico can churn out turbo-charged automatic vacuums just as well as American workers can, and for far lower wages. Indeed, today Henry is as likely to license a South Korean or Taiwanese company to manufacture the vacuum as he is to sell out to Westinghouse. If Westinghouse does get hold of Henry's Big Idea, it is apt to build its own factory overseas.

In a world where routine production is footloose and billions of potential workers are ready to underbid American labor, competitive advantage lies not in onetime breakthroughs but in continual improvements. Stable technologies get away. Keeping a technology requires elaborating upon it continuously, developing variations and small improvements in it that better meet particular needs.

The Japanese are skilled at using the essential insight of a Big Idea as the starting point in such an ongoing process of elaboration and refinement. To return to Henry's Big Idea, the Japanese knack for modification and improvement would likely foreshorten the profitable life of the turbo-charged automatic vacuum cleaner. Within one or two years after it hit the market, Hitachi would likely come up with a *super* turbo-charged automatic vacuum cleaner that can be programmed to suck up all the dirt and dust in your whole *house* in one minute flat. Anticipating this, Westinghouse is likely to sell the patent on the basic turbo-charged vacuum to Hitachi early on in return for an exclusive license to sell and distribute Hitachi's super version in the United States. Thus Westinghouse would be able to offer American consumers a full line: cheap, basic turbo-charged automatic vacuums made in South Korea, and *super* turbo-charged automatics made in Japan.

The specific example may be fanciful, but the general tendency is not. Americans continue to lead the world in scientific discoveries and Nobel laureates. But we often have had difficulty elaborating upon our inventions and turning them into streams of commercial products. We get bogged down somewhere between big breakthroughs and their applications. Americans invented the solid-state transistor. Then, in 1953, Western Electric licensed the technology to Sony for $25,000, and the rest is history. A few years later RCA licensed several Japanese companies to make color TV production in America. Routine assembly of color TVs eventually was shifted to Taiwan and Mexico, but Sony and other Japanese companies continuously refined the technology into an array of continuously evolving consumer electronic products.

In 1968 Unimation licensed Kawasaki Heavy Industries to make industrial robots; the nascent American robotics industry never quite recovered, as the Japanese developed ever more elaborate versions. Americans came up with the Big Ideas for video-cassette recorders, basic oxygen furnaces and continuous casters for making steel, microwave ovens, automobile stamping machines, computerized machine tools, and integrated circuits. But these Big Ideas—and many others—quickly found their way into Japanese production, where they were steadily improved upon, step by step.

In this integrated world economy, Americans must live by their wits. If they hope to command a premium wage, their labor must generate more value. They must produce goods that continuously embody new innovations that workers in less complex and more distant economic systems cannot easily or quickly match. Such products may comprise standard components put together in unique ways, like a communications network custom-designed for a particular corporation. Or they may incorporate standard hardware but specialized software, like an "intelligent" credit card that lists credit balances, or a work station for developing and testing alternative engineering approaches. Or the products may involve particularly high standards of precision. Or they may require custom-tailoring, like made-to-order semiconductor chips, or special chemicals prepared for particular end uses. (I have elsewhere referred to these products and the means of producing them as "flexible systems.")[3]

Where innovation is continuous, and products are ever more tailored to customers' particular needs, the distinction between goods and services begins to blur. Thus when robots and computerized machine tools are linked through software that allows them to perform unique tasks, customer service becomes a part of production. When a new alloy is molded to a specified weight and tolerance, service accounts for a significant part of the value added. IBM is in the business of providing bundles of high-technology goods and services. Of its 400,000 employees, only a comparative few are engaged in "manufacturing" in the traditional sense. The rest provide services—putting together packages of hardware, software, financing, and maintenance. What IBM and other advanced companies provide are best described as "service goods." Reports that American workers can no longer compete in manufacturing and must shift to services are only half-right. More precisely, they can keep high wages only by producing goods with a large component of specialized services or, to state the same thing differently, providing services integral to the production and use of specific goods.

The point is this: In the new global economy, nearly everyone has access to Big Ideas (and the machines and money to turn them into standardized products) at about the same time, and on roughly the same terms. The older industrial economies have two options: They can try to match the wages for which workers elsewhere are willing to labor. Or they can compete on the basis of how quickly and well they can transform ideas into incrementally better products. This second and obviously more appealing option implies a fundamentally different approach to entrepreneurialism. Instead of a handful of lone entrepreneurs producing a few industry-making Big Ideas, innovation must be more continuous and collective.

4

To compete on the basis of rapid improvements in product and process, rather than on the basis of the scale economies of mass production, means a new emphasis on the innovative skills of workers—the productive services they deliver—and on the organizational structure of production. Consider these evolutionary paths followed by successful firms (a few American, mostly Jap-

anese or the Japanese parts of Japanese-American corporations):
Vacuum-tube radios become transistorized radios, then stereo
pocket radios audible through earphones, then compact disks and
compact disk players, and then optical-disk computer memories.
Color televisions evolve into digital televisions, capable of showing several pictures simultaneously; videocassette recorders into
camcorders. A single strand of technological evolution is embodied in electronic sewing machines, then in electronic type-
writers, and then in flexible electronic work stations. Basic steels
give way to high-strength and corrosion-resistant steels, and then
to new materials composed of steel mixed with silicon and cus-
tom-made polymers. Basic chemicals evolve into high-perfor-
mance ceramics, to single-crystal silicon, and high-grade crystal
glass. Copper wire gives way to copper cables, and then to fiber-
optic cables.

These patterns reveal no clear life cycles with beginnings,
middles, and ends. Instead of Big Ideas that beget standardized
commodities, these series display a continuous process of incremental change and adaptation. Workers add value not solely or
even mostly by tending the machines and carrying out routines,
but in the analysis, experimentation, and the application of creativity. They are paid for the services they embody in goods. In
this context, it makes no sense to speak of an "industry" like
steel or automobiles or televisions, or even banking, because
there are no clear borders around any of these service-goods. When
products and processes are so protean, firms grow or decline not
with the market for some specific good, but with the adaptive
capacity of their work force. One thing leads to another. Producing the latest generation of automobiles involves making electronic circuits that govern fuel consumption and monitor engine
performance; improvements in these devices lead to improved
sensing equipment and software for monitoring heartbeats and
moisture in the air. Producing cars also involves making flexible
robots for assembling parts and linking them by computer; steady
improvements in these technologies, in turn, lead to expert production systems that can be applied anywhere. What is considered the "automobile industry" therefore is really a variety of

technologies evolving toward all sorts of applications that flow from the same strand of technological development but toward different markets.

And because there are no preordained life cycles, and machines and workers are not locked into producing long runs of any single standardized good, the firm has less need to hedge its bets. Experimentation and development are occurring constantly, so it is not necessary for the firm to leap into deliberately unrelated lines of business as insurance against declining demand in any one.

5

This pattern of ongoing, incremental evolution depends on the cumulative expertise of a great number of people. Workers within the firm garner experience in the process of product design, fabrication, engineering, and production. Expertise *outside* the firm itself is also important; suppliers of key components share intimately in the evolution. The path of change is governed by continuous feedback from consumers, sometimes spread around the globe, whose needs and priorities shift over time.

There are no sharp distinctions between goods and services, between invention and production, between entrepreneurs and drones. Because production is a continuous process of reinvention, entrepreneurial efforts must be focused on many thousands of small ideas rather than a few big ones. As the speed and precision of response become more important, so does the potential of each member of the enterpise as a source of innovation. Workers who design the software, make the hardware, or sell and service the resulting product are cultivated as fonts of valuable up-to-the-minute information about how things can be improved. Because the information and expertise are dispersed throughout the organization, top management does not solve problems nor set specific direction; it creates an environment in which people can identify and solve problems for themselves.

Collective entrepreneurialism requires close working relationships among people at all stages of the process. If customers' needs are to be recognized and profitably met, designers and engineers must be familiar with marketing and sales. And salespeople must have an intimate understanding of the enterprise's capacity to design and deliver specialized products. The system can adapt quickly to new opportunities only if information is widely shared, and everyone involved is actively looking for opportunities to improve, adjust, and upgrade.

Most of the training for this type of work can only occur on the job. Formal education prepares people to absorb and integrate experience; it does not substitute for experience. This is because the precise skills to be learned cannot be anticipated in advance. Opportunities cannot be foreseen. Any production process that can be taught on the basis of textbook procedures can be moved to low-wage areas or programmed into robots and computers.

Individual skills are integrated into a group whose collective capacity to innovate becomes something more than the simple sum of its parts. Over time, as group members work through various problems and approaches together, they learn about each others' abilities. They learn how they can help one another perform better, who can contribute what to a particular project, how they can best gain experience together. Innovation is inherently collective and incremental. Each participant appreciates what the others are trying to do; he is constantly on the lookout for small adjustments that will speed and smooth the evolution of the whole. The net effect of many such small-scale adaptations, occurring throughout the organization, is to propel the enterprise forward. Because such cumulative experience and understanding is so critical, this network of people must be maintained over time. Their collective capacity, by assumption, cannot be translated into standard operating procedures and transferred to other workers. The capacity to add value resides in the whole, and this capacity is what the enterprise seeks to preserve and develop. This is in sharp contrast to the pattern in standardized production, in which drone workers are seen as interchangeable, and extruded when the industry or product approaches the end of its life cycle.

6

Enterprises designed primarily to reduce the cost of mass-producing Big Ideas are organized into a series of hierarchical tiers, so that each superior can ensure that subordinates are acting according to plan. But enterprises designed to continuously discover and apply incremental advances have a relatively flat structure. Here it is far less important that workers follow preordained rules than that they gain new insights into how products or processes can be improved. Coordination is achieved both through common experience—working together long enough so that signals are relatively clear—and through common understandings about what sorts of small-scale refinements are likely to improve products and processes. There are thus few middle-level managers and only modest differences in the status and income of senior managers and junior employees. Individual performance cannot be monitored and evaluated through simple accounting systems, because the quality of work is often more important than the quantity. Tasks are often so intertwined, moreover, that it becomes impossible to evaluate them separately. Since each worker necessarily relies on many others, success can be measured only in reference to collective results.

In this very different world of work, automation poses no threat to employment, as some liberals have feared. Computers are used less to reduce the cost of labor than to enhance its value. Rather than simplify and standardize jobs by preprogramming every task, computer-based information provides a means of expanding workers' discretion. It gives workers more feedback about what they are doing and how what they do affects other aspects of the production process. Computerized data might reveal, for example, that a particular component, if slightly modified, could exactly meet the needs of a product on a different line, thereby reducing the number of parts that need to be produced overall. Or the data might show that one piece of equipment is using up a great deal of energy, and could be redesigned to be much more efficient. Or that with a slight alteration in pressure or composition, a batch of material could be put to very different end uses.

These sorts of information help workers discover ways to improve product and process. They give them the means to use their imaginations—to experiment in rearranging the data to provide new insights into what is being produced and how it can be refined.[4]

7

Collective entrepreneurialism is not as unusual as it may at first seem. Rarely do even Big Ideas emerge any longer from the solitary labors of genius. Modern science and technology is too complicated for one brain. It requires groups of astronomers, physicists, and computer programmers to discover new dimensions of the universe; teams of microbiologists, oncologists, and chemists to unravel the mysteries of cancer. With ever more frequency, Nobel prizes are awarded to collections of people. Scientific papers are authored by small platoons of researchers.[5]

Nor is collective entrepreneurialism the sole province of Japanese enterprise. Some corners of American enterprise, too, have long been premised on the ideal of collective entrepreneurialism. This is true for professional partnerships—lawyers, doctors, accountants, management consultants, architects, investment bankers—for which the value of the enterprise rests almost entirely in the knowledge and experience of its members. Within the most successful and innovative of these enterprises there is little hierarchy and few established routines; all members have a stake in improving the performance of the entire group.

Collective entrepreneurialism also has characterized many small firms producing service-intensive goods. Coalitions of designers, engineers, fabricators, marketers, and salespeople and financial specialists race to get new product generations to market. A comparable pattern could be observed for a time in some of the notable geographic centers of technology-based production. In the late 1970s and early 1980s the areas around Route 128, which encircles Boston, and California's Santa Clara County both represented diffused but often effective entrepreneurial networks. Technical specialists tended to be familiar with one another's work and knew who to tap for help when a specific sort of problem arose. Firms and projects came and went, but the underlying network evolved and developed, at least for a time. Shared experiences were cultivated and preserved, and technological competence accumulated. (The divergence between private and social returns on these activities, however, eventually would threaten these learning communities, as will be recounted shortly.)

But many Americans have continued to work in enterprises that conform to the standard pattern, in which drones mass-produce Big Ideas—be they automobiles or hamburgers. Why? If collective entrepreneurialism offers higher returns in the future, why would Americans cling to the old ways?

Consider: In 1985, soon after the Reagan administration arranged for quotas on the importation of foreign steel, the U.S. Steel Corporation dropped plans for new investment in a Utah facility. Instead, it opted to import semifinished slabs from South Korea to feed its West Coast finishing mills. Soon thereafter it spent $3.6 billion to purchase Texas Oil and Gas Corporation, on top of the $6 billion it spent a few years before to buy Marathon Oil. In mid-1986 it dropped "steel" out of its name and became USX—with the last letter serving as an indelible reminder that what the corporation now stood for was unknown and unknowable. By that time energy accounted for two thirds of its revenues and all of its profits, and thousands of workers had lost their jobs.

The ensuing political debate centered, as usual, on the benefits and the pains of economic change. Unionized workers, and not a few liberals, complained that U.S. Steel was abandoning steel, and so it was. They lamented the resulting unemployment of steel workers and the decline of traditional steel towns. On the other hand, conservative disciplinarians pointed out, correctly, that there was no future in making basic steel. South Korea's Pohang Iron and Steel Company, for instance, operated one of the most modern mills in the world, which generated over 9 million tons of steel a year; Pohang's workers earned an average of $2.50 per hour, or about a tenth of U.S. Steel's pay scale.

Another example from the opposite end of the industrial spectrum: In the 1970s the Zenith Corporation invested several hundred million dollars trying to implement a potentially revolutionary Big Idea: using lasers to play sounds recorded on a plastic disk. The lasers would "read" information encoded and compactly stored on the disk and reproduce sounds far more faithfully than conventional tapes or records. But by the end of the decade, Zenith had abandoned the effort. Production was simply too risky and expensive. Zenith opted to import videocassette recorders—a comparable but simpler technology—to sell under its own brand name. Sony, meanwhile, soon introduced the first successful minisized, laser-operated compact disk player, which swept the American market.[6]

Both U.S. Steel and Zenith made rational calculations of the cost of pursuing a market and, following the logic of standardized mass production, opted out. In principle, however, each had other options. U.S. Steel could have eased out of steel and into new alloys and plastics that combine high strength with light weight. Or it could have moved into advanced ceramics that resist corrosion and heat, or into any number of other new materials that do what steel does but better or cheaper. In most of these areas, no foreign producer was yet ready to compete. U.S. Steel could then have maintained its marketing links to its customers making cars, buildings, and appliances; American automakers, for example, were beginning to turn to Japan for ceramic engines and carbon-fiber chassis. Had U.S. Steel moved in this direction, it could have retrained many of its workers—already skilled in making one kind of durable material—to meet the same needs with new products. It would have become U.S. Advanced Materials, a robust descendant of its former self. Zenith, likewise, could have regarded the laser disk not just as one potential product but as the wellspring of a stream of potential products flowing out of the collective experience gained by making the first—items like optical computer memories, disks containing information services, videodisks that could be erased and revised. In this way, Zenith too could have evolved as its work force, and its surrounding network of suppliers and customers, also evolved.

Yet neither firm followed any such path. What are we to conclude from this? One possibility is that the notions of high-value service-goods and collective entrepreneurship are pipe-dreams, and that the only realistic options for most American workers are protection, idleness, or wages as low as their competition abroad. Another possibility is that the managements of U.S. Steel and Zenith were simply too blind to spot the sources of future profits. Neither of these explanations holds true, however, for Zenith and U.S. Steel nor for the many other American companies who cling to the logic of standardized mass production and balk at a strategy of collective entrepreneurialism. The problem is rooted in a deeper dilemma, to be taken up in the next chapter.

CHAPTER 11

THE GENERAL THEORY
OF GRIDLOCK

1

So long as the economy remains divided between a few entrepreneurs and many drones, the political choice can be neatly posed: How much should entrepreneurs be rewarded? How can drones be kept busy, and kept in line? American political leaders and citizens, with different notions of fairness and different preferences for social wealth versus social harmony, have long debated the proper balance. But if our future happens in fact to lie in a collective form of entrepreneurialism, in which these two species are no longer distinct, the issue is subtler, at once more challenging and less grimly divisive. The question becomes: how can we structure a political culture and an economic system that allows collective entrepreneurialism to flourish?

Collective entrepreneurialism requires mutual investment. Owners continuously invest in workers by giving them training and experience in new technologies. Workers invest in one another by sharing ideas and insights. Workers invest in the overall enterprise by moderating their wage demands. Suppliers of materials and parts invest by committing to produce specialized components. Creditors supply capital without requiring a rigid projection of how the funds will be used.

What distinguishes these types of investment from the standard form is that they rest primarily on trust. Each party trusts that its contributions will eventually be reciprocated, and that ultimately all will gain from the mutual commitments. Uncertainty and constant change make it impossible to fully specify roles or formalize obligations. Trust is required because reciprocal performance cannot be completely assured in advance through the legal device of contract. This—an essential characteristic of collective entrepreneurialism—is its greatest weakness. For in a system that primarily encourages individual exploits, trust is a particularly fragile commodity. This explains the difficulty in shifting away from standardized mass production.

2

In a system of stable mass production, most responsibilities could be delineated in advance. This meant that simple contracts could suffice to bind obligations. Drone jobs involved a limited number of repetitive activities that could be reduced to standard operating procedures. Suppliers delivered standardized parts and materials. Banks and other creditors could know with reasonable certainty how their money was to be used and what was to be produced. Shareholders could anticipate their risk and probable return. The communities to which these enterprises gravitated could expect a certain level of economic activity over a certain stretch of time. And because all the cars, steel sheets, or insurance policies that emerged from the enterprise were identical, consumers could be reasonably assured what they were buying and how it would perform.

In this stable world, there was little need for trust. Firms, workers, and investors shopped around for the best deal they could find, and then entered into contracts that specified precisely what each party owed the other. When commodities were more or less standard, parties usually could switch their allegiances at the end of the contract without disrupting the system. Drone workers who welded automobile parts together, for example, could leave the enterprise and find other welding jobs. Those who supplied the parts could supply the same parts to another firm. Consumers could try a competitor's product; shareholders could put their money elsewhere; senior managers might come and go. The entire enterprise, and the network of relationships that surrounded it, was like a machine with replaceable parts.

Stability broke down only with the advent of Big Ideas that rendered obsolete what had come before. The invention of the electric light bulb came as a rude shock to those who owed their livelihoods to the kerosene lamp. When a Big Idea like this emerged, contractual relationships had to be reordered. There were bankruptcies; those with specialized skills no longer in demand faced long periods of unemployment; purchasers and suppliers were inconvenienced. But stability was soon reestablished, as the Big Idea was translated into mass production. The light bulb soon became a standard, stable commodity. And this translation allowed a new set of expectations to be encoded in contract. Big Ideas, moreover, did not arise often enough to call into question the idea of an economy of individual agents united only by contractual obligation.

3

The enterprise that is continuously evolving through collective entrepreneurial efforts, however, is inherently unpredictable. Because it is not organized to repeat what it did before, parties can rarely rely on the past as a guide to the future. Responsibilities cannot be described in advance, within contracts and rules, because no one can anticipate precisely where the pursuit of markets will lead, or exactly what level and form of effort will be required. The cumulative effect of incessant incremental change is to continuously render former expectations obsolete. Suppliers, workers, financiers, and even customers are often leaping together into uncharted domains. The entrepreneurial network rests on imperfectly enforceable understandings that if one party contributes now, others will reciprocate in the future. And these understandings are based, in turn, on the conviction that collective enterprise offers richer rewards for each participant than does more individualistic endeavor.[1]

Even were roles defined and predictable, it would be difficult to contractually establish individual obligations and expectations in a system of collective entrepreneurship. The value of what each party contributes to the enterprise, and what each derives from it, turns on what others also contribute. One party cannot simply switch allegiances after a time without imposing hardships on others who had relied upon the deserting party's participation. The supplier of ball bearings customized for a particular purchaser, for example, must dedicate special equipment to making them, and train his workers to meet unique specifications. A profitable return on these investments depends upon how successful the purchaser is at putting them to use. Supplier and purchaser have a mutual interest in working together to develop the customized bearings, apply them to the new product, and perhaps discover other uses for them. Should the purchaser pull out, or suddenly insist on a much lower price, the supplier would lose much of his investment.

Trust is by no means foreign to American enterprise, of course. Trust is apparent even in standardized mass-production enterprises when they face the vagaries of the business cycle. There is evidence, for example, that employers commonly maintain wages and employment during downturns in the business cycle at higher levels than a strict reading of supply and demand would warrant. Employers are eager to maintain workers' loyalty, lest employees depart during upturns in the cycle. It is simply too expensive to find and train good employees with every uptick in the economy. Similarly, sellers often allocate scarce goods to steady customers when supplies are tight—rather than charge the customers higher prices—to reward and reinforce customer loyalty during downturns.

These "invisible handshakes," as the economist Arthur M. Okun has called them, help explain why wages and prices do not move smoothly up and down with the overall economy—and may also explain, incidentally, why inflation sometimes threatens even when the economy is lukewarm.[2] For our purposes, the important point is that loyalty has its own economic value. Even traditional firms often find it prudent not to squander goodwill in pursuit of a single period's profit. For enterprises embracing collective entrepreneurialism, the role of loyalty is more central still.

4

Trust is a brittle organizational adhesive, however. Even if each member of a common endeavor stands to gain from a policy of trust, the perception that any one member can do even better by exploiting the others' trust tends to undermine the policy.

Imagine, for example, that the chief executive of an American firm buys the idea of collective entrepreneurialism. He decides to invest in the production experience of the firm's workers. Instead of relying upon a Japanese supplier for a complex component, this executive decides to produce it inside the firm. Since the Japanese supplier has already learned to produce the item cheaply while the firm's work force has not, internal procurement will cost about $1,000 more per worker than buying it outside. But our enlightened executive looks upon this added expense as an investment in his firm's workers. He figures that once his workers master the challenge of making this one component, they will be better equipped for further innovations. The firm's capacity to innovate, adapt, and improve will be expanded. The manager estimates that the total present value of this learning will come to about $1,500 per worker. So the initial $1,000 investment—with a 50 percent return—is well worth it, and the company opts for internal production of the component.

A year later, the executive is delighted to discover that his prediction was dead right. After figuring out how to make the component, the firm's workers are far more knowledgeable about this area of technology. They can see all sorts of ways to apply their hard-won expertise to new products and improvements to existing product lines.

But there is a problem. The workers *know* that they are now more valuable to the firm than they were before—about $1,500 per employee more valuable. When it comes time for salary talks, each worker demands a raise worth, say, $1,499. If the company won't deliver, the workers announce they will simply go to work for a competitor who *will* pay what the workers are now undeniably worth. Triumphant Individuals are not bound by ties of loyalty; they strike out on their own. Our enlightened executive has no choice but to accede to their demands, even though it wipes out the gain from his investment. But he sadly vows that from now on he'll buy advanced components from Japan.

Investments in knowledge cannot be protected like investments in real estate or machinery. Investors can assert and defend their stakes in tangible assets, but not in value that resides in people's minds. They cannot require workers to stay with the firm; the Thirteenth Amendment to the United States Constitution, after all, bars involuntary servitude. Patents are no answer when the learning cannot—like Big Ideas—be reduced to technical specifications in a patent application, but rather takes the form of increased intuition and judgment that yield a stream of future innovations.

This dilemma explains, in part, the rise of the Japanese-American corporation, which I referred to earlier. For many American firms, buying complex parts from the Japanese was more economical than training their own employees to make them precisely because firms could not guarantee themselves any harvest from investing in experience. Why go to the expense of giving your design and production engineers such valuable experience if almost half of them would leave the firm within two years to become Triumphant Individuals on their own?[3] In Japan such an investment was worth its price because engineers could be expected to spend their lifetimes with the firm.[4] There, the myth of the Triumphant Individual was less rooted than that of the Loyal Teammate. Thus when the Sperry Corporation announced in 1985 that it would stop making its own small computers and begin to rely on Hitachi for the computers it sold under the Sperry name, investment analysts welcomed the news. They noted that Sperry would save tens of millions of dollars that it otherwise would have to spend on developing technologies for its next generation of machines—an investment that it could not be sure it would ever recoup.[5] Some critics charged that the stock market was forcing a shortsighted view on Sperry. But both the market and Sperry were behaving rationally, in terms of the anticipated return to Sperry's shareholders. The decision was irrational only from the standpoint of the American economy as a whole, which otherwise would have benefited if more scientists, engineers, technicians, and production workers were trained in the next generation of small-computer technology.

By the 1980s this disjuncture between the private and social returns of investment in people was widespread. When Guardian Industries wanted to get into the fiberglass insulation business, it simply hired away six Manville Corporation employees, who knew all about how to produce the material. Manville had spent $9 million over seven years to gain that expertise; Guardian was selling its own brand in just eighteen months. Next time, Manville (and others like it) would be more reluctant to make such large investments.[6]

American companies were energetically but seldom successfully suing former workers for walking off with hard-won expertise. In the mid-1980s even California's famed Silicon Valley was embroiled in such litigation. It was not uncommon to throw a good-bye dinner for a key employee one night and then serve legal papers on him the next morning. When Steven Jobs, co-founder of Apple Computer, left the firm to start another—taking with him his cumulative experience and that of several other engineers whom he brought along—the action reverberated throughout Santa Clara County. What would become of Apple's shareholders and other employees who had relied on the expertise of Jobs and the defecting engineers? All over the Valley, the entrepreneurs who had founded the major high-technology companies were being succeeded by second and third generations of entrepreneurs who wanted to found their own. In 1985, one out of three of the Valley's skilled engineers left their companies. As each successive group peeled off from the former—carrying away the experience necessary for devising future products—it became ever more difficult to reap full rewards on the initial investments.

This in turn caused investors to be more wary. And as fewer investments were made, Silicon Valley began to falter.[7]

5

The risk of exploitation runs the other way as well. Consider a company that makes die castings for automobiles, appliances, and factory machines. The market for standard castings is shrinking, as ever more of these end products are produced abroad. The future lies in doing precision casts for computer parts and missile components, a process requiring substantial collective investment. Suppose the firm's chief executive asks his material supplier to develop an unusual blend of aluminum and silicon, which will be easier to cast into small sizes and intricate shapes. He asks his employees to forego wage increases for the next two years, so that the firm has enough cash to pay for the new molds and computers it will need. He asks the towns and cities where the firm's factories are located to reduce the firm's tax bill to free up funds for the retooling. His reputation for solid investments earns the firm's bonds a good rating, and creditors buy up a new issue despite its unspectacular interest rate. The implicit promise made to all these parties is that, once the transition is complete, the firm will survive and prosper, and all who depend on it will be better off. Suppliers, workers, creditors, and city officials go along.

Two years later, the new precision die casting operation earns gratifying returns and is relatively safe from foreign competition. The future looks so bright, in fact, that the firm is acquired by a group of investors who offer the firm's shareholders a hefty premium over the current market price of their shares. The new group of investors pays for these shares with money borrowed from pension funds and savings and loan companies at relatively high interest rates. These loans are secured by the value of the firm's assets.

The chief executive who orchestrated the retooling promptly resigns, and the new group takes over the management of the firm. They inform the firm's employees that they are expected to continue working at the low wages to which they agreed two years before. They announce that because the firm is now so much more efficient, some of the employees will be let go. The new management demands a price cut for the hybrid material its suppliers developed; otherwise, it will contract with another supplier at the same price. The city gets a similar message: more tax abatements, or the firm decamps to another city. The company's creditors got the news via the bond market: The firm's additional indebtedness has substantially increased the risk of eventual default and reduced the value of the bonds.

No party reaps the return it anticipated when it made its investment; none has any certain recourse in contract law. All would have done better by cutting their losses in the first place and refusing to cooperate in the firm's renewal. The new owners have, in effect, expropriated the benefits that were to go to these parties under the tacit agreements made with the former chief executive.[8]

Three years later, when the South Koreans begin producing precision castings, the firm's new owners realize that to stay competitive they must offer customers still greater value. They prepare a plan to incorporate customized services into the product—milling, drilling, plating, trimming, and finishing the precision casts according to the customer's special needs. But the employees, suppliers, and other constituents will not be fooled again. They balk at participating in new investment without elaborate formal contracts that complicate and constrain retooling efforts. Covenants on the new debt limit investment options. Each participant insists that every obligation be spelled out in advance, every contingency clearly described. It should come as no surprise that the contract-bound organization proves incapable of the sort of quick, creative responses to customer needs that will keep it competitive.

This story, too, has been replayed across America. The Chrysler Corporation, for example, received concessions from employees, suppliers, bank creditors, and the government during its near collapse in 1979 and 1980. Everyone contributed out of fear that the company would lapse into bankruptcy if they did not. But

Chrysler continued to close plants and lay off workers. By the end, the firm employed one third fewer people than it had at the start, and many of the cars it sold were being made in Japan. Thus the largest beneficiaries of the sacrifices were Chrysler's managers, who enjoyed magnificent bonuses, and its investors, whose shareholdings increased substantially in value as the firm recovered.[9] Those Chrysler workers who survived until the austerity campaign paid off with spectacular gains in profit received only moderate pay increases. It seemed doubtful that Chrysler workers would willingly sacrifice again.

Other enterprises experiencing competitive strains followed a similar route. In 1982 the management of General Motors persuaded GM workers that to keep the company competitive they had to scale back their wage and benefit expectations. Workers agreed to sacrifice for the long term, but on the very day the new contract was ratified, GM announced a new and more generous executive bonus program. Eastern Airlines faced bankruptcy in 1984. Its workers, challenged to help save the company, agreed to reduced wages and benefits in exchange for a seat on the board of directors and a chunk of common stock. But two years later, when one of Eastern's unions refused further reductions, Eastern's board accepted a takeover offer from the Texas Air Corporation. Texas Air's chairman was notorious with labor for a ploy he pulled off with an earlier acquisition: After buying Continental Airlines he had filed for bankruptcy, which let him repudiate union contracts, lay off two thirds of the labor force, and cut wages by half.[10]

Some contracts were simply disavowed when they became burdensome. Pipeline companies that sell natural gas wholesale had expected in the 1970s that the demand for natural gas would continue to rise. So they agreed to pay escalating prices to natural gas producers, who in turn invested in more production capacity. But when energy prices plummeted in the 1980s, several pipeline companies promptly walked away from their agreements without making any effort to negotiate new terms and left the gas producers with excess capacity and substantial losses. In the summer of 1983 the Washington Public Power Supply System merely defaulted on interest payments due on $2.25 billion in bonds held by tens of thousands of investors.[11]

Tacit understandings were breached when they became inconvenient. Employees in many companies assumed that they would receive any surpluses that might accumulate in their pension funds' investment portfolios, over and above minimum sums required to be paid out to them as pensions. But this assumption was based upon informal agreements; the pension plans did not stipulate precisely what would be done with any surpluses. So firms with surpluses in their funds cashed them in, converted the minimum sums to annuities, and kept the surpluses for themselves and their shareholders. By the mid-1980s corporate raiders were on the prowl for firms that had not yet exploited this easy source of cash; when they found one, they offered shareholders a premium over the market price of the shares, reflecting this windfall.

6

Nor were shareholders immune from exploitation by the stewards of their wealth, corporate managers. The erosion of good faith was amply illustrated, for example, by the device of the "golden parachute," which became routine during the merger wave of the early 1980s. This was a generous severance payment, often totaling a large multiple of the executive's annual salary and bonus, which was awarded—the parachute automatically opened, as it were—when a takeover became successful. The telling point is the justification invoked: The protected executives suggested such insurance was essential to preserve their impartial judgment about unfriendly takeover bids. Without the parachute, so the argument went, the executive would be tempted to fight the takeover even if it was in the best interests of the shareholders. This logic suggested that the only way shareholders could trust corporate executives not to feather their nests at the shareholders' expense was to provide them a prefeathered nest at the shareholders' expense.

By the mid-1980s another technique known as the leveraged

buyout had come into vogue. The process was quite simple. Executives borrowed money from banks or the credit market to buy up their company's stock. The loans or bonds, which carried high interest rates, were backed by the company's assets. The executive then owned the company. The argument was that once managers' wealth was tied up in the company, they would adopt a more efficient, more entrepreneurial managerial style and improve the firm's performance; executives who owned their company would work harder and better. Yet from the standpoint of the company's shareholders, this was a curious argument indeed. If ownership would so improve management, it had presumably been deficient in the past. Perhaps the managers, unmotivated by their salaries alone, had lounged around the executive suites daydreaming about how energetic they would be if only the company were theirs. Or perhaps they had developed some new product or marketing scheme, but delayed releasing it until they could reap the full reward. Executives proposing to buy their companies had an inherent conflict of interest. How could they advise owners on whether to sell their shares when they themselves were the aspiring purchasers? If a small group of top managers could borrow to the hilt to buy their company and still expect a handsome return, it would seem wise for the original shareholders to hang on to their stakes in order to gain some of the action.

7

When is it economically rational to violate a trust? Those who renege on informal promises and understandings surely bear a burden: They must live with a sullied reputation. Notoriety has its costs; parties who once repudiated obligations will find it harder to gain trust in the future. Employees who abandon a firm after gaining valuable experience, managers who abandon suppliers and employees after gaining concessions, suppliers who walk away from burdensome contracts, managers who feather their nests at shareholders' expense—all must live with the long-term consequences of their onetime gains. But these consequences may be more than balanced by the onetime gains of exploitation. This is especially likely in a highly mobile, anonymous society. Reputations, like unpaid bills, often cannot keep up with those who move quickly.

For many Americans a lifetime of work entails relatively few repeat dealings. The typical American curriculum vitae records an unattached self who advances from job to job, organization to organization, place to place—as horizontally mobile as upwardly. By 1985 the average corporate manager stayed put for four and a half years; the average chief executive, four years; the average employee, even less.[12] Corporations themselves changed hands at a rapid pace, often altering their names, locations, and images in the process. Mergers and acquisitions remained a favorite sport, and nearly half of all senior executives left their jobs within a year after their companies were taken over.[13] When Esmark absorbed Norton Simon, Inc. in 1983, for example, many key Norton Simon executives departed. A year later Esmark itself was acquired by Beatrice Companies, which proceeded to slash Esmark's staff. Two years after that, Beatrice, in turn, was taken over by a group of investors that included several former Esmark executives, who promptly dismissed the latest regime. In these games of corporate musical chairs, the underlying production process typically remains unaltered.

Trust breakers thus stand a good chance of dodging the full consequences of their behavior in part because they outrun them, and in part because the damage is inherently cumulative and systemic. Rather than attaching solely to the offending person or firm, the effects are likely to be diffused—resulting in a general reduction of trust in all commercial dealings. Managers who feel exploited by departing employees are less forthcoming with subsequent employees. Suppliers or workers who are mistreated by one set of managers do not make the same mistake again when they deal with a different set. Shareholders are more meticulous in their choice of firm. Like jilted lovers, these parties are far more cautious next time. And their caution is shared by others who, although they have had no direct experience of being exploited, learn by observation to keep their guards up. No one wants to be a sucker.[14]

This systemic erosion of trust precipitates all manner of precautions. Commercial dealings are hedged about by ever more elaborate contracts. There is a proliferation of work rules, codes, and standards to be followed. Requirements and expectations are well documented in advance; enforcement procedures are minutely delineated. Laws are spelled out in greater detail, so that next time no party will be surprised by the opportunistic move of another. Rules governing bankruptcies, pension plans, the fiduciary responsibilities of corporate officers, and corporate takeovers, among other transactions, are rendered ever more specific. Reciprocal rights and obligations are codified in ever more voluminous detail.

As a result, the opportunistic behavior of a relative few reduces the flexibility of the entire system. Collective entrepreneurialism becomes impossible. Because no one can be sure that someone else might not violate a trust, everyone takes precautions. Like a university honor code that, once transgressed, is replaced by a book of detailed stipulations, the exploitation of tacit commercial understandings results in a stifling profusion of contractual particulars.

8

When opportunism becomes an accepted feature of commercial life, no legal formulation can fully deter it. Language is never free from ambiguity. Loopholes can be discovered even in the most detailed of contracts or rules. The exploitation of such loopholes invites, in turn, still more tedious and constraining rules the next time around. As purchasers slip out of supply contracts, future supply contracts become longer and more complex. As takeover defenses proliferate, takeover tactics become ever more intricate. As corporate borrowers manage to pile new debt upon old, earlier creditors demand burdensome new guarantees for additional loans. As corporations smoothly circumvent pension plans or wage agreements, subsequent pension and wage agreements grow ever more specific.

The principle is understood by every practicing lawyer, accountant, and investment banker in America: Red tape multiplies with the profusion of finagles it seeks to contain, and vice versa. And as contractual refinements progress, litigation over them also escalates, for each party feels compelled to contest adverse interpretations of the ever more convoluted contracts and rules. Employees sue managers, shareholders sue directors, creditors sue those who audited the corporate books, everyone sues the companies that insure everyone else against liability.

Those who get paid for rearranging economic assets, rather than enhancing their value, have a not inconsiderable pecuniary interest in the continued deterioration of commercial trust. The business pages of the morning paper offer continuous news of novel ploys and counterploys, as paper entrepreneurs seek to outmaneuver one another. Every new thrust invites a more sophisticated parry, requiring an ever larger number of lawyers, accountants, and financial advisers to execute it. Between 1970 and 1985 the yearly total of private contractual disputes brought before federal courts tripled, to 35,400.[15] And the number and remuneration of lawyers and financial specialists steadily rose through the ups and downs of the real economy.[16]

The party that refuses to take part in the game is at a distinct disadvantage. Self-righteousness is a poor substitute for strategy. The probability that others may try to exploit a relationship inspires a widespread resolve to be the exploiter rather than the exploitee. Taking immediate advantage of ambiguities in contracts and rules, for example, makes eminent sense when the other party, given a chance, can be expected to twist them to serve its own purposes. Similarly, in a context of suspicion and opportunism, information is transformed from a tool to a weapon. Withholding technical and economic data that, if shared, could boost joint productivity can be the only logical strategy for individuals who have learned to distrust their coworkers and managers.

Such stratagems, while rational from the standpoint of the parties involved, absorb time and effort and undermine joint endeavors. They make it far more difficult for enterprises to shift and evolve in response to new commercial opportunities. They reduce the system's capacity to generate wealth.

A culture of opportunistic individualism aborts collective entrepreneurialism. It induces collective gridlock. When drivers going north and south opportunistically crowd into an intersection as the light turns red, they block the drivers moving east and west from going through on the green light. The maneuver is perfectly understandable from the standpoint of the first motorists, who thus ensure they will not be the ones trapped by other drivers using the same ploy. Gridlock violators seldom suffer directly from their opportunism; city driving is a sufficiently anonymous activity that they are likely to get through with their reputations intact. But the cumulative effect of such behavior is to ensnarl traffic, and the greater the pressure on the traffic system, the more tightly gridlock takes hold.

Collective entrepreneurialism depends on commercial trust. Collective gridlock ensues when trust breaks down. The American economy, now in transition, generates countless opportunities for mutual endeavor and joint gains, but at the same time countless invitations to opportunism. Each participant, knowing this and wary of being victimized, foreswears trusting collaboration. Thus the system's evolution is stymied. This—not the contest between lone entrepreneurs and regiments of drones—is the dilemma we face.

CHAPTER 12

TRIUMPH
RECONSIDERED

1

The Triumphant Individual has been a permanent character in American mythology. He has appeared in different guises throughout our history: the pilgrim, the minuteman, the explorer, the pioneer and homesteader, the cowboy, the inventor, the path-breaking aviator, the combat hero. During recent decades the parable has been retold with the business entrepreneur cast in the lead role. In this version, it is his daring and imagination that propels the economy. His is the role to which we all aspire but which few of us can ever hope to attain. Most of us are fated for routine tasks implementing entrepreneurs' Big Ideas. The prevailing economic debate, accordingly, has turned on how to induce the entrepreneur to unleash his efforts, and how sternly to discipline the drones and how briskly to keep them moving out of obsolete functions and into more productive jobs. The question, in short, has been the proper balance between economic growth and fairness. Conservative disciplinarians have tended to put more stress on growth; liberal conciliators have emphasized fairness.

But this debate, like that over the Mob at the Gates, has been strangely out of sync with the new challenges America confronts. Global competition and rapid technological change have strained the system of stable mass production. Big Ideas devised by lone entrepreneurs—major inventions, scientific breakthroughs, dramatically new ways of doing things—can now move readily to the far reaches of the globe, where huge pools of willing low-wage labor await. The alternative to matching Third World wage bids—or to opting out of the competition through protectionism—lies in seeking the future not in stable mass production, but in continuous refinement and elaboration. These two paths entail quite different choices.

The first path—toward stable mass production—relies on cutting labor costs and leaping into wholly new product lines as old ones are played out. For managers this path has meant undertaking (or threatening) massive layoffs, moving (or threatening to move) to lower-wage states and countries, parceling out work to lower-cost suppliers, automating to cut total employment, and diversifying into radically different goods and services. For workers this path has meant defending existing jobs and pay scales, grudgingly conceding lower wages and benefits, shifting burdens by accepting lower pay scales for newly hired workers, seeking protection from foreign competition, and occasionally striking.

The second path—toward collective entrepreneurialism—involves increasing labor *value*. For managers this path means continuously retraining employees for more complex tasks, automating in ways that cut routine tasks and enhance worker flexibility and creativity, diffusing responsibility for innovation, taking seriously labor's concern for job security, and giving workers a stake in improved productivity via profit-linked bonuses and stock plans. For workers this second path means accepting flexible job classifications and work rules, agreeing to wage rates linked to profits and productivity improvements, and generally taking greater responsibility for the soundness and efficiency of the enterprise. The second path also involves a closer and more permanent relationship with other parties that have a stake in the firm—suppliers, dealers, creditors, even the towns and cities in which the firm resides.

On this second path, all those associated with the firm become partners in its future. The distinction between entrepreneurs and drones breaks down. Each member of the enterprise participates in its evolution. All have a commitment to the firm's continued success. Both paths can boost profits and improve competitiveness in the short run. But only the second can maintain and improve America's standard of living over time.

The problem is that the first path is easier to follow, at least in the short term. It economizes on that perilously rare commodity, trust. In the more fluid and more dangerous commercial world of the late twentieth century, each group has been ever more anxious to preserve its status, even at the expense of others. Claimants have dug in. They have sought to immunize themselves against change by defending their grip on the status quo and shifting risk to others. Managers have sought stability by resorting to intricate, economically sterile legal and financial dodges that dump risk on employees, suppliers, or investors. Investors, meanwhile, have rewarded managers who cut short-run labor costs and abrogated burdensome contracts. Unionized workers have doggedly demanded increases in wages and benefits, even at the expense of more junior workers whose jobs may have to be sacrificed. Other workers have absconded with valuable training and experience. Each party has spent ever greater time and effort trying to outmaneuver the others.

The frequent result has been collective gridlock. The resulting loss is largely invisible, because we cannot see the potential in our economy that remains unfulfilled. The only evidence is circumstantial: a failure to improve productivity, stagnant incomes, a loss of competitiveness. We blame the shadowy "them" for our problems and also fret over the federal deficit or the supply of money. But the failure lies deeper, and closer. Our productive organizations are too often marked by suspicion, insecurity, and opportunism. Employees know they can be sacked at any time. Executives are dumped in response to a short-run drop in earnings, or they preemptively walk off with the goods. This fearful atmosphere inhibits the flow of accurate information. Bad news is buried below until it blossoms into a major crisis or scandal; good ideas rarely surface. Job insecurity discourages cooperation even among employees at roughly the same level. Why help your junior colleague if there is a risk he will displace you when he learns his job? Since the system appears to be rigged, the only rational response is to be self-seeking and cunning. Within a productive system that depends ever more on cooperation and good faith, we have spawned a dominant work ethic characterized by cynicism and manipulation. Its most visible symptom is shoddy workmanship. Its more insidious manifestation is paper entrepreneurialism.

2

There is no ready technique for overcoming gridlock. Collaboration cannot be enforced. (Not even police officers stationed at every intersection during rush hour can always keep the way clear.) The central challenge is to foster collective commitment and reduce exploitative maneuver. Outside incentives can help. (If I'm convinced the police will keep the intersection open, I'm less determined to block it lest I be blocked.) But incentives are not central; culture is, the deep culture that shapes and is shaped by our common mythology.

In recent years we have been treated to a number of inspirational management texts that instruct executives to be kinder to employees, treat them with respect, listen to them, and make them feel they are part of the team. Bookstores bulge with new volumes of anecdotes about creating, achieving, or becoming impassioned about excellence—preferably within one minute. Managers are supposed to walk around, touch employees, get directly involved, effervesce with praise and encouragement, stage celebrations and indulge in hoopla. Some of this is sound, some of it is hogwash. But most of it, even the best, is a matter of atmospherics, superficial, and treated as such. The effervescent executive will be gone in a few years, many of the employees will be gone, and the owners will be different as well. The hoopla is transient; the praise and involvement, mere devices to motivate people. The firm itself is assumed to be an instrument for making money, nothing more. When times require it, employees will be sacked. Contracts will not be renewed. Everybody knows this. Everybody responds accordingly.

Indeed, the legal and economic foundations of the American corporation support this instrumental view. Within the network of contractual relationships that comprise the firm, managers are formally empowered to act on behalf of the investors of capital, to maximize the value of their shares, and nothing more. Internal working relationships have value only insofar as they are directly instrumental to this goal. Productive alliances are simply the temporary devices by which Triumphant Individuals may eventually triumph. American culture accepts, even encourages the breaking of commercial relationships when they get in the way.

But collective entrepreneurialism rests on a different set of cultural premises. The firm is a community. The relationships that comprise it have a value in themselves; they are not merely instrumental. Personal satisfactions derive, in part, from commitment to this community. And such commitments transcend contractual agreements. Thus when the relationships sour, the first responsibility of all those involved with them is to try to adapt them and restore their value. By this view, the market is a signaling device to the organizations that inhabit the economy, not their reason for existence. Membership within such organizations entails reciprocal responsibilities and mutual benefits. Loyalty, trust, and cooperation matter more than the ease of exit.

The myth of the Triumphant Individual may have been appropriate to a simpler and more insular economy. But within a complex system such as ours, there are so many potential bottlenecks and critical levers, so many transactions to be coordinated among so many people, that opportunistic individualism more often short-circuits progress than advances it. The fear of exploitation, firmly founded on experience, mandates defensiveness and preemptive exploitation. Each party is led to limit his own responsibility and commitment, and to take refuge in explicit contracts, rules, and other guarantees. Such a culture inhibits economic flexibility.

The skeptic warns that collective entrepreneurialism is at odds with American culture; we should stick to the individualistic variety we do best. But there's a catch. The Triumphant Individual's Big Ideas are now footloose, and can be turned into realities by drone workers anywhere; his Big Finagles are likely to remain at home, and confound collaboration. Thus the current version of the American myth of the Triumphant Individual may have outlasted its time. It is no longer useful as a guide to our place in the world.

PART THREE

THE
BENEVOLENT
COMMUNITY

THE SYSTEM OF
SOCIAL BENEVOLENCE

1

The parable of the Benevolent Community speaks of the nature and the degree of Americans' obligations to one another. Like the other myths, this one has altered over time. During wars and depressions, the theme has been social solidarity, mutual sacrifice, and joint progress. In more recent years, however, it has been a tale of our charity and compassion toward the poor, and of their dependency and the stubborn persistence of poverty.

Yet as the stories we tell about obligation and benevolence have shifted, the instruments of benevolence—the programs we enact and fund—have come to have less to do with aid to the poor and more to do with redistribution among the relatively comfortable majority of Americans. As with the other myths, the reigning version of the Benevolent Community may be too far adrift from reality to reliably guide our discussions and debates. We do indeed transfer large sums of money to one another to avoid or compensate for hardship. But little of this goes to the groups we think of when we refer to "the poor." We talk a good deal, and sincerely, of charity and compassion. But most of the social programs we support are based on the idea of insurance. We worry about welfare dependency and the irresponsibility of the poor, but—as with the other mythic realms—we have paid

scant attention to the mutual responsibilities that should un-
dergird these relationships, and to the reciprocal benefits that
could emerge from them.

Our ideas about benevolence are inchoate, and in some ways
simply mistaken. The instruments of benevolence are poorly considered and unexamined in their effects; some of the flows of
resources are much too large, some much too small. There are
yawning gaps. The system continues to evolve, without much
public awareness or debate about the whole of it, in ways unrelated
to the nation's emerging needs in a radically different world.

2

The Benevolent Community's most well-endowed and popular
efforts have not been for "the poor"; they have been for all of us.
These include Medicare and Social Security's cash benefits; unemployment insurance; tax-favored pensions, tax-free health insurance, and other social services delivered through corporations;
and even liability awards in tort suits. Together, they comprise
the system through which most Americans have insured themselves, their families, and their compatriots against adversity.

We have distinguished these forms of benevolence from "welfare," on the rationale that their purpose is not to eradicate poverty, but rather to avoid a precipitous decline in anyone's standard
of living brought on by hardship. On closer examination, however, the distinction begins to blur. Both social insurance and
welfare redistribute income in response to perceived need. Under
both schemes, the most obvious redistribution is from those who
have avoided a particular hardship to those who have not. Moreover, because hardship is only rarely just a matter of bad luck,
both welfare and social insurance to some extent shift resources
from the prudent to the careless.

Aside from levels of funding, and intimately linked to them,
the principal difference between the two sets of programs lies in
the degree to which most of us identify with those in need. Americans do not perceive Social Security, Medicare, and other forms
of social insurance as taking money from "us" and giving it to

"them." We think of ourselves as among the beneficiaries of social insurance. Most of us assume that we face the same risks as do those who draw upon these programs—any of us could die, leaving spouses and children behind; we could reach old age without adequate savings to see us through; we might succumb to illness or disability, or suffer temporary unemployment. By the same token, the weaknesses and foibles of our fellow recipients of social insurance are somehow familiar and understandable, and thus forgivable: Those who have not taken good care of their health, or willingly subjected their bodies or their savings to larger than normal risks, with the result that they are now in dire straits, perhaps have been foolish and negligent. But we have been willing to support them nonetheless. By pooling our resources we spread these potential losses widely among us, so that each of us ends up bearing only a small part of the burden. Such loss spreading is presumed to be one of the advantages of living in civilized society. Such expenditures are legitimized by a pervasive sense of "there but for the grace of God go I."

The lot of "the poor" seems different. We all know we face some risk of accident, unemployment, or debilitating disease; we all expect to grow old. But we know we will not be born into poverty, and we assume that our children will not be. Welfare, accordingly, is thought to be for "them"—entailing a transfer of wealth from us. Expenditures on welfare are justified by a sense of "there but for my charity they'd go under."

3

Together, welfare and social insurance comprised almost half of the federal budget in 1985; one dollar out of every nine that Americans spent that year went to pay for these programs. But 83 cents went for social insurance; only 17 cents for welfare. Social Security and Medicare alone accounted for over 6 percent of America's national product; cash assistance for the nonelderly poor, substantially less than 1 percent. America paid out less in food stamps for the poor than in pensions for its retired civil servants. As a proportion of national product, programs aimed at

157

the poor did not grow at all since 1972, while social insurance mushroomed. Aid to Families with Dependent Children, the centerpiece of welfare, declined by one third.

The two largest social insurance programs, Social Security and Medicare, have remained extremely popular. By 1985, 39 million Americans were receiving government checks providing financial support and health care. These recipients were elderly, disabled, or dependent on breadwinners who had died. More than 22 million of them relied on such payments as their primary source of income. The programs were well-regarded because they benefited "us." Opinion polls confirmed their popularity: In contrast to welfare, which the public treated with growing suspicion, at least two thirds of the nation supported Medicare; 90 percent favored Social Security.[1] Ronald Reagan's early proposal to cut Social Security benefits elicited such an outcry that his later budgets carefully sheltered Social Security and Medicare, just as they protected defense. There was not much left to cut, except for the relatively small welfare system.

4

Social Security came to America as a descendant of Otto von Bismarck's insurance schemes for old age, sickness, and unemployment. The German leader had put them into effect in the 1890s, in an attempt to maintain the loyalties of the German working class in the face of the rising Social Democrats. The idea was later adopted by Britain's Lloyd George in a similar effort to woo the working class away from the Labour party. The insurance schemes were to be universally applied and compulsory.

Franklin D. Roosevelt emphasized these qualities when he brought the idea to America. "I see no reason why every child, from the day he is born, shouldn't be a member of the social security system," he said. Every child should be protected against misfortune, from cradle to grave. "When he begins to grow up, he should know he will receive old-age benefits direct from the insurance system to which he will belong all his life. If he is out of work, he gets a benefit. If he is sick or crippled, he gets a benefit."[2] Roosevelt never embraced the idea of welfare; he repeatedly denounced "the dole." His New Deal involved no major redistribution of income from rich to poor, but only emergency relief designed to tide people over until the economy rebounded, and aid to the chronically ill, homeless, and abandoned. Even Social Security, in its initial stages, was limited to those who worked.[3] It was sold to the American people as a system of insurance, not welfare: There would be a trust fund. Each American would have his own Social Security account, recording the amounts of money that he and his employer had contributed through payroll taxes. Retirees, disabled workers, or dependents would have a right to collect on these accounts. Charity had nothing to do with it. "Those [payroll] taxes were never a problem of economics," Roosevelt recounted. "They are politics all the way through. We put those payroll contributions there so as to give the contributors a legal, moral, and political right to collect their pensions and their unemployment benefits."[4]

The initial concept proved so popular that the Social Security system grew over time. Its benefits were extended; its coverage was broadened. In 1950 only 16 percent of Americans over sixty-five years of age had been eligible for Social Security. By 1970 over 90 percent were. And as it expanded, its redistributions grew, while the principle (and the perception) of insurance endured. Widows and children were added early on, then the disabled. Beneficiaries who had had relatively low average earnings in their working years were deemed entitled to a higher return on their contributions than beneficiaries who had contributed more. Hospitalization benefits were added, in the form of Medicare. Workers could retire earlier than age sixty-five. And finally, as a hedge against inflation, benefit levels were tied to consumer prices. Together, these changes comprised a major system of redistribution. And they were expensive, requiring that payroll taxes go up, steadily, from 1 percent of a worker's wages in 1935 to about 7 percent by the mid-1980s. (In fact, if employers' contributions are counted as coming at the expense of higher wages, as they probably should be, the payroll tax rose to over 14 percent.)

5

By 1985 the biggest flow of income redistribution in America was from younger workers to the elderly. Social Security benefits had increased almost by half since 1970 in real terms, while average wages had hardly increased at all.[5] Retirees who had had relatively high incomes during their working lives received (in real terms) about three times what they had contributed to the system; poorer retirees collected up to fifteen times their contributions. Medicare benefits ballooned too, as more Americans lived longer and tended to die of chronic conditions like cancer and heart disease rather than quick killers like pneumonia. By the 1980s the average retired person received an additional 50 cents of health care benefits for every dollar received of retirement payments.

The idea of an insurance pool, funded by the same people who would later draw on it, was a mirage, and indeed had been from the start. The little-understood premise of the Social Security system, even as Roosevelt designed it, was that it was funded by the *next* generation of workers. Their contributions went directly to pay the benefits of those who had already retired. For most of the system's history, the buckets have been emptied as fast as they were filled. The trust fund was primarily a bookkeeping device. There were no personal accounts; nothing was being accumulated by individual contributors. So as Social Security benefits were expanded over time, current workers had to contribute that much more to keep the buckets filled. They did so willingly on the supposition that they were in fact saving for themselves. But as they did so, their take-home earnings declined; and as average earnings stagnated through the 1970s and 1980s, they became ever more resistant to paying out additional sums in welfare to "them."

The result was a shift, over time, in the distribution of American poverty. As late as 1970 an elderly person was more likely to be living in poverty than a child. But by 1985 a child was nearly six times more likely to be poor than an elderly person. This shift occurred imperceptibly, without public discussion or deliberation. It was a natural consequence of our prevailing social philosophy, our governing myth. The elderly were "us"; they had earned their social insurance. Poor children—many of them black or Hispanic, living in central cities—were "them." They were the objects of our charity.

This distinction was illuminated in the 1980s by what was perceived to be a remaining gap in the system of social insurance for the elderly. Over 5 percent of Americans over age sixty-five lived in nursing homes. Nursing home care was expensive—costing over $30,000 a year. And many elderly found themselves facing huge medical bills, far in excess of what Medicare would reimburse or retirement benefits support. But no help was available to pay these sorts of expenses, outside of welfare. And to qualify for welfare, in the form of Medicaid, it was first necessary to join "the poor." You had to use up your accumulated savings and accept the stigma of poverty and charity. Since its inception under the Johnson administration, Medicaid had been Medicare's poor stepchild. Rather than being financed by payroll taxes, it was supported by general revenues. Part of its financing came from the states, which meant that it was subject to differing state regulations. And it remained politically vulnerable. Medicaid was for "them"; Medicare, for "us." Medicaid was charity; Medicare, social insurance. To become an object of charity was too humiliating for many Americans. Many swallowed their pride.[6] But they wanted "insurance" instead. Accordingly, politicians of all stripes, including many enemies of welfare, duly pledged to expand the social insurance system to deal with these hardships.

Roosevelt had appreciated from the start the mythic importance of casting redistribution as insurance rather than welfare. In 1939 one of his advisers noted that Social Security could be streamlined by dispensing with all the clerks who distributed Social Security cards, assigned numbers, maintained files on how much each cardholder and employer had contributed to date, and responded to personal inquiries about specific accounts. The adviser argued that these costly chores were a waste of time, since there were no real accounts to start with; money was simply transferred from contributors to beneficiaries. Roosevelt heard the argument and then patiently explained why all the clerks were necessary. They were not there to maintain the individual accounts. They were there to maintain the perception of social insurance.

> Your logic is correct, your facts are correct, but your conclusion's wrong. Now, I'll tell you why that account is not useless. That account is not to determine how much should be paid out and to control what should be paid out. That account is there so those sons of bitches up on the Hill can't ever abandon this system when I'm gone.[7]

And they never would.

6

Most Americans also benefit from a third major instrument of the social benevolence. These benefits are delivered to employees by the companies they work for. Like Social Security and Medicare, employee benefits have ballooned in recent years. In 1983 they comprised over 14 percent of employee compensation, up from just over 5 percent in 1950.[8] And like Social Security and Medicare, employee benefits have been enormously popular. Tax reformers periodically have tried to limit them, to no avail.

Most people tend to think of these benefits as private insurance rather than social spending. But they have been financed substantially by the income taxes all of us pay. Corporations provide these benefits in place of higher wages precisely because their employees do not have to pay income taxes on them.[9] Since a dollar's worth of tax-free health care is worth more to an employee than a taxable dollar of income destined to be spent on health care, for example, the company can save money by paying more in benefits and less in wages. The gap is filled by other taxpayers, who must pay more income tax to make up the difference. Thus this system of benefits has all the characteristics of social benevolence—a broad pooling of risk, financed through government, entailing substantial redistributions.

The public costs of this form of social benevolence have been high—below the cost of Social Security and Medicare, but a good deal higher than welfare spending. In 1984 Americans paid out $115 billion in income taxes to finance employee benefits.[10] This was almost twice the amount we paid out that year to finance all welfare programs for "the poor."[11]

Taxpayers spent about $18 billion to subsidize corporate health plans in 1984, or roughly as much as they spent on health care for the poor through Medicaid. But the two programs were never considered as alternative means of meeting the same goal. Political controversy swirled around Medicaid; but tax-free employee health insurance, by contrast, was seen as something that workers earned; the public contribution, when it was understood at all, was seen as self-evidently justifiable. A similar comparison could be drawn for other categories of aid. Tax-free day care for employees has never been subjected to budget review and continues to grow; Head Start, a comparable program for impoverished preschoolers, has been chronically vulnerable to budget cuts. Tax-free group life insurance for employees cost taxpayers about $2 billion. The welfare cost of supplemental food for poor women, infants, and children was half that sum. Tax-free pension contributions and earnings cost taxpayers over $50 billion; the total cost of cash aid for the poor was less than half that. All these welfare expenditures, and others like them, were declining or barely hanging on; their political legitimacy was eroding amid demands that the federal deficit be reduced. Employee benefits, meanwhile, were expanding.

By the mid-1980s most Americans were collecting at least one form of social benefit financed directly or indirectly by tax funds. About 65 percent of the population was covered by tax-favored employee health plans. Half the workers were employed by firms with pension plans. But a significant minority enjoyed no such benefits. Many small companies and self-employed workers found insurance premiums and pension plans to be too expensive, even with government's indirect support. Many of the nation's working poor, engaged in temporary or part-time jobs, had no access to company plans. Workers who were laid off from their jobs often lost their coverage. Thus millions of people fell through the gap—ineligible for welfare but detached from the system of tax-favored employee benefits. One result of this gap was that one out of five American children had no health insurance whatever.[12]

7

The fourth broad category of social benevolence comprises liability judgments against firms whose products or services cause injury. By the 1980s the nation's courts had embarked upon an unmistakable trend: Judges and juries were less concerned with whether the company that caused the injury was negligent than with how best to compensate the victim. Like the other instruments of social insurance we have been considering—Social Security, Medicare, and employee benefits—liability judgments mushroomed. In 1975, 1,500 product suits were filed in federal courts. Only 25 of them resulted in judgments over $1 million. Ten years later the number reached 11,000, and over 400 of them passed the million-dollar mark.[13]

This instrument of compensation should be considered of a piece with other forms of social insurance because we all pay for it. Doctors, ski resorts, and toy manufacturers, among many others, have sought to insure themselves against the possibility that one of their customers would sue them and collect a large award. As the risks and costs of such lawsuits have mounted, insurance premiums have risen. The costs of the higher premiums have been passed on to consumers in the form of higher prices for medical services, ski tickets, and toys. It was as if, in purchasing the item, we also purchased a small insurance policy against the possibility that we might be injured while using it.[14]

Liability suits are inherently inefficient instruments for insuring ourselves against injury. As total awards mounted, many victims received nothing, either because they lost in court or because they were unaware of their right to sue. And the victims who did get compensated ended up giving more than half their awards (on average) to their lawyers, who had instituted the suits on condition that they would receive a healthy fee upon winning.

8

We all know the world is a perilous place. Some people reach old age without adequate savings. Some die, leaving dependents without the wherewithal to fend for themselves. Some fall prey to sickness, which prevents them from working or requires expensive medical care. Some are seriously injured. Some lose their job and are unable to find another for a long time. Some lack the skills and child support to get a job in the first place. Many of these hardships can precipitate a long-term fall in economic status, or perpetuate poverty.

Which of these risks should we insure ourselves and our fellow citizens against? Which are the proper justifications of welfare or of charity? Does it matter which label we apply?

The choice matters a great deal. The idea of social insurance is inclusive. Its premise is that we all, mutually, depend on and contribute to the system, because we are all subject to the risks it secures us against. Social insurance reminds us of our interdependence. We are all in the same boat. By contrast, the idea of welfare is exclusive. Its premise is that some rely on the compassion of others. This logic emphasizes our differences. We are safely on the big ship, while they—the objects of our beneficence—are barely staying afloat on the life rafts we toss out.

In 1934 the framers of the Social Security system hoped that it would one day replace welfare. The idea of social insurance was both consistent with current versions of the American mythology, and compelling in a time when one quarter—and a quite representative quarter—of the nation was unemployed. Then, nearly everyone's boat was leaking. This was also a time when most blacks and millions of very poor whites lived invisibly on southern farms far removed from urban centers, and when most American families had two parents. Relatively few Mexicans and Puerto Ricans had reached our shores, few blacks had streamed into our cities from the South. Perhaps it was easier then, under those circumstances, to envision one comprehensive system of social benevolence, rather than two—one for "us" and one for "them"—and the accompanying patchwork we have contrived.

But the subsequent discovery of "the poor" bifurcated the system. This discovery inspired antipoverty programs and eligibility formulas that sharply distinguished the needy from the rest of us.

In the last decades of the century, social insurance was expanding its benefits while welfare was contracting. The system of social benevolence was tilted less toward bringing those born into poverty out of it, more toward sheltering the rest of us from insecurity.

CHAPTER 14

THE LIMITS OF
BENEVOLENCE

1

In America the principle of compassion toward the poor is non-partisan and nonsectarian, regularly proclaimed by preachers and politicians. The parable of the Benevolent Community informs endless rounds of exhortation and self-congratulation. Walter Mondale and fellow Democrats tried to seize the rhetorical high ground of righteousness in 1984, declaring "we're fair, we're decent, we're kind, and we're caring. We insist that, as we care for ourselves, there are some in America who need our help. There's a limit to what Americans will permit to happen in this good country of ours."[1] Ronald Reagan matched him, sentiment for sentiment, and scored extra points on style: "How can we love our country and not love our countrymen; and loving them, reach out a hand when they fall, heal them when they're sick, and provide opportunity to make them self-sufficient so they will be equal in fact and not just in theory?"[2]

No nation talks more about the importance of charity toward the less fortunate. No people organizes more concerts, bake sales, telethons, walkathons, and national hand-holdings to raise money for the hungry and homeless. None takes as seriously the problem of poverty or the ideal of equal opportunity. But few Western industrialized nations fail as miserably to bridge the gap between their richest and poorest citizens.[3] The irony is not incidental. During the last quarter century a consistent majority of Americans has believed that the income gap between the nation's rich and poor is too wide and should be narrowed.[4] But an equally consistent majority has been deeply suspicious of the basic tenets of welfare.[5]

"Welfare" was a dirty word for a long time before Ronald Reagan entered the White House. Conservatives had long assailed the welfare system for corroding the work ethic and retarding capital accumulation. They were gradually joined by liberals disenchanted with a system they saw as stigmatizing the poor. Both sides worried that welfare induced permanent dependency. Jimmy Carter campaigned against the welfare system's inefficiencies. State and federal welfare agencies symbolically transformed themselves into departments of "human services," disdaining the dreaded word "welfare." The stories that Americans began telling one another were of a welfare system run amok, draining the paychecks of working citizens, perverting the people it was meant to help, and ultimately harming the nation.

Compassion and generosity are still sentiments that Americans endorse and act on when it's a matter of concerts, bake sales, and other such voluntary activities. But when it comes to government welfare programs, the consensus has dissolved. It is widely accepted that welfare does not work, but there is no alternative vision of public action that might. The Benevolent Community is bereft of any guiding philosophy for demarcating public and private responsibilities. As private individuals, we understand our obligations toward the poor; as citizens, we are frequently baffled, disappointed, and suspicious.

2

There has been confusion, first, about the definition of the community within which benevolence should take root. Franklin D. Roosevelt's boldest innovation had been designating the *nation* as a community. At a time when the whole nation was stricken, and only a massive common campaign could hope to prevail over depression and fascism, this designation was compelling to the American people. But it was not until the mid-1960s, when Lyndon Johnson declared war on poverty, that Roosevelt's notion of a national community became linked to welfare. The marriage was not easy and never gained widespread political support. Public generosity could readily be mustered for the needy living nearby, in the same town or even the same state. These poor could be seen and heard; their plight was palpable. But the poor of another state or region—many of them black, filling central cities thousands of miles away—had less of a purchase on the citizens' sympathy. Generosity is a powerful sentiment, but its strength drops as distance and differentness from its object increase. And as guilt was pushed more prominently as a motive for aiding the poor, especially the black poor, welfare spending felt more like grim duty or even compulsion than like the embodiment of generosity. As a new wave of immigrants from Latin America and the Caribbean swarmed into the nation's cities in the 1970s and early 1980s, the ideal of national community seemed an even feebler motive. To many Americans, there seemed no principled difference between poor Hispanics—some of them illegal aliens—living in Los Angeles and poor Hispanics living in Mexico City. What were the purposes and proper limits of benevolence? The idea of national community offered no guidance.

By the 1980s, accordingly, a not insubstantial portion of the American public was ready to hear a new story about the Benevolent Community, one that defined benevolence as voluntary charity and defined community as the local neighborhood rather than the nation. It was to be a "renaissance of the American community, a rebirth of neighborhood," according to Reagan. The Republican platform for 1984 emphasized the new definition and encased it within a narrative that explained what had gone awry: "By centralizing responsibility for social programs in Washington, liberal experimenters destroyed the sense of community that sustains local institutions." It was necessary to put responsibility back where it belonged, in the neighborhood, where natural bonds of friendship and shared aspirations would nourish and guide generosity. By the end of his first term, Reagan could point to several of his initiatives that were premised on this idea—the "New Federalism," the block grant components of the 1981 tax and spending package, the private-sector initiatives task force, and, of course, his hostility to forced busing. Reagan declared that the new "emphasis on voluntarism, the mobilization of private groupings to deal with our social ills, is designed to foster . . . our sense of communal values." Reagan explicitly repudiated Roosevelt's vision: America was a nation of local communities, not a national community.[6]

This vision was emotionally appealing, mythically resonant, and profoundly out of sync with changing American reality. By the 1980s rather more Americans lived on military bases than lived in what could be called "neighborhoods" in the traditional sense (card games on the front porch, kids running over lawns and fields, corner soda fountains, town meetings, PTAs, and the friendly, familiar policemen and postmen). The majority lived in suburban subdivisions that extended helter-skelter in every direction, bordered by highways and punctuated by large shopping malls; or they lived in condominiums, townhouses, cooperative apartments, and retirement communities that promised privacy and safety in the better urban enclaves; or they inhabited dilapidated houses and apartments in the far less fashionable areas. Many worked at some distance from their homes and socialized with friends selected on some other basis than proximity. The people who happened to inhabit the geographic area immediately surrounding their homes had no special claim on their allegiances or affections. The average family, moreover, moved every five years or so.[7] These ersatz neighborhoods contained no shared history, no pattern of long-term association.

Even if they had the time or inclination to get to know their neighbors, most Americans would meet people who shared the same standard of living as they. If they were very poor, their neighborhood was likely to be populated by other very poor people; if very rich, by others who enjoyed the good things in life; if young and professional, then by other well-heeled, upwardly-mobiles. In sum, by the 1980s the meaning of neighborhood had changed. What had once been small towns or ethnic sections within larger cities had given way to economic enclaves whose members had little in common with one another but their average incomes.

The idea of neighborhood benevolence—of neighbors looking after one another—had little practical meaning in this new context. The sentiment remained attractive partly because of its nostalgic and romantic qualities, like a stroll down Main Street in Disneyland. But it was also attractive for a more insidious reason. The idea of community as neighborhood offered a way of enjoying the sentiment of benevolence without the burden of acting on it. Since responsibility ended at the borders of one's neighborhood, and most Americans could rest assured that their neighbors were not in dire straits, the apparent requirements of charity could be exhausted at small cost. If the inhabitants of another neighborhood needed help, they should look to one another; let them solve their problems, and we'll solve our own. The poor, meanwhile, clustered in their own, isolated neighborhoods. By the late 1980s many of America's older cities—forced to take ever more financial responsibility for the health, education, and welfare of their poor inhabitants—were becoming small islands of destitution within larger seas of suburban well-being.[8]

3

There were other confusions concerning our collective obligation to the poor. Most Americans subscribed to the ideal of equal opportunity. But what did this mean? Surely it included the notion that no citizens should endure legally enforced discrimination against their race or religion or national origin, in the form of segregated schools and public transportation. Many would extend the proscription to private discriminations by employers and sellers. But it was something else again to enforce equality of opportunity by imposing what many Americans saw as penalties against themselves: forcing them to bus their children to distant and more dangerous parts of town, or giving jobs and promotions to minorities ahead of other worthy candidates.[9]

The revolt of blue-collar and middle-class Americans against these liberal policies is generally explained by simple self-interest; suddenly, they were bearing the burden of providing the poor with equal opportunity. But to attribute all of the resistance to selfish motives misses an important part of the tale. These policies were neither explained nor justified by reference to any broader principles that fit them into a philosophy of social obligation. There was no convincing story to explain why this burden should fall so heavily upon the shoulders of working-class Americans.

A third confusion concerned the objects of benevolence. Who was needy? Conservatives argued that the only people who should be eligible for public assistance were those *unable* to care for themselves. Persons capable of working but who chose not to, or who worked but collected low incomes, did not deserve help. This argument, however, offered incomplete guidance. Even a mentally retarded teenage mother might be considered capable of living without public assistance if she shared a home with relatives, left her child with them or with friends each day, and traveled several hours to a menial job in a distant part of the city. Through most of human history, most people somehow managed to take care of themselves without public assistance, including many who lived with handicaps that most Americans would consider wholly debilitating. Thus the criterion of potential self-sufficiency remained thoroughly ambiguous. What should America expect of its poor and disadvantaged? What were the appropriate limits of public benevolence?

4

Before the mid-1960s America was inhabited by many poor people, but not by "the poor." Those who suffered material deprivation were not sharply differentiated from the rest of us because poverty was relative, mostly a matter of degree. With one quarter of the work force unemployed during the Depression decade of the 1930s, poverty was demonstrably not a condition that some morally flawed subgroup was solely subject to or responsible for. The subsequent wars, recessions, and demographic bulge of young postwar families with limited incomes confirmed America's collective experience of struggling to make ends meet.

The nation began to perceive "the poor" as a separate group only once the majority of Americans achieved relative economic security. New stories began to be told: The public was shocked to discover entire cultures of poverty, as revealed, for example, in Michael Harrington's tellingly titled book, *The Other America*,[10] journalistic accounts of life in Appalachia, dramatizations of the urban poor, like *Blackboard Jungle* and *West Side Story*, and the early rhetoric of antipoverty policy, which linked the movement for black civil rights to the plight of the poor.

In these new stories, the poor were different from the rest of us. They lived in exotic and mysterious environments; they sang their own songs and danced their own dances; their skin was often a different color, and they spoke in strange languages or with odd accents. Many of these groups, we discovered, had been poor for generations as the rest of us grew prosperous. The poverty of neglected minorities became a national scandal.

As with all such moral campaigns in America, the issue easily became a constitutional one. Many blacks were poor, and the two sets of deprivations, one based on deep-seated prejudice and the other on economic exclusion, were so entwined that welfare rights and civil rights came to be seen as much the same thing. This merger of newly asserted rights was argued in the courts. It was institutionalized in the community action agencies and the antipoverty bureaucracy that grew up around them. And it was dramatized by the urban riots of the late 1960s. These developments, in turn, served to further accentuate the differences between the poor and the rest of us. Just as blacks were entitled to affirmative remedies for the racial discrimination to which they had been subject, it was urged that the poor were entitled to a certain minimal standard of living. Welfare benefits were cast as *rights*. These claims implied a corresponding duty of the majority of Americans who were neither poor nor black to pay for them. But even before this logic was traumatically extended to busing and affirmative action, the poor were indisputably "them."

Government analysts, dutifully responding to the demands

of federal poverty agencies for a criterion by which to dispense the benefits now due, came up with the elegant notion of a "poverty line." This was the minimal amount of income that calculations revealed an American family would require to escape unacceptable want. Families whose total income fell below this theoretical line were in poverty; families above it were not.[11] The line distinguishing "us" from "them" was now defined with an accountant's apparent precision.[12]

The poverty-line definition of the needy, however corrosive of the ideal of mutual obligation, did serve to remind us of how many Americans were unable to support themselves. When the poverty index rose, we knew that the problem was getting worse. That explicit signal provoked comment and debate. A president who presided over a large increase in the poverty index had some explaining to do. But the price we paid for adhering to this symbolic definition, and the separation it implied between the poor and the rest of us, was significant.

Within American political discourse, the problem of poverty was now as neatly delineated as was the poor population itself. The boundary allowed the rest of us to distance ourselves emotionally. There was relief in the notion that the real poor were different from us. We could put aside discomfiting speculation that our comfort and their distress reflected luck as much as anything else. We could also escape the distress that comes in identifying oneself and family with others experiencing hardship. We may acknowledge a moral obligation to alleviate their lot, but we did not share their experience.

5

But in fact, most of the poor were not very different from the rest of us. Between 1975 and 1985 one out of three Americans fell below the poverty line at least once. Half of all who did remained there only one or two years. The poor did not shun work or live off welfare: Two thirds of the nonelderly poor lived in households where someone worked, and most of these families received no welfare payments at all. Two thirds of the very poor were white, living in rural or suburban areas of the country.[13] This is not to suggest that the "culture of poverty" was illusory. About 20 percent of the poor remained permanently submerged below the poverty line, trapped within urban ghettos and pockets of rural poverty. The problem of permanent poverty was smaller than commonly understood, however, and the line separating "us" from "them" far less distinct.

Nevertheless, the boundary drawn around "the poor" in the stories we told one another had transformed our understanding, perpetuating many of the problems we sought to solve. When the poor could be any one of us, public assistance was assumed to entail reciprocal benefits and responsibilities. Now it was a matter of charity, assigning no response and presuming no responsibilities on the part of recipients. This emphasized the redistributive nature of the transaction—our magnanimity and their dependency. This perception tended to project itself on us and them alike, undermining whatever sense of reciprocity there might otherwise have been. Poverty programs were chronically subject to the charge that government was doing too much or too little for "them." The programs seemed inadequate whenever large numbers of people were recorded as being under the poverty line. The programs seemed too generous whenever budget deficits or economic sluggishness seemed to require that government reduce its scope, or whenever "they" seemed undeserving of the benefits they received.

As the separateness of the poor became reinforced through racial, ethnic, or geographic isolation, a widening range of public services took on the character of welfare. As affluent urban dwellers deserted the public schools for private alternatives, public education came to be seen as a means of promoting equal opportunity rather than as an affirmation of our common culture. As middle-class Americans built vacation homes and joined private sports clubs, expenditures for public parks and playgrounds were justified by reference to the needs of poor children for outdoor recreation. As private hospitals—scrambling to cut costs— stopped subsidizing uninsured patients, support for public hospitals was cast as mostly a matter of aid to the poor.

By the 1980s the debate over welfare was essentially a series of variations on the question of how tough we should be on "them." Ronald Reagan answered it in the way an increasing portion of the public thought it should be answered: very tough. In the name of concentrating resources on the "truly needy," the administration proceeded to tighten eligibility requirements for food stamps, child nutrition, housing assistance, and Medicaid. It cut back on programs that dealt with anything beyond the bare necessities of life—programs like Head Start (preschool for poor four-year-olds), the Job Corps (work training for unemployed youngsters), vocational schooling, compensatory education, and the like.[14]

The debate would not end here, however. Americans would continue to be shocked, periodically, by dramatic revelations of hungry and homeless people across the land—many of them small children. At the same time, Americans would continue to be outraged by exposés of welfare fraud and dependency. The issue would remain bitterly contested, but unresolvable.

A more fruitful course would be to understand the issue not as unique to "them," or to the "problem of poverty," but as part of a larger set of questions about the nature of the Benevolent Community in modern America: What responsibilities do we owe one another? What should the deprived expect from the fortunate, and what should the fortunate expect of the deprived? How can we express our solidarity without rendering ourselves vulnerable to exploitation by those who would take advantage of our charity? It is to these issues that we now turn.

CHAPTER 15

A MATTER OF RESPONSIBILITY

1

The problem of irresponsibility is endemic to the Benevolent Community. Any system of social benevolence involves pooling the perils of a precarious existence. Because both fate *and* individual decisions determine who will require the community's assistance, any instrument of collective obligation—whether founded on the principle of insurance or that of welfare—offers individuals a device for shifting the cost of their own irresponsibility onto others. Knowing this, they may be less inclined to responsible behavior and well-considered choices in the first place. Irresponsibility can be infectious. As the community's members learn that risks are shared while pleasures are personal, more may be tempted into laxity and recklessness. The result is analogous to the economic gridlock discussed earlier: Without a potent sense of accountability, any system capable of conferring mutual benefits may be exploited. The greater the tendency toward irresponsibility and exploitation, the greater the costs of guarding against it, and the less capable the system is of realizing the ideals of community.

Americans appreciate this basic dilemma, but in a way that appears curiously unbalanced. The potential for irresponsibility inherent in social insurance programs has been largely neglected, with the result that spending on these programs has ballooned. The potential for irresponsibility in programs thought of as welfare, conversely, has come to dominate the debate about poverty, with the result that efforts to eradicate "waste, fraud, and abuse" have gone so far as to deny help to the destitute.

2

Fear and insecurity focus the mind. People who know that the consequences of their actions will fall on themselves or their families tend toward prudent behavior. Any social device that makes people more secure by protecting them against hardship will in general cause them to relax their vigilance, at least a bit. The certainty that the rest of the community is pledged to keep harm at bay or compensate victims can entice individuals into irresponsibility.

When the Social Security Act was first proposed in 1935, opponents argued that it would induce dependency and sloth. If people knew in advance that they would be insured against unemployment and poverty in old age, so the argument went, they would see no reason to work hard or save money. The National Association of Manufacturers laid out the logic succinctly:

> Legislation which from its very nature tends to increase dependency and indigency decreases individual energy and efficiency of individuals in attempting to take care of themselves. It would thereby decrease the sum total of national productive effort in the country, and in the long run thereby decrease the aggregate income available for distribution among the body of citizens, and hence inevitably lower the standard of living.[1]

A comparable protest emerged a half century later, as some economists argued that Social Security reduced individuals' incentives to save during the course of their working lives. Americans who had come to expect generous Social Security checks on retirement lost the will to save and invest, they said, because these people considered their payroll taxes a sufficient sum to dedicate to their old age. The problem was that these payroll taxes had simply paid for the previous generation's retirement. The present generation, in turn, collected far more from the system than its contributions had earned. From society's standpoint, then, Social Security was no savings system at all. When people acted on the illusion that it was, and cut back their savings as payroll taxes rose, the total amount the economy could draw on for investment shrank. As a result, American industry suffered from a shortage of capital for the investment that would have to pay for the *next* generation.[2]

Similarly, the soothing certainty of Medicare might reduce individuals' inclination to take care of their bodies. Studies revealed that one fifth of Medicare patients accounted for nearly 70 percent of the expenses. This high cost group was not simply older than other recipients; the same skewed pattern held at every age. But a significant portion of this high-cost group had bad health habits. They smoked, they were alcoholic, or they were obese.[3] Without the promise that the rest of us would pay their health-care bills, irresponsible souls like these might be more strongly motivated to foreswear their dissolute ways.

The underlying problem plagues all forms of insurance: When the risk of misfortune is related in any way to individual choices, compensating people when bad things happen will increase the incidence of bad things. Any promise of rescue encourages risk taking. If the government offers cheap insurance against flood damage, more people will build houses in low-lying flood plains. Bankers and businessmen who know that federal insurers and the public at large will come to their aid if bankruptcy looms are more likely to go for the long shot. Workers secure that unemployment compensation will keep them solvent may choose jobs less carefully in the first place, and may balk at seeking retraining or moving in search of work. Doctors with insurance against malpractice may be a bit more cavalier in the treatments they prescribe; patients who anticipate liability awards in the event of error may be less careful in choosing and evaluating their doctors.[4]

How can we enjoy the benefits of *mutual* responsibility without eroding *individual* responsibility? Welfare dependency and mushrooming health care and pension costs are part and parcel of the same phenomenon. But the answer is no more to abolish all forms of social insurance than it is to abandon the very poor to hunger and homelessness.

3

It has been an article of faith in liberal circles that the poor are not really responsible for their plight; society is. They are poor because they have been deprived of good schools, good jobs, adequate diets and medical attention, safe neighborhoods, and all the other things that equip someone to cope. We should attack the root causes of poverty rather than blame its victims. In the meantime, the poor are entitled to a decent standard of living.

This argument has never been particularly compelling to a majority of Americans, who stubbornly cling to the belief that people are, and should be, responsible for themselves. Even at the height of the Great Society in 1967, fully 42 percent of Americans thought that poverty reflected mostly a "lack of effort," and another 39 percent felt that lack of effort had something to do with it. Only 19 percent concluded that poverty was due to "circumstances beyond the control" of the poor.[5]

By the 1980s the uneasiness about absolving the poor of all responsibility had grown. Two decades of antipoverty programs seemed to have done little good, and in one respect the poverty problem had become worse. The nation discovered a large and growing population of poor, unmarried teenage mothers living off welfare in our central cities. Many of these teenagers were the children of welfare mothers, and their babies seemed destined to live out their lives on the dole and spawn another generation of dependents.[6]

Conservative disciplinarians concluded that welfare itself caused this situation. Since the welfare payments a woman collected rose with the number of dependent children in her care, the system encouraged teenage girls to have babies and live off the dole, and teenage fathers to abandon them. The misguided principle of paying girls to have babies made welfare perversely alluring, and once dependent on it, recipients lost all motivation to better themselves. They remained trapped in their own incompetence and irresponsibility. The only solution, by this view, was to get rid of welfare altogether. We should, in the words of one influential commentator, "leave the working-aged person with no recourse whatsoever except the job market, family members, friends, and public or private locally funded services. It is the Alexandrian solution: cut the knot, for there is no way to untie it."[7]

The disciplinarians thus invoked a version of the liberals' old argument: The poor should not be blamed for their situation; it was not a matter of congenitally bad character. The environment they lived in was largely responsible for what had become of them, and we were all at fault for creating that environment. But—and here the conservative story departed sharply from the liberal one—the most damaging part of the environment was welfare itself, which condemned the poor to lives of permanent dependence. The welfare system had allowed people to survive without making any effort to work or to improve themselves.

Liberals took issue with this story on the seldom compelling grounds of empirical fact. Most of the poor, they said, were clearly incapable of taking care of themselves however willing they might be; fully 40 percent were children, and another 15 percent were old or disabled.[8] Liberals pointed out that cash benefits for the nonelderly poor hardly rose at all during the 1970s, when teenage illegitimacy began to rise precipitously. They noted that teenage mothers comprised only a relatively small proportion of welfare recipients, and that the highest increases in illegitimacy occurred in states with relatively low welfare payments. The lure of welfare may be one minor cause of the plight of some of the poor, they conceded, but it was a minor factor within the more important environment of deprivation.

The curious thing about these two stories—the liberal one about deprivation and the conservative one about dependency—was that both were told as if the much larger system of social benevolence did not exist. Surely *some* poverty was attributable to the lure of welfare. But precisely the same dilemma of personal responsibility plagued social insurance programs. In walling off welfare as a separate system, premised on charity rather than mutual obligation, we emphasized the passivity of the poor and neglected the inevitable dilemma of accountability. Thus liberal conciliators set themselves up to be surprised when the poor behaved like anyone else—like beneficiaries of Social Security, Medicare, or unemployment compensation—and exploited a system with few bulwarks against exploitation. Conservative disciplinarians, equally oblivious of the parallels between welfare and social insurance, could envision no approach to welfare dependency except for eliminating the system. Had we considered welfare as one strand of the network of community support by which we all guard each other against adversity, however, we might have contemplated other ways of encouraging responsibility short of abandoning people to their fates.

4

One common approach to preserving individual responsibility in an insurance system has been to make support contingent on private behavior. Victims are compensated for hardship only if they have conformed to reasonable standards of prudence. If their plight is mostly due to recklessness, they must live with the consequences.

Examples of this approach can be found in both public and private sectors. Judges and juries refuse to award damages (or scale down the awards) if an accident victim's negligence contributed to the mishap. Banks often refuse to loan money (or charge higher interest rates) to people who have defaulted before. Private insurers typically decline to insure (or charge higher premiums to) people who have had several accidents in the past. It has even been suggested that people who are addicted to cigarettes or alcohol, or are chronically obese, should pay higher premiums for health insurance and higher payroll taxes for subsequent Medicare protection.[9]

The problem with all such attempts to condition help on personal responsibility has come in defining exactly what responsibility means. Alcoholism and gluttony, for example, shade easily into heavy drinking and overeating. Where should the line be drawn? Contributory negligence has been so difficult to determine that courts have all but given up; by the late 1980s many judges and politicians were urging that we abolish personal-injury lawsuits altogether in favor of a system that would automatically compensate accident victims.[10] Even private insurance companies have found it too expensive to draw fine categories of risk and responsibility; instead, they employ broad criteria like age and location, which have been found to be rough indicators of the degree of personal responsibility to be expected of the populations they describe.

"Workfare" schemes have been subject to a similar ambiguity. Programs that simply require able-bodied recipients to take any job offered or assigned to them, regardless of the skills it conveys or the salary it pays, are not so much a screen to sort the willing from the shiftless as they are a simple penalty on requiring aid. The purpose of such programs (like the workhouses in nineteenth-century England) is to deter misrepresentation by making welfare less attractive to all recipients. To the extent that beneficiaries are capable of work but aspire to a life of leisure, such requirements might indeed enforce responsibility. But they do nothing to increase people's capacity to take active responsibility for their fate.[11]

"Workfare" schemes informed by the ideal of reciprocal responsibility, however, have been organized quite differently. The idea is not to penalize dependency, but to make work a more feasible option—that is, to penalize not low attainment but only willfully low aspiration. Assistance is conditioned upon the recipients taking steps to improve their prospects by, for example, finishing high school or obtaining vocational training. Along the way they might be counseled in how to find a job and perform reliably in it, and assisted with day care for their small children and with transportation to and from work. Regardless of the specific features of the program, the basic logic is to impose requirements that improve recipients' odds for a more self-sufficient future, and are understood to do so by the recipients themselves.[12]

In the late 1980s both approaches were being tried. Both were labeled "workfare" and justified as campaigns against chronic dependency. But one was designed to get "them" off the welfare rolls primarily by making welfare harder to obtain. The other was designed to cut the welfare rolls by turning recipients from dependents into productive members of society. The public philosophies underlying the two could not have been more different.

5

A second broad approach to the problem of reconciling social insurance with personal responsibility has been to rely on the groups in which people live to guide individual behavior. This is hardly a new device; for much of human history, the extended family or ethnic community has been the principal monitor of individual conduct and the cardinal check on careless or dangerous behavior. These traditional social units functioned as rudimentary systems of insurance all their own. Parents took care of children until the children were responsible for themselves, and then the children took care of the parents when the parents were no longer able to. When a fire consumed someone's house, the community rebuilt it, with the understanding that the beneficiary would respond in kind when the next house succumbed. Sick or temporarily disabled members were cared for, in the expectation that they would care for other victims of misfortune. Those who had saved money lent it to members who aspired to start businesses, with the understanding that the recipient acknowledged the obligation to foster community enterprise once he gained the means.

Traditional social units—the extended family, the village, the clan—were notably, even notoriously efficient at monitoring behavior and enforcing norms of acceptable conduct. This was of course absolutely required by the premise of mutual responsibility. A member who failed to exercise industry, prudence, or self-discipline imposed a cost on the entire group. He also menaced the tradition of reciprocal obligation itself; if his irresponsibility went unchecked, it could undermine the motivation of others to act responsibly. Each member thus had a personal stake in fostering, and enforcing, every other member's sense of responsibility.

But with the displacement of the traditional community and family as central social institutions, these older forms of control became less effective. The decline was both a cause and a consequence of the creation of a broader system of social benevolence. It was a cause in the sense that, as these traditional social units disintegrated and many communities and families found themselves unable to care for their members, they sought help from society at large. But the decline was also a consequence, in that the very availability of public support made it less necessary for the communities and families to bear the burden. Once it was clear that the profligate man could rely on Social Security when he retired, for example, his children, siblings, spouse, or neighbors needed no longer worry that his imprudence might impose a burden on them later on. To this extent, they could ignore his behavior with impunity.

One solution to this problem, in principle, would be to shift authority for monitoring behavior to the new source of support— to have the public at large, through the agency of the government, enforce appropriate conduct among recipients. This is what some conservative disciplinarians have meant by "tightening" welfare eligibility. Welfare agencies in a few states, for example, have been authorized to ensure by whatever means necessary that a beneficiary is unable to work, or that a single mother is not living with an employable man. But such nitpicking surveillance is both inefficient and invasive. Americans would never stomach it for the social insurance programs that benefit the majority. Another approach, equally draconian, would be to concede that the problem of personal responsibility is insoluble, and thereby give up on all forms of social insurance, including Social Security and Medicare, as some disciplinarians have urged we do with regard to welfare. But there is no turning back; the public is unwilling to give up the freedom that social insurance allows. The traditional, tightly knit neighborhood and family exacted unquestioning allegiance and conformity; its members intruded conspicuously on one another's affairs. Social insurance lifted the yoke.[13]

There is, in any event, a middle course between jettisoning all forms of social benevolence and imposing strict government surveillance. This is to merge the principle of collective obligation with the advantages of smaller groups as agents for inculcating responsibility among their members. By insuring the smaller group as a whole rather than the individuals who comprise it, the group becomes an intermediary in the system of social benevolence. The costs of any specific hardship are still pooled; society continues to be insurer of last resort. But because the other members of the group share a significant portion of the cost, they have a strong incentive to look out for one another and take preventive action.

By the 1980s the American corporation fulfilled this role for a portion of the population. Its willingness to take on this responsibility was not due to any outbreak of benevolence on the parts of top management or shareholders. As we have observed, the advantages of tax-free employee benefits had pushed many corporations into the business of insuring their workers and workers' families against all sorts of adversity. But while American taxpayers funded a portion of these benefits, the corporations financed the rest. The bill could be high. In 1982, for example, over $600 of the cost of a new Chrysler was attributable to payments on employee health insurance.[14] Companies that did a better job than their rivals of controlling these costs could gain a competitive advantage; those whose employees led more dissipated lives would end up paying the bill. Corporations were thus motivated to encourage employees to avoid the risk of costly afflictions.

Accordingly, American corporations invested ever larger sums on preventing risks. One company, Johnson & Johnson, encouraged its employees to quit smoking and to eat and exercise properly; after five years the program slashed hospitalization costs by 35 percent and recaptured three times the cost of the effort.[15] Other companies were providing their employees with counseling for alcoholism and drug abuse, advice on how to deal with financial and legal problems, therapy for coping with family crises and emotional problems, and lessons for improving personal safety and hygiene. The American corporation was fast becoming the community service agency of the 1980s. But unlike the older version, it was an agency with a direct financial stake in helping people to become more responsible for themselves.

Prepaid group health plans, prepaid group legal plans, and other forms of collective insurance generated similar incentives. Because the costs of insurance to the entire group depended upon the responsibility that each member assumed for avoiding large expenses later on, all such plans emphasized prevention as well as compensation. Health maintenance organizations educated their members in good health habits, legal plans offered guidance in avoiding costly litigation, hospitals counseled their doctors in how to reduce carelessness and thereby stem future malpractice claims.

6

In its own way, the welfare system was groping toward the principle of group liability as well. By the 1980s welfare agencies were imposing financial responsibility on people other than those directly in need—on those who could help prevent hardship from occurring in the first place.

One example was the man (or boy) who might father a child and then abandon it. His cooperation was induced by a simple strategy: Welfare agencies agreed to provide aid to the mother and child on condition that the agency be authorized to seek out the absent father and, if he had a job, dock his pay for child support. This innovation had rather the opposite effect of another rule, still in effect in several states, which denied mothers and children aid if an employable male were found on the premises. Instead of encouraging fathers to leave, the new rule encouraged them to take more responsibility from the start.[16]

Alternatively, welfare agencies held the *parents* of the unmarried teenagers financially liable for their childrens' plight. The boy's parents would bear an equal share of the responsibility with the girl's. (A sponsor of such legislation in one state offered a modest hope that the provision would induce parents to "at least talk about the subject [with their children] before there's an unwanted pregnancy.")[17] A third, related approach involved assigning partial responsibility to family members when calculating the aid due to the claimants. Childrens' assets would be considered, for example, in deciding whether their elderly parents needed welfare.[18] The intent and effect here was to induce the family to help its wayward members take greater personal responsibility in advance of any difficulties, and simultaneously to render their insistence on such responsibility highly persuasive.

In all these instances, public welfare remained a last resort. The idea was not simply to cut costs to the public budget—although that was an aspect as well—but rather to tap the potential of the recipient's family to encourage responsible behavior, and at the same time to affirm these relationships by sharing responsibility. There remained one central problem, however: Those who were asked to share the responsibility for the needy were often in the same desperate straits as recipients. Runaway fathers, the parents of wayward teenagers, and the children of the elderly poor were apt to be as needy as those whom they were to influence. A group comprised primarily of needy people may not have the resources to both ameliorate hardship and inculcate responsibility. It is *differences* in condition—the coexistence of prosperity and want within the same community—that makes social insurance workable. Thus the principle of group responsibility is of limited utility so long as it is confined to the welfare system.

Many of the poor in America have remained outside the groups in society with resources to help them gain responsibility. Being unemployed, or at least unsalaried, they have had no access to corporate-sponsored prevention programs. Living together in poor communities, they have been too readily shunned by health maintenance organizations or other group insurance plans, which regard them as too risky. So long as "the poor" exist as a separately identifiable population, therefore, they continue to be locked out of the very organizations that might otherwise best help them avoid perpetual dependence.

CHAPTER 16

THE FABLE OF THE FISHERMAN (REVISED)

1

The reigning version of the basic American myth of the Benevolent Community tends to neglect the responsibilities that must accompany social membership. This invites inefficiency and, often, unfairness. It also tends to lose sight of the function of community itself, and the benefits that come to all with a broadening of the concept of membership. In the transformed world that America inhabits, the second oversight is particularly dangerous.

As has been observed, the elderly poor have been entitled to social insurance; poor children, to welfare. The two spheres have been separated by more than different legal and bureaucratic trappings. They have rested on different rationales. Aid to the elderly is perceived as a means of spreading the risks of ill health and poverty in old age. Aid to children is seen as a redistribution of income, justified by social benevolence. The former appears to benefit all of us. The latter, it is assumed, benefits the recipients at the expense of everybody else who transfers his income to them (although some of us might take considerable satisfaction in the thought of our culture's benevolence).

Yet the perceptions of these two sets of programs—the one a matter of charity, the other motivated by self-interest—has come to be quite precisely the reverse of reality. Aid to the elderly has become, as we have seen, a massive redistribution from current workers to their predecessors. Contributors are not "investing" in their own retirement, except in the sense that they are perpetuating a system of redistribution from which they hope to gain in the future. But the political *will* to retain a system whereby workers pay a bonanza to retirees is one thing; the economic capacity to retain it is quite another. The prosperity in retirement of each generation of workers depends on the productivity of the *next* generation. So it had been for the early waves of Social Security recipients. So it would be for current workers. Yet by mid-1980s it was clear that the *number* of new workers destined to pay Social Security taxes in the future was destined to fall and the *productivity* of each was stagnating. The ability of the next generation of workers to support the current generation—in the way the current generation was supporting its predecessors—was imperiled. Social Security for current retirees was more like charity than like insurance. Conversely, aid to the young was less a matter of redistribution than an investment in our future. Only by cultivating the future economic capacity of today's children—and, equally importantly, by enlisting them into a culture of mutual obligation—could today's workers provide for their own retirement.

2

This warped allocation of aid, between the young poor and elderly poor, could be explained in part by the simple logic of politics. Elderly Americans vote; children do not. There is more to it than that, however. Liberalism's standard rationale for aiding the disadvantaged turns on charity. To the extent liberalism appeals to collective self-interest, it argues that to accept continued poverty among the young is to threaten domestic tranquility—to invite robbery, random violence, and vandalism. Conservative disciplinarians have never found this line of argument terribly convincing. In their view the best method of achieving domestic tranquility is to punish miscreants. (That America imprisons a larger fraction of its citizens than any other industrialized nation but South

Africa and the Soviet Union, and still suffers the highest crime rate, has not dissuaded disciplinarians from this line of reasoning.[1])

But this debate has steadfastly overlooked the central self-interested argument for public attention to the problems of troubled and impoverished children. In addition to their potential for wreaking havoc, poor young people also have a capacity for generating future wealth. Like all of us they have brains and energies that can be tapped and put to use, or perverted and left to wither. The standard debate has focused on the peril of young minds gone wrong, and how to defend ourselves against them. It has neglected the ghastly waste of young minds left idle.

Part of this oversight is due to the way we are accustomed to think about people in the productive system. Economists have long regarded the economy as a bundle of resources—land, labor, and capital—which are turned into goods and services. If some able-bodied workers are jobless and factories and machines stand idle, the economy is not living up to its potential, and some corrective measures are needed. But it is assumed that so long as all people who want to work are in fact punching a time clock somewhere five days a week, the potential of the labor force is being fully tapped. People too discouraged to look for work, or who lack the rudimentary skills necessary to hold down even a simple job, are not included in the definition of under-utilized resources. Nor are people who work in menial jobs, whose capacities for creativity and insight lie fallow or never have been developed.

The idea that people's capacities are as rigid and immutable as a factory or piece of equipment is incorrect, however. The human brain is the most capacious and flexible of instruments, capable of far more learning and synthesizing than its users typically demand of it. Indeed, if one is to believe neurobiologists, every brain is under-utilized, relative to its capacity when exercised and challenged. A two-year-old child—too young to be bored with life or disengaged from learning—absorbs at a breathless pace. To waste this asset is not only a tragedy for the individual who possesses it, but a loss to us all. Thus we tend to

191

dwell on only the most invisible features of the wastage—the welfare dependency and crime—and not the wasted opportunity.

There is a fable whose origins remain obscure, but whose moral is familiar to most people who have thought about the problem of poverty: Give a man a fish and he will beg for another tomorrow. But teach him to fish and he will feed himself forever. The metaphor neatly confirms conventional notions about the means and ends of welfare policy. The goal is to make people more independent. But the fable misses an equally important consequence: The new fisherman joins and thus enriches the productive system. Once he learns to catch more fish than he can eat himself, or tires of an all-seafood diet, he starts to trade with the gardener, the butcher, the vintner, the baker—with the rest of us. He expands the network of mutually beneficial interdependencies. Our initial contribution to his education was thus not simply a donation meant to ease his dependency; it was also an investment in our own future prosperity.

3

Muscle was once more important than brains for generating wealth. When work literally meant "labor," when employees were accurately termed "hired hands," physical strength was a prime asset. But as machines came to be powered by more efficient sources of energy, the importance of muscle receded. The wealth of a society has come over time to depend ever more on the value added by thought. As the world economy has grown more integrated, brains have become the determinists of international advantage. Modern machinery, technologies, and money are increasingly footloose; the only factors of production that remain unique to a nation, and determine what it can sell on favorable terms to the rest of the world, are the minds of its citizens—how they are utilized and interconnected. The capacity of its citizens to generate conceptual value-added is the source of a nation's standard of living.

Consider that in 1986 the average Mexican was willing to work for about a tenth of the average American wage. Many of the machines with which he worked were identical to those that equipped his American counterpart; the money to buy the machines came from the same international capital markets; the factories were often similar to American factories, and were sometimes located within a few miles of American cities. Yet Mexico was a much poorer society; had the United States suddenly annexed Mexico, by far the majority of the new American citizens would have been counted below the poverty line. What was the explanation for this striking disparity in wealth? What did American workers have to offer that their Mexican counterparts lacked? Little beyond their membership in a more supportive productive culture. The innate capacities of United States citizens and Mexicans were no different. The difference lay in how this potential was developed and applied. It depended on such advantages as good prenatal care, attention to the acquisition of early skills, good basic education, sound nutrition, good health care, the accessibility to specialized training later on, and a culture of mutually reinforcing, productive relationships.

By the late 1980s, however, there was disturbing evidence that an increasing proportion of American children were growing up without these advantages. Almost 30 percent of American teenagers did not finish high school. In our largest cities, the dropout rate reached 50 percent. One in five of our young adults was functionally illiterate, unable to perform simple tasks like reading help-wanted ads or writing grocery lists.[2] More disturbing still was evidence that growing numbers of American children were suffering from inadequate nutrition and health care, the grim consequences of which would plague them in later life.[3]

One answer has been to resign ourselves to this deterioration and simply look for ways to keep even the most inept and unambitious youths busy once they reached working age. Some have argued that we should reduce the minimum wage and create "enterprise zones," sheltered from taxes and regulations, where the untalented could undertake the sorts of jobs that would otherwise drift overseas to low-wage nations. But to compete with places like Mexico, while doing the same jobs as Mexicans, these new entrants into the work force would have to accept wages far below the present minimum. There is no reason why customers would be willing to pay any more. Our poor young people would end up with jobs, but the jobs would lead nowhere except to further types of Third World employment.

Others have preferred to place their faith in the service sector of the American economy, which has remained largely sheltered from international competition. It was here that America had created millions of new jobs during the 1970s and 1980s. Many of these jobs were challenging and rewarding positions as doctors, architects, and so on; most were not. The majority involved the kinds of mindless tasks that the uneducated poor could perform—as custodians, security guards, waitresses, clerks, and orderlies. Jobs like these would provide a modicum of financial independence. But they lacked any possibility for future advancement or learning. More to the point, these types of jobs offered "us" little in return. Compared to the production of service-goods whose added value was primarily conceptual (involving design, engineering, programming, customizing), menial tasks like these contributed only marginally to our common wealth. The scope for continuous productivity improvements was limited; they made our lives less troublesome but hardly richer; they did not summon goods and services from abroad.

The core challenge has been misconstrued as finding something for the disadvantaged young to do forty hours a week in lieu of plotting mayhem. It has never been difficult to come up with almost any number of menial chores. The real challenge, if we were to take seriously the idea of national economic wealth, is to develop the potential in all of us for creating value. A society whose young were taking on thoughtless jobs in ever greater numbers squanders its most precious resources. But this loss, again, has remained invisible.

4

Rather than view public expenditures on the health, education, and well-being of America's poor children as a form of "welfare" motivated by magnanimity or a prudent fear of the resentful and idle young, they are more accurately cast as investments in our collective future. A number of studies have suggested that certain kinds of expenditures on the health and education of children offer substantial public returns. Participants in one preschool program for poor children who were tracked through their teenage years and then compared with a set of otherwise similar children were found to have remained longer in high school and enjoyed significantly better job prospects. (They were also less often involved in crime or teenage pregnancies.) The program had cost $4,000 per child; the return on the investment was calculated to be many multiples of that sum.[4] Another study found that young people who had been enrolled in the Job Corps, a program designed to socialize disadvantaged youth into the world of work, subsequently earned higher wages and needed fewer unemployment and welfare benefits than those who had not been.[5] Title I of the Elementary and Secondary School Act of 1965, providing extra aid to poor school districts, was found to have had a positive effect on the achievement of disadvantaged children, particularly in their earlier years.[6] Public funds spent on diet supplements and checkups for poor pregnant and nursing women and their children were demonstrated to cut the rate of premature births, lower infant mortality, reduce long-term child disability, and lead to larger head (and brain) sizes among babies.[7] Community health centers were found to have reduced infant mortality and childhood disabilities.[8]

Not all such programs tested out so well as collective investments, of course, since so many were inspired by the narrow ethos of charity. And, at least as importantly, the success of those that did work represented only *potential* benefits. It was still up to the individual to realize them. Our complex and rapidly evolving society offers many opportunities to use intelligence to beat the system—exploiting public benefits, circumventing rules and laws, taking advantage of others' gullibilities, turning to crime. To be motivated to contribute rather than exploit, a young person needs more than good health and a solid education; he also must feel that he is a member of a society that respects him, and whose respect is worth retaining. Thus investment in American youth has meant not only efforts to guarantee their health and improve their technical competence, but also measures to initiate them into a culture of shared responsibility and mutual benefit.

These notions of investment are far removed from how we normally use the term. Most economists regard investment as an activity undertaken exclusively in the private sector of the economy, a matter of accumulating artifacts. In the United States national accounts, where the economy is officially weighed and measured, no public expenditures whatsoever are tallied in the "investment" column—not even those for health and education. They are all lumped in with consumption.

This peculiarity in the way we do the accounting had profound implications for one of the central policy preoccupations of the 1980s: the perceived shortage of investment capital. Orthodox economics attributed the chronic slowdown in economic growth to inadequate conventional investment—too little money devoted to buildings and equipment. The prescription was to reconfigure economic rules to encourage more of everything entered on the books as investment and less of everything entered on the books as consumption. Measures meant to achieve this result included across-the-board tax cuts coupled with extra-low tax rates on savings and capital investment, and corresponding reductions in government spending. The imperative was to cut back the "welfare state" and expand the productive sector of the society. The rationale could be easily summarized: Charity was a fine sentiment, but it must be balanced against the more compelling goals of growth and productivity. Expenditures on all manner of public goods—schools, day-care centers, parks, recreational facilities, clean air and water, museums, libraries, health facilities, prenatal care—were moral luxuries to be afforded when and to the extent we could. Beginning in 1981, the federal government withdrew support from all these areas.

Consider the implications of redefining investment to include not just bricks, mortar, and machines, but also spending on the health and education (both technical and moral) of our nation's children. First, cutting taxes solely to increase the pool of savings available for investment is a dubious strategy in a world of global capital markets—domestic savings are no longer the key determinant of the rate of investment. Second, reducing government spending on the capacity of the next generation to produce wealth means cutting a crucial investment that is nowhere reflected in national economic accounts. Third, under this broader definition of investment, a larger part of the public debt should be counted not as an excess of current consumption over current receipts, but rather as capital spending. Because the U.S. government, unlike corporations, makes no distinction between current expenses and investment, the assault on public spending indiscriminately cuts both categories. Far from constituting luxuries to be traded off against growth and productivity, investments in human capital ought to be viewed as a central means of achieving prosperity.

5

In the early part of the nineteenth century, when Britain set out to reform its Poor Law, the debates were both furious and fundamentally inconclusive. According to historian Gertrude Himmelfarb,

> Even as the ideological battles were being most seriously waged . . . there were significant respects in which most of the parties in the dispute were in agreement, sharing the same moral and intellectual assumptions about poverty, making the same distinctions among the poor, focusing on the same group of poor as "the social problem" and using the same vocabulary to describe that group and that problem.[9]

The debates over social benevolence that raged in America during the 1980s could be characterized in much the same terms. Casting the issue as how tough or compassionate we should be toward "the poor" obscured more central questions. Both conservatives and liberals focused the argument on the appropriate level and means of transferring income from the majority of Americans to a separate and distinguishable minority in need. Both endorsed the ultimate objective of making them independent of us, either by eliminating their need or our obligation. It was an argument merely over the extent and instruments of public charity.

Again, the mythic view has distracted us from the heart of the matter. Our Benevolent Community in fact faces a set of moral and intellectual challenges more complex and universal than how to guard "them" against hardship while also helping "them" gain independence. Pooling risks and investments can offer common benefits only when such policies are founded on a shared sense of social obligation. Thus the challenges: How to spread the risks of hardship without inviting laxness? How to pool our investments in the next generation while also inspiring them to fulfill their potential?

A society premised solely upon the principle of selfish interest, even of the enlightened variety, cannot summon the shared responsibility upon which any scheme of social insurance or social investment must depend. But it is equally true that a society premised upon altruism and compassion toward others cannot sustain these noble sentiments when the going gets tough. The former arrangement asks too little of its citizens; the latter, too much. A truly Benevolent Community must both inculcate mutual responsibility and simultaneously celebrate the resulting mutual gain.

PART FOUR

THE ROT
AT THE TOP

CHAPTER 17

THE CYCLES
OF RIGHTEOUS
FULMINATION

1

A readiness to suspect Rot at the Top—a conviction that our major institutions are prone to corruption and irresponsibility—is an enduring aspect of the American character. Like the other American myths, this one changes over time, and its varying versions have manifested both the best and the worst features that distinguish our culture, from a healthy vigilance against abuse of authority to occasional hysteria over fiendish plotting by the devils of the day. Previous chapters have examined how prevailing versions of the other myths have drifted away from current realities, so that they are less faithful guides to the challenges we now confront. In emphasizing either toughness or magnanimity, they have ignored the central challenge of seeking joint benefits and avoiding joint losses. So too with the tale of Rot at the Top. This mythology, however, has a special feature. The other myths generally evolve in responses (albeit often delayed or distorted) to our collective experience; today's version of the Triumphant Individual is quite unlike that which prevailed fifty years ago, which was in turn different from that of one hundred years go. But the myth of the Rot at the Top tends to cycle, alternating its indictment between the two major realms of authority: political power and economic power.

The liberal version of this tale typically concerns itself with the depradations of business; the conservative, with the bloat and meddling of government. As with the other stories, this one clearly has roots in reality. Both public and private bureaucracies have on occasion been impervious to the wants and needs of those whom they were established to serve. Neither has been immune from corruption, and both political and economic elites are often cushioned against the consequences of incompetence. At the highest reaches of either realm of authority—here as elsewhere—arrogance is often endemic.

Yet our readiness to lay the blame for any ills that beset us at the door of the most visibly powerful among us—while it spares America the passivity and subservience that plague other cultures—risks obscuring the responsibility of citizens at large and our collective power and obligation to make choices. As we lament a pattern of failing farms, shuttered factories, or rising unemployment, our mythology comfortingly but insidiously blinds us to the fact that the fault lies not solely with "them"—with corporate or governmental leaders—but with us, in our failure to come to grips with the choices we face about what rules will govern our economic system. As the world becomes more complex and integrated, these choices become at once more daunting and more urgent. The temptation to avoid them increases, as does the cost. In excoriating in turn the demons of corporate or government control, we have fabricated a false dichotomy between economic and political leadership. We have paid scant attention to how the "market" should be organized and maintained to engender a productive working relationship between public and private spheres. As the global economy shrinks, this oversight has constrained our capacity to adapt.

2

By some accounts, public suspicions of Rot at the Top have deepened in recent years. In 1966, 42 percent of Americans surveyed expressed a "great deal of confidence" in congressional leaders, 41 percent were equally confident about the president and his cabinet, 55 percent expressed great confidence in corporate executives, and fully 62 percent felt the same way about top-level military officers. Even labor leaders (22 percent) and the press (29 percent) summoned a fair degree of confidence. But by 1981 a different picture emerged: Confidence in government and business leaders had fallen by about 20 percentage points; leaders in the military, labor unions, and the press suffered comparable declines.[1] The drop was even more precipitous when the public was asked about the relationship between government and business. In 1958 more than three out of four Americans believed that their government was run for "the benefit of the people"; only 18 percent thought it was run "by a few big interests looking out for themselves." By the end of 1972 opinions had reversed: Now more than half believed that the "big interests" were in control.[2]

One could look upon this decline in confidence as a unique event in American history, attributable to the Vietnam War, the Watergate scandal, and economic stagnation. Left-leaning liberals, no less than conservatives, recoiled from the corruption and incompetence they saw at the top of American government. Daniel Ellsberg's jeremiad to a crowd of students in the fall of 1971 exemplified nonpartisan scorn: "If there is one message I have gotten from the Pentagon papers, it is to distrust authority, distrust the president, distrust the men in power, because power does corrupt, even in America."[3] Modern liberals may defend government, and conservatives decry it, but when discussion turns to the latest adventure of the Central Intelligence Agency or the Pentagon their positions are often reversed.

The recent decline in confidence is not unique to American history, however; what is more unusual, perhaps, is the high degree of confidence Americans felt for their leaders in the decades immediately following World War II. The subsequent decline has been more like a return to the normal level of suspicion that had been there from the start—against the imperial power of the British Parliament and Crown in the late eighteenth century; against the fragile central government established in Philadelphia and then in Washington; against the Bank of the United

States, chartered corporations, and the caucus system in the 1830s; against Eastern plutocrats and bankers in the 1880s; against the urban machines and the trusts at the turn of the century; against the "economic royalists" of the 1930s. Dwight Eisenhower conjured up a specter of Rot at the Top that would haunt subsequent decades: "the military-industrial complex."

What precisely is the source of the Rot? Not great wealth alone. America's rich have always claimed a large portion of the nation's productive resources.[4] But this has by no means always inspired general resentment or alarm. Opulence in America has provoked more ambition than hostility. In this, too, we are different from older cultures with feudal origins and histories of class conflict. For most of us, the rich are not "them"; they are what we aspire to become.[5] We worry only when private wealth exercises political power. It was here that Theodore Roosevelt and Woodrow Wilson drew the line on the trusts, and Franklin D. Roosevelt damned the "economic royalists." Private wealth applied to ostentatious consumption is perfectly appropriate; applied to the purchase of political power, it becomes diabolic.

Nor is the Rot attributable to our political-economic system. In neither Marxism nor the fantasies of the far right have Americans found a plausible diagnosis of what ails the nation. For the most part, we have been proud of our system of government and we like capitalism. The Constitution, checks and balances, free speech, the right to vote, autonomous corporations, the free flow of capital, the profit motive, the free market—all of these features of democratic capitalism are held in deep regard. We may seek to improve them from time to time, but the basic principles remain sacrosanct. We worry only when the system is exploited by individuals or groups bent on accumulating power—when authority is misused. Nothing is held in lower contempt in America than "the interests"; nothing more reviled than monopolists, influence peddlers, and political cabals. Other nations, with parliamentary systems and deep social and economic cleavages, explicitly organize their politics around blocs of economic interests, whose leaders openly bargain on behalf of their constituents. In the United States, such corporatist negotiations are anathema.

Pluralism—the play of competing groups for political influence—may provide an apt description for how policy actually gets made in America; but it is not how we choose to see ourselves. No one trusts the big boys negotiating in the back rooms.

The cause of the Rot is assumed to be concentrated power. Our enduring crusade has been to check power wherever it occurs, whether in public or in private spheres. We have been less certain, however, about how we should go about the task, and what structures of leadership and organization should remain after we harness this danger.

3

When the myth takes up the depredations of business, the moral is that we must contain corporate malfeasance through strong government action. When the tale turns to the encroachments of government, the lesson is that we must liberate ourselves from meddling bureaucrats. Occasionally the two themes have been merged in a cautionary tale about collusion between business and government, but usually one or the other is seen as the source of the perversion. Casting issues of organization and authority as essentially moral struggles, though perhaps invigorating, tends to leave murky the question of how we are to arrange our common affairs once the miscreants have been routed. Thus each purging has appeared to invite a surge of unconstrained power on the other side.

For most of this century, conservative Republicans have sympathized with business; liberals and Democrats, with government. These affiliations have rarely rendered the parties or their candidates durably attractive to the majority of the electorate. Rather, political campaigns most commonly have been waged *against* one or the other of these demons; American politicians do not bid for power, they beg the electorate's aid in ejecting the rascals that currently hold power. Republicans and conservatives have spoken darkly of the threats to liberty posed by government and labor; Democrats and liberals, of the threats to democracy and equality posed by business.

The pendulum of righteous fulmination has tended to swing back and forth as business, then government, alternate in ascendancy. It was business's turn in the 1880s, with the advent of large-scale enterprise. Progressivist activism followed in the early decades of this century with the first large wave of government regulation, culminating in the establishment of the Federal Trade Commission, laws governing hours and working conditions, health standards for medicines and meat, and antitrust legislation. The pendulum swung back again in the 1920s, as business regained its preeminence, and government duly receded.[6] Efforts to enact welfare and labor legislation, or to expand farm supports, failed or were vetoed. The courts found social reform legislation to be unconstitutional. The Harding, Coolidge, and Hoover administrations busied themselves dismantling what was left of the previous decades' economic controls.

With the New Deal, government again held sway, and business was once more on the defensive. Industrial production in 1932 was 52 percent of its 1929 level, and industry's ability to deliver the goods was thrown into doubt. Meanwhile, well-publicized disclosures of corruption and gross privilege undercut its legitimacy. Out of this environment came a wave of regulations, imposing on business the obligations to engage in collective bargaining, offer employees minimum wages (and maximum hours), pay for part of Social Security, open the books to prospective shareholders, and pay taxes on undistributed profits.

It was not until the 1970s that the pendulum swung firmly once again. The effusion of regulations and expenditures of the 1960s was largely a continuation of what had begun thirty years before; government—its status bolstered by victory over fascism and depression—had remained ascendant. But in the 1970s America was stymied by a massive and novel set of economic phenomena as inexplicable as the Depression had once been: low productivity growth and stagnating real incomes, coupled with spiraling inflation. It was easy to blame the crippling effects of regulation, and the excessive spending of the welfare state. Amid growing public apprehensions, the long ascendancy of government came to an end, and the myth reverted to a former set of villains.

Beginning in 1968 no one became President of the United States, and few were elected to Congress, without denouncing the government. It became a staple of campaign rhetoric to rail against unresponsive bureaucrats, Washington insiders, arrogant public officials, and cumbersome intervention with the market. Every successful contender was an "outsider"—like the rest of "us"—campaigning against "them" in the nation's capital. Every successful bid for public office was cast as a crusade to "send a message" to Washington.

Even before Ronald Reagan entered the White House, the public's attention was focused on the perils of centralized government: Solutions were sought in tax revolts; "privatization" of services; deregulation of the transportation, communications, and securities industries; block grants and revenue sharing that delegated authority to the states; a scaling back of antitrust prosecutions; and efforts to pare environmental and health regulations. Federal expenditures did not shrink, nor did the number of federal personnel substantially fall. But the rate of increase was stalled, and the terms of debate fundamentally altered. The burden was now on government to justify its interventions into the economy, rather than on business to justify its power in society.

Each of these swings of the pendulum marked a shift in the core definition of the economic problem: It was due either to the unregulated and unaccountable power of business or to the overreaching of government. Each swing marked a corresponding shift in the pronouns of political discourse: "They" were, respectively, Wall Street moguls or Washington politicos; "we" were, respectively, common folk ground under the heel of big business, or entrepreneurs trapped in the clutches of big government. Each manifestation of the mythic warning was silent about the other demon lurking in the shadows: When business was indicted, there was little mention of the failings to which government was prone; when blame shifted to government, we forgot what had ever troubled us about private economic power.

4

By the 1980s the pendulum had swung all the way. Not since the 1920s had business been so unconstrained. In 1965, for example, corporate tax payments had accounted for 26 percent of federal revenues; by 1983 the portion was down to 6 percent. The biggest corporations enjoyed their lowest effective tax rates in fifty years. General Electric, for one, paid no taxes at all between 1981 and 1983, on profits of $6.5 billion. John Kenneth Galbraith had written reassuringly in the 1950s of the "countervailing power" within the American system, which offset the influence of large corporations. But in the America of the eighties, these counterweights were all but removed. Health, safety, and environmental regulations were deferred or cut back; consumer groups and environmentalists no longer claimed the influence or the media attention they once did. Organized labor was all but routed; union membership was down to 17 percent of the private-sector work force, and wage concessions were the order of the day.

Few voices any longer broached the subject of corporate responsibility to the poor or to the communities and nations in which they did business. With increasing alacrity, American-based corporations abandoned communities and laid off workers as they shifted their production abroad. Egregious displays of corporate negligence provoked little public outrage or regulatory response. A Union Carbide plant spewed poisonous fumes that killed 2,000 Indians in Bhopal and injured many thousands more. Johns Manville retreated into the shelter of bankruptcy law to dodge the claims of workers sickened by exposure to its asbestos. A. H. Robbins continued to market a contraceptive device it apparently had known for years could cause sterility and worse. In earlier eras, and surely in times to come, such revelations would inspire denunciation and legislation, but not while it was government's turn in the dock.

America's defense contractors similarly continued to display stunning greed and incompetence: General Electric admitted to defrauding the U.S. Air Force by forging workers' time cards;

McDonnell Douglas produced fighter jets whose tail fins cracked; General Dynamics overcharged the Pentagon and was indicted for fraud. By 1985 forty-five of the nation's hundred largest military contractors were under criminal investigation for kickbacks, illegal overcharges, and other sins, although none was long barred from profitable Pentagon contracts.

Corporate lobbyists swarmed over Capitol Hill. Political action committees (PACs) upped their contributions to congressional candidates from $16 million in 1978 to $57 million in 1984.[7] Access and influence flowed in return for these contributions. Governors and mayors eagerly offered tax breaks and subsidies to any company that might locate within their jurisdictions; not a few firms learned the art of playing off desperate localities against each other.

By the close of 1986, Wall Street was awash in scandal. Many millions of dollars had been pocketed by trading on "insider" information unavailable to the general public.

The point of this catalogue of iniquities and improprieties is not to inspire yet another swing of the pendulum; if the pattern holds, the cycle will not easily be either hurried or retarded. What is remarkable about this list is the failure of such examples, individually or as part of a pattern, to excite any appreciable protest from a chronically suspicious citizenry. Such displays of unaccountable power would surely have inspired a general indictment of business in an era when the pendulum of righteous fulmination was swinging in a different direction. But in the 1980s, with government cast as the demon, there was little interest in attacking business. It is the *purity* of the myth of Rot at the Top that is here so strikingly displayed; Americans are determined to take their devils one at a time. Editors and politicians occasionally pontificated indignantly about this or that corporate enormity. But until the spell of antigovernment fervor had run its course, business would remain largely proof against abuse.

If the past offered any guide, business would eventually overreach. Public tolerance, or indifference, would invite ever more egregious displays of power until one day—with the economy once again in shambles—America would swing to the other side. Campaign orators would once again fulminate against "them" in the boardrooms of corporate America. There would be talk of "sending a message to Wall Street." A new set of regulations and restrictions, doubtless hastily assembled and ill-considered, would be invoked. And the corruption, incompetence, and arrogance of government would pass for a time from American consciousness.

5

Placing blame is among the most comforting cognitive acts, for it allows one to cast away responsibility. The cycles of righteous fulmination, first against corporate malfeasance and then against government intervention and then back again, have enabled us to keep at bay some troubling questions regarding how a complex economy is to be organized, and how responsibilities should best be divided between public and private realms. Perhaps we could once avoid answering those questions. But as we lose the luxuries of economic isolation or preeminence that we once enjoyed, the costs of dodging these issues increase.

The first legal function of the modern corporation is to generate profits for those who risk their money supporting it. No serious person who has thought about the issue, however, believes that the unfettered pursuit of profit will always be consistent with the public's best interests. Economic activities have social consequences, for good or ill, that go beyond returns to shareholders. But contrary to the condemnation of profit seeking per se that periodically erupts in American politics, corporate executives do not necessarily behave irresponsibly when they ignore these social consequences in the pursuit of private profit—unless these social concerns are codified in law. In the absence of laws and rules that tell corporate executives where the public interest lies, they should be under no obligation to guess. They are neither trained nor selected to make such choices.

Corporations, and those who lead them, *do* have a public responsibility to obey the law, however. This obligation is meaningless if it applies only to the literal letter of the law and scorns its spirit and purpose. Government agencies, and those who lead them, for their part, *do* have a responsibility to address the social consequences of business activity—to constrain and channel economic endeavors in accordance with the public interest. But this does not mean that government is authorized or competent to organize the economy through commands and controls. The roles and responsibilities of business and government to together define and animate our market economy is the broad topic to which we next turn.

CHAPTER 18

THE MIASMA OF REGULATION

1

Ask any business executive about government regulation, and he will tell you a horror story of bureaucratic excess. This is his version of the Rot at the Top. But the executive will not, most likely, object to the goal of regulation. Most executives agree that the public deserves protection from toxic wastes, nuclear accidents, air and water pollutants, unsafe products, fraudulent claims, and monopoly. Even in eras like the present, when business is ascendant and government suspect, the public supports these broad objectives. The complaints of American business center not on the purposes of regulation, but on the ways they are designed and implemented: Statutes are overly complicated; the rules devised to fulfill them are excruciatingly detailed, comprising voluminous rulings and interpretations, interpretations of interpretations, opinions and dissenting opinions of interpretations of interpretations. Even the simplest public goal spawns an imposing herd of rules requiring exhaustive filings, reports, nitpicking inspections, and picayune compliance with every jot and tittle of the law. And they are subject to constant alteration, elaboration, and ever more detailed explication. Under the spell of congressional committees, regulatory agency officials, hearing examiners, administrative law judges, appellate judges, and scores of zealous government lawyers, inspectors, and bureaucrats, regulations grow more complicated by the hour. They multiply in the *Federal Register*; they engorge the *Code of Federal Regulations*; they inundate companies with their petty requirements.

Tales of bureaucratic atrocities abound. The chairman of one large pharmaceutical firm complains that his company spends more hours filling out government forms and reports than it does on research for cancer and heart disease combined.[1] Others tell of trivial, often silly requirements, like giving loan applicants pages of detailed information that nobody ever reads, or putting a toilet within one hundred yards of each employee. The laws are impenetrable: The Employee Retirement Income Security Act, which regulates private pension plans, runs to more than two hundred pages. It has been estimated that federal agencies each year require American businesses to fill out 4,400 different forms, together consuming 143 million hours of executive and clerical time, and costing $25 billion.[2]

Nitpicking regulation has been blamed for slowing America's productivity and impairing the nation's competitiveness.[3] Yet other advanced industrial nations require that their companies achieve similar regulatory goals. Environmental, health, and safety requirements in Japan and most of Western Europe are no less stringent than in the United States.

There is one significant difference, however. Although the *results* of regulation are about the same among all advanced nations, the *means* of regulating are quite distinct. In these other nations, regulations are far less detailed than they are in the United States. Their regulations involve fewer rules and interpretations, impose less paperwork, entail only informal inspections and reports, and generate significantly lower compliance costs. If American business is conspicuously burdened by government regulation, it is not due to the ends that regulation seeks, but to the means employed. Among advanced industrial nations, the regulation of American business is uniquely picayune.[4] Why should this be so?

2

Many who speak from or for American business attribute the trouble to the attitudes and values of the people who inhabit government regulatory agencies: These people *want* to be nettlesome. In this story, the Rot at the Top is traceable to a "new class" of college-educated social planners and public policy professionals who disdain economic growth and abhor private enterprise. In the words of Irving Kristol, a principal exponent of such views, regulators and their fellow travelers "find it convenient to believe the worst about business because they have certain adverse intentions toward the business community to begin with." They seek "the power to shape our civilization—a power which, in the capitalist system, is supposed to reside in the free market." Their ambition is "to see much of this power redistributed to government, where *they* will have a major say in how it is exercised [emphasis in the original]."[5]

In this story, many denizens of the new class populate the staffs of regulatory agencies—surviving administration after administration. These individuals relish any chance to harass American business with endless, trivial commands, to clog the channels of commerce with their piddling requirements and endless forms. They take delight in transforming commonsensical regulatory goals into reams of irritating detail. According to Kristol and others who share his views, the new class is waging a war of attrition against capitalism.

> The New Regulation [to protect the environment, safety, and health] is the social policy of the new class. . . . They have merely transferred power from those who produce material goods to those who produce ideological ones—to the intellectuals, policy professionals, journalists, and "reformers," who are arguably much less representative of the American people as a whole than those whose influence has been curtailed. . . . With each passing year it becomes clearer that the real animus of the new class is not so much against business or technology as against the liberal values served by corporate capitalism and the benefits these institutions provide to the broad mass of the American people.[6]

This conspiracy has proven to be an oddly comforting phantom for American businessmen. First, it provides a ready explanation for why business has felt so besieged. It is not any serious failings or erosion of legitimacy on the part of industry, but rather the machinations of a group bent on undermining free enterprise. It is an enemy within, an ally of the Mob at the Gates that seeks to substitute centralized planning for free markets. Second, the story suggests a plan of action. All we need do is to expel from government these ideological traitors and put in their place teams of levelheaded and unbiased civil servants. (Hunting out the miscreants should be no problem; they leave a trail of red tape wherever they wander.) Finally, the story promises a happy ending. Once these saboteurs have been ejected, the present regulatory miasma will be transformed into simple, sensible rules. The public will continue to be protected—as it should be—from the irresponsible acts of a few misguided managers. The rest of American business will be freed of the nitpicks, technicalities, and meticulous excesses of the present system.

Unfortunately for those who find the story satisfying, it wilts in the face of the facts. To begin with, the "new class" of interventionist zealots who are supposedly responsible for the picayune character of so much modern regulation have been far harder to track down than expected. Both the Carter and Reagan administrations were committed to reducing the burden of government regulation. The latter, indeed, installed its own counterzealots at the controlling levels of government agencies to track down the guilty parties. The Reagan administration did succeed in abandoning some regulatory efforts. But—and here is the important point—it did nothing to change the *way* in which the remaining regulations were administered. Notwithstanding its concerted efforts, the *Code of Federal Regulations* continued to swell with detail, the *Federal Register* bulged with new interpretations and elaborations, and American business continued to writhe under the burden of pettifogging directives from Washington. The underlying problem had nothing to do with nefarious forces hidden within regulatory agencies; it was inherent in the American regulatory process itself. A probusiness administration might succeed in rescinding particular regulations, but not in reducing the amount of niggling minutiae surrounding any regulatory goal that survived.

In addition, it turns out that the vast majority of regulatory agency lawyers and middle-level managers aspire not to undermine American capitalism but to live off it. After gaining experience in government, they move on to the private sector. They gain jobs in law firms, representing companies before regulatory agencies. They join consulting firms, accounting firms, research institutes, and public relations firms. They move into government affairs offices of large corporations, and into trade associations. Some have even been known to join university faculties, from where they sell extracurricular insights to corporations. Their experience in government makes them valuable to the private sector, and they are not reluctant to trade upon that value. Far from comprising a "new class" of intellectuals animated by an antibusiness bias, these former civil servants prove themselves adept at making money off what they have to sell—their inside knowledge of how regulations are made. They bring as much zealousness to their newfound corporate jobs as they did to their former ones.

If America's regulatory miasma is not due to a covert war against capitalism waged within government agencies, then what is the real cause?

3

Let us return to our inventor friend, Henry, and his turbo-charged automatic vacuum cleaner. (You remember: Just leave the vacuum on a shelf for five minutes and—presto!—the room is spanking clean.) Imagine, as before, that the product proves enormously popular. But this time imagine that it suffers from a small flaw: It emits a roar something like a jet engine at full throttle, but louder. Every time the machine is switched on, the noise loosens tooth fillings and induces deep neurosis in dogs within a radius of two hundred yards. This flaw does not deter consumers from using the vacuum; following operating instructions, they simply set the timer, sedate the dog, and go off to the movies while the machine cuts loose. Soon in neighborhoods all over America the vacuum's roar issues from empty houses, causing flocks of passing birds to fall stunned from the sky and neighbors at table to drop plates and fling drinks into the air. Henry would like to make a quieter version of the product, but so far has had no luck; adding an adequate muffler would triple the cost of the vacuum.

Now suppose that several years before all this Congress had instructed the Environmental Protection Agency to take steps to "ensure no household appliance emits excessive noise." That was all the legislation said. Congress decided to leave it to the EPA to devise and enforce regulations concerning neighborhood noise pollution. Since then, the agency has issued only one broad rule: "No consumer product shall generate noise in excess of 110 decibels." That's it—nothing more specific than this, no reporting requirements, no interpretations, no elaborations. The EPA publishes the rule and considers the problem settled.

Henry has hired a Washington lawyer named Seymour, who informs him of the EPA's regulation. Worried about the threat to his company, Henry asks Seymour if he can think of some legal way to continue selling the turbo-charged vacuum cleaner. Seymour is a smart lawyer who specializes in federal regulations. "Not to worry," Seymour assures Henry. "I can think of two hundred ways to dodge this regulation." Henry rests easier.

Two months later, the EPA inquires about the vacuum. It seems they have been getting complaints about its noise. Seymour meets with the EPA's attorney. "The regulation doesn't apply to the turbo-charged automatic vacuum," says Seymour, matter-of-factly. "It says no *consumer product* should emit a sound in excess of 110 decibels, but this isn't a consumer product. It's designed for industrial applications, although consumers happen to use it. And it's not even a *product*, but a service, since under our unique payment plan it is leased rather than purchased outright." The EPA attorneys silently take off their hats to Seymour and go back to their law books and word processors.

Two months after that, the EPA announces a more detailed set of rulings, which define "consumer product" as "any product or service sold or leased to industrial or consumer users." They then return to Seymour's office. "Still doesn't apply," says Seymour calmly. "The regulation prohibits sounds in excess of 110 decibels. But our automatic vacuum records only 95 decibels when we've tested it outside in the middle of a field during a hailstorm. Here's the proof." He hands the EPA attorneys computerized results of the experiment. They take off their hats again, solemnly shake his hand, and drag back to the office.

Two months later, the EPA announces precise specifications for how such products are to be tested to determine decibel levels— the kind of sound chamber in which testing is to occur, the type of testing equipment, scientific definitions for "decibel," and detailed requirements for when the testing must be done and under whose auspices. The agency also announces that hereafter all manufacturers of a new product "designed for or adaptable to household use" must file a report with the agency indicating its decibel level according to the prescribed test. All over America, developers of new cat beds, corn poppers, and sock matchers fume as they pay for the premarketing decibel tests Washington demands.

Over the next several years Seymour meets with the EPA attorneys innumerable times. Each time, he claims that the burgeoning regulations, rules, and interpretations still do not apply. Each time thereafter, they become more detailed. Seymour also disputes their applicability before administrative law judges and he appeals their rulings to the federal courts. He argues, as the occasion warrants and the spirit moves him, that the EPA has exceeded its mandate from Congress, or that the agency has acted arbitrarily in singling out the turbo-charged automatic vacuum, or that the company's constitutional rights have been violated. The administrative judges and appellate courts issue opinions that further elaborate upon the EPA's regulations and interpretations, and its authority to regulate in this area. Meanwhile, the original statute has been amended by Congress to avoid the loopholes and ambiguities that Seymour (and others like him) have discovered. The new law is far more detailed and complex, spelling out in excruciating specificity what is required.

Five years later, Henry meets with Seymour. "I'm afraid," says Seymour, "we've reached the end of the line." Seymour points to a bookshelf sagging under the weight of statutes, EPA regulations, rulings, advisory opinions, interpretations, court opinions, and appellate decisions, all concerning noise pollution. "But at least I got you more than five years of delay." Henry is downcast nonetheless. "Does this mean we have to stop selling the turbo-charged automatic vacuum, or else install the muffler?" he asks. "Either that," Seymour warns, "or you'll have to pay the fine every year you violate the regulation." "How much?" Henry asks, trembling. "A full twenty-five hundred American dollars," Seymour says as he grins and takes off his hat to himself. Henry jubilantly goes back to his company, where he asks his secretary to organize a bake sale to cover the fine.

This example exaggerates, but not much, the typical fate of a regulatory effort. It describes a familiar dynamic between American business and government. American corporations are not reluctant to test the limits of the law. They pay lawyers handsome sums to discover loopholes, technicalities, and elegant circumventions. In many instances the investment is worth it to the corporation. It buys the firm at least temporary relief from a regulation, enabling the company to profitably continue doing what it was doing before. Nor do American lawyers recoil from the challenge. They relish it. They cultivate reputations for their elegant pirouettes around statutes. The art of Washington practice is to stake out an area of government regulation and then become expert at outwitting those who administer it. Talented people have been known to spend entire careers circumventing a single, arcane area of regulation for the benefit of a few corporations.

This ploy may be rational from the standpoint of the lawyer and his client, but it is often irrational for American business as a whole. Each such maneuver generates a countermaneuver from within the regulatory bureaucracy and Congress; every feint and dodge, a more complicated prophylactic for the next encounter. The result, over time, is a profusion of legislative and regulatory detail that confounds American business. The underlying dynamic is analogous to the commercial gridlock examined earlier, and the crippling dilemma of irresponsibility in social programs, which was also explored. American business finds itself strangled by the red tape that government uses to seal the loopholes through which American business repeatedly tries to sneak.

The profession of discovering and exploiting loopholes is both intellectually and financially rewarding. It is also eminently respectable. Some of the nation's most erudite and honorable people do it. Those who play the game on the other side—the lawyers and middle-level bureaucrats within regulatory agencies and pertinent congressional committees—are simply trying to realize a simple and often sensible congressional mandate. Honor and financial reward will come to them later on, moreover, if they have gained a reputation for expertise and adroitness. The best law firms and largest corporations will hire them out of government, paying them many times their government salaries, to outwit their successors.

Washington lawyers who advise American business have a certain stake in the profusion of regulatory detail. When an area of regulation, like noise pollution, is compounded by such maneuver and countermaneuver into volumes of detailed statutory language, rules, interpretations, and opinions, it becomes accessible only to those, like Seymour and his tenacious opponents inside the agency, who have spent long hours refining it. The very complexity of the area generates new business and further elaboration. Soon every major corporation whose activities touch upon the area of law must have tactical advice about it. Seymour and his younger partners (who had once enforced EPA regulations on noise pollution) are sought out. Their practice mushrooms.

Unlike the story of the "new class," there are no plotting villains to this tale, which makes it far less satisfying. Seymour and other lawyers like him have no intention of confounding American capitalism. Seymour does his job as he understands it, and is good at what he does. Henry and other chief executives are no revolutionaries either. Henry also is trying to do his job, protecting his company's interests. Indeed, Henry has a responsibility to his shareholders to do whatever he can, within the limits of the law, to maximize the firm's profits. If he did not hire good lawyers to maneuver around statutes and regulations that were open to such circumnavigation, Henry might be found liable for breach of fiduciary duty to his shareholders, or he might be taken over by someone with fewer scruples about exploiting every possible route to higher profits. Every actor in this sad and silly tale is simply carrying out the responsibilities assigned him within a set of rules that we all have accepted.

The story, exasperatingly, suggests no obvious plan of action. For any fundamental improvement to occur would require a broader definition of responsibility by which businesses would not simply yield to the letter of the law but endorse its spirit, or else openly challenge the goals underlying the laws. And the story promises no happy ending, because such a change in attitude and practice will be difficult to achieve. Business executives like Henry, lawyers like Seymour, shareholders and regulatory officials alike, act on the expectation that American business will try to outmaneuver government. As thrust meets parry, the miasma of regulation thickens.

CHAPTER 19

THE MYTHOLOGY
OF THE MARKET

1

American political rhetoric often frames the decision in the dramatic terms of myth: Either we leave the market free, or the government controls it. The starkness of the choice thus posed infuses issue after issue with mythic overtones, and excites debates over where we dare and where we must abandon other social concerns in favor of the vigor of the market, or abandon free enterprise to pursue a higher public good. The debates have generally failed to help the public understand the options and the stakes of each issue.

Two truths underlie the grand debate; each side tends to emphasize one to the exclusion of the other. First, government efforts to dictate economic outcomes are inherently inefficient; they stifle innovation and concentrate decision making within imperfectly accountable bureaucracies. Second, unfettered profit seeking inherently neglects both the broader costs and the potential benefits that do not figure in individual tallies of profit and loss. This is true *to the extent* the rules that define the market fail to induce profit seekers to take such effects into account. Posing the debate in mythic terms, as a moral choice between the security combined with stagnation of bureaucratic control and the vitality combined with rapacity of capitalist enterprise, obscures the more prosaic but central choice, the real choice, of how we make the rules.

The idea of a free market somehow separate from law is a fantasy. The market was not created by God on any of the first six days (at least, not directly), nor is it apparently maintained by divine will. It is a human artifact, the shifting sum of a set of judgments about individual rights and responsibilities. What is mine? What is yours? What is ours? How do we define and deal with actions that threaten these borders—theft, force, fraud, extortion, or carelessness? What should we trade, and what should we not? (Drugs? Sex? Votes? Babies?) How should we enforce these decisions, and what penalties should apply to transgressions? As a culture accumulates answers to these questions, it creates its version of the market.

These answers are not found in logic or analysis alone. Different cultures, at different times, have answered them in different ways. The answers depend on the values a society professes, the weight it places on solidarity, prosperity, tradition, piety, and so on. In modern societies, government is the principle agency by which the culture deliberates, defines, and enforces the norms that structure the market. Judges and legislators, as well as government executives and administrators, endlessly alter and adapt the rules of the games—usually tacitly, often unintentionally, always under the watchful eye and sometimes under the guiding hand of interests with clear stakes in the outcomes of particular decisions.

To the extent that rhetoric frames the issue as one grand choice—between government and market—it befogs our view of the series of smaller choices about the wisest and fairest of an endless set of alternative ways to structure the rules of ownership and exchange. The myth of Rot at the Top, which indicts in turn profit seekers and policy makers, blinds us to the real source of so many economic inefficiencies and outrages—bad choices about rules, flawed procedures for making such choices. Complicated codes of laws and regulations lack the emotional charge of mythic struggle, but they are where the action is.

2

Economic activities often have consequences for people not immediately party to them. Some of the consequences are unwelcome: private ponds flood neighboring fields, locomotives ignite prairie fires. Some are socially useful: a beekeeper's swarm pollinates his neighbor's orchards; knowledge gained in developing a new product proves relevant to a range of other endeavors.[1] As the world shrinks and the pace of economic change quickens, many of these side effects loom larger. Industrial pollution, unsafe products, community abandonment, and sudden unemployment all take a toll. Simultaneously, new knowledge, skills, and experience are ever more central determinants of a culture's prosperity. How to deal with these social effects? The mythic contest between the free market and government intervention forces us either to ignore them, or to rely on countless government directives to pull corporations, and on subsidies to push them, onto paths other than the pursuit of profit. Each of these alternatives invites abuse and inefficiency, as we have observed, which tend to launch the pendulum of righteous fulmination in the opposite direction.

There is a third alternative, however. It is to reorganize the market to bring these broader effects into consideration as private agents decide on transactions. This is not a utopian proposal. It suggests merely that the government concern itself with designing the right market rules, rather than trying to dictate the right market results. Consider how the most recent swing in the pendulum has obscured government's role for dealing with the unwanted side effects of corporate action in just this way.

"Deregulation," a term that had a heyday in the late 1970s and 1980s, was broadly seen as a manifestation of a decisive swing toward the free market, away from government intervention. In fact, deregulation represented only a shift in the nature of government action, from commanding specific outcomes to creating and maintaining new markets. By 1980, for example, the airline industry was deregulated in the sense that the Civil Aeronautics Board no longer passed judgment on air fares or routes. Carriers could compete on prices and services, to the delight of passengers. This reform did not eliminate the government's involvement in the air travel business, but rather shifted government responsibilities. Government was now charged with organizing a new market, whose development called for all sorts of decisions: Under what conditions should mergers and acquisitions among airlines be barred because they might stifle competition? How should airport landing slots be apportioned among competing airlines? On what terms should airlines gain access to their competitors' computerized reservation systems? What kinds of standard, comparative information should airlines provide prospective passengers about their flights and services? How should the airlines handle overbooking, or the sudden cancellation of flights? Beyond these issues lay new concerns about safety. With so many more flights, more passengers, and more airlines competing far more furiously against one another, there was a greater risk of accident. The government now had to expand its safety inspections—and also restructure industry incentives to guarantee the proper degree of care. This prompted some liberal interventionists to talk about "reregulating" the airlines. But that option was irrelevant to the issue at hand. In continuing to view the choice as between government intervention and the free market, the more subtle questions of market *design* were often obscured.

The control of air pollution offered another example. Since the passage of the Clean Air Act in 1970, the federal government had issued mounds of regulations determining the maximum concentrations of air pollution throughout the nation and how much airborne toxin could be emitted by each of tens of thousands of industrial facilities. Enormous amounts of data had to be accumulated and analyzed, and even then it was possible only to issue uniform and inflexible rules for whole industries and regions. The uniform rules took no account of individual needs or deviations and were altered only slowly or more often not at all as circumstances changed. They were almost impossible to enforce.[2]

Free marketeers (including not a few trade associations and large businesses) periodically argued that because the costs of enforcing the Clean Air Act far exceeded its benefits, the regulations should be scaled back. Environmentalists (and, if polls are to be believed, a majority of the American public) disagreed. The debate centered on the value of clean air versus the costs and inefficiencies of regulations to achieve it. But posed in this way, the debate left out a far more useful line of inquiry: How could government better organize the market to attain the cleanest possible air at the lowest possible social cost? This way of framing the debate may have invited consideration of numerous options, such as a system of transferable pollution permits. Such permits, issued in numbers equal to the maximum amount of pollution allowed in a particular region, could be bought and sold by polluters. Thus each polluter could decide which was cheaper, in light of its own special circumstances: cutting pollution or buying permits. As a result, the air would be as clean as before, but most of the cost of curbing emissions would fall on firms that could do it most cheaply. In addition, all firms would have an incentive to develop more efficient methods of cleaning up in the future.[3]

Or consider the question of how tall and wide buildings should be in a crowded city. For years American cities struggled with complex zoning regulations designed to assure adequate sunlight and fresh air for their inhabitants, notwithstanding office construction that was rapidly depleting the air space downtown. As the price of office space increased and developers became cleverer and more demanding, the regulations typically grew more complicated and less effective. But the answer was neither to bar further development, as some argued, nor to abandon all efforts to save some modicum of fresh air and sunlight. It was for government to organize a market in air space, featuring a three-dimensional form of property that could be purchased and sold, like any other. Some of this property would be reserved for the public's fresh air and sunlight (rather like a three-dimensional park). Thus as developers purchased the air space that their proposed buildings would displace, construction would occur on sites where it was most valuable, and fresh air and sunshine would be retained at least cost.[4]

A final example concerns product safety. Here again, the most important choice is not between government intervention and the free market. In the absence of regulations governing product safety, consumers injured by a faulty product would not simply take their business elsewhere. They would seek compensation for their injury from the producer or from their insurer. The practical choice, then, was between (1) regulations specifying how safe products should be, (2) lawsuits by injured consumers against the firms that produced the products, and (3) a more comprehensive system of insurance that would fully compensate injured consumers for any lost wages, pain, and suffering they endured. To the extent that government withdrew from the task of regulating product safety directly, it would find itself more involved in the latter two alternatives. Indeed, by the mid-1980s there was some evidence that the Reagan administration's disinclination to regulate had prompted a rise in product liability lawsuits. The action had simply moved from the regulatory agencies to the courts. The central question, however, remained: Which response, or combination of responses, comprised the most efficient and equitable way of coping with products that caused injury?

As these examples suggest, the absence of government regulation does not necessarily mean an abrogation of government authority nor the abandonment of public goals. It often calls for a different governmental role—organizing and maintaining decentralized markets that can align the publicly desirable with the privately profitable. The debate over the relative merits of government intervention or free enterprise has obscured this more difficult and subtle task. It has distracted the attention of the public and of opinion leaders, who continue to fulminate against either government incompetence or corporate irresponsibility. Because neither free marketeers nor interventionists are accustomed to view the challenge in terms of market design, this potentially more fruitful course has often been left unattended.

3

Precisely the same lesson applies to corporate activities that have positive social effects, such as creating new knowledge and skills.

Here again, the mythic choice between government intervention and an unfettered market has obscured the central issue. Our debates often have degenerated into diatribes about whether government should attempt to steer the direction of the nation's economy by selecting for favorable treatment certain "industries of the future," or leave it to the market to decide who comes out the winner. Some liberal interventionists have talked wistfully of tripartite boards comprised of business, labor, and government, which would plot industrial strategies and outcomes. Free marketeers have argued in response that the government is incompetent to pick winners, and that any such attempt would just end up as another trough at which the special interests fed. The debate has been less than edifying.[5]

The debate should be about how the market can be better organized to stimulate new knowledge and skills. The government has already tipped the scales in certain directions: Countless decisions about taxes, publicly sponsored research and development, the enforceability of commercial contracts, defense procurement, the organization of banks and securities markets, labor, patents and copyrights, antitrust, and international trade (to name only a few pertinent areas) influence how the American economy is evolving. Because each industry[6] has a distinct competitive position relative to all others—based upon the costs it bears and the markets it serves—any seemingly evenhanded rule is likely to affect it differently from others. The notion of "neutral" policy is simply fantasy. Even something so apparently neutral as tax depreciation rules for plant and equipment alters the relative prospects of industries whose competitive success hinges on the careful hiring and training of personnel or on the use of sophisticated marketing techniques (the costs of which can be deducted in the year they occurred) vis-à-vis those that depend on factories and machines. Gross disparities in effective rates of corporate income tax among industries[7] have been due not so much to tax breaks targeted to particular groups of firms as to differences in the ability of firms to take advantage of superficially neutral deductions and credits. Notwithstanding the determined efforts of tax reformers—which in 1986 did indeed manage to eliminate some of the less rational disparities—no conceivable tax system can raise revenue with no effect on the structure and dynamics of the economy. The same general point applies for every other rule of the game. Most industry lobbyists—and not a few legislators and government officials—well understand that no rule, however neutral in appearance, is neutral in competitive effect.

Disparities in effect are inevitable as new circumstances impel the design of new rules. A sampling: Should copyright protection be extended to cover computer software? This decision would profoundly affect the development of computers and semiconductors. If no copyright protection is granted, then each semiconductor and computer manufacturer will have a strong incentive to copy another's software rather than invest money in designing its own. This in turn will create winners out of smaller or more backward segments of the industry, including upstarts in South Korea and Taiwan, at the expense of industry leaders like IBM. It could also be expected to reduce the ardor with which inventors devised new software. On the other hand, a decision that software *can* be copyrighted would make it difficult for smaller firms to produce peripheral equipment or programs compatible with leading computers, whose innards they could no longer copy. This would have the effect of shouldering them out of the market, and boosting the market power of IBM. Either way, the pace and direction of technological change (and work force experience) will be affected.[8]

Should coal slurry pipelines be authorized to lay their pipes beneath railroad lines?[9] An affirmative answer would alter both the energy industry (enhancing the competitiveness of coal, reducing that of oil) and transportation (boosting the pipelines, hurting the railroads, which would then carry less coal to market). Should the government grant fiber-optic cable systems rights of way along interstate highways? An affirmative decision here would spur fiber-optics, but stall the development of communications satellites, which compete with fiber-optic cable for data transmission.

The list of such questions can be extended indefinitely. Each decision affects how the economy evolves and the sorts of skills and knowledge that will be generated as a result: What computer language should the Defense Department adopt so that its complex networks of military hardware can "talk" to one another? This choice would alter the relative competitiveness of several high-technology industries and firms, each of which has invested in different computer languages and standards. How long should proprietary drugs maintain their patent protection? A decision here would shift the balance between proprietary and "generic" drugs, and determine both the cost of prescriptions today and the pace of drug research and development. Should large firms be permitted to band together in research joint venture, which might spur the pace of technological advance but cut competition? And so on.

America's competitiveness is directly at stake in many of these choices. In 1982, for example, a federal judge approved the settlement of a government antitrust suit to break up AT&T, the world's largest corporation, into seven regional holding companies—"Baby Bells"—and a new, but far smaller, AT&T. This decision boosted competition and reduced prices on long-distance telephone service. It also opened a vast new market to Japanese producers of telecommunications equipment. They could now sell their private-branch-exchanges, fiber cables, cellular phones, digital networks, and other gadgets to the new Baby Bells, who before had got all their equipment from Ma. The decision to dismember AT&T also altered Bell Labs, AT&T's research arm, which had functioned as a kind of national laboratory for developing new technologies in transistors, semiconductors, and advanced electronics. Before the breakup, Bell Lab's research had been financed, in effect, by all of us through our telephone bills. But the new, more competitive AT&T could no longer afford such luxuries. Bell Labs shrunk, and much of its work was redirected toward more immediate applications. Thus a national telecommunications policy with major consequences for America's place in the world economy was set by a solitary unelected judge.

None of these decisions turn on whether the government

should "intervene" in the market, but on how competition within the market should be organized. It is impossible for government *not* to make these sorts of decisions. A decision not to decide simply forces private parties to rely on prior decisions, or else creates uncertainty in areas where the prior decisions offer no clear guidance for what the market rule should be. Because technologies, tastes, and industries are forever changing, new questions are always arising, and prior decisions are often inadequate.

The debate over whether government should embark upon a centralized "industrial policy" has tended broadly to miss the point. Our government and every other is continuously engaged in devising industrial policies through their market-structuring decisions. Indeed, the key to Japan's successful industrial policy has lain not in any elaborate plans emanating from MITI, but in an industrial structure that has been designed and redesigned for the express purpose of pushing Japanese industry (and Japanese workers) into ever more complex and efficient production, thereby enriching their experience and extending outward the frontier of their production possibilities as quickly as possible. Their rules of the game (taxes, public procurement, the organization of banks and labor, and so on) are tilted in favor of the rapid accumulation of new knowledge and skills.

In the United States, by contrast, the pattern of winners and losers that has resulted from our implicit industrial policy is typically of the "do-it-yourself" variety—spearheaded by the most politically active and sophisticated industries, firms, and labor unions. The pattern bears no particular relation to those economic activities that could be expected to advance as the American work force gained experience and skill in applying new technologies. Our resulting industrial policy has lain fragmented and hidden from view while the larger choices it embodies have never been clearly posed.

4

The problem is one of focus and interpretation. The deregulation of airlines *has* benefited consumers, but so has the regulation of toxic chemicals. The point is that many of the most important choices have nothing to do with the grand mythic division between free markets and control. When almost every discussion about the unwanted or the desirable side effects of corporate activity becomes shoehorned into a debate over the relative merits of centralized planning or a decentralized market, we lose the capacity to design the market in accordance with our values. We thus miss opportunities to better match corporate conduct to public goals *through* the market. Our cycles of righteous fulmination against, in turn, meddling bureaucrats and irresponsible executives have tended to elicit the worst of both worlds—a rigid tangle of rules that fails to enforce effective accountability. This is particularly lamentable, since it is entirely within our organizational and analytic powers to achieve a good deal more of the best of both.

EPILOGUE

RETELLING THE AMERICAN STORY

CHAPTER 20

NEW VERSIONS,
NEW VISIONS

1

Political culture in America—as it always has been and will be, as it is anywhere else—is permeated by myth. Mythology is an indispensable conceptual shorthand, the means by which we comprehend, come to terms with, and talk about complicated social realities. Mythology is the vehicle by which we bequeath our political culture to our children, and teach them lessons about what our society is for. This book has suggested that America's political mythology can be rendered, with only slight gaps, exaggerations, and overlaps, as a set of four core parables: the Mob at the Gates, the Triumphant Individual, the Benevolent Community, and the Rot at the Top. The basic outlines of this mythology are enduring and uniquely characteristic of our culture; the American mythology of today more closely resembles the American mythology of a hundred years ago than it resembles that of France or Germany in any age, for example. Yet within these broad outlines there has always been a good deal of room for adaptation, evolution, and shifts of emphasis. Myths change— quickly or otherwise, successfully or otherwise—as the cultural environment they interpret also changes.

I have argued that certain peculiar postwar developments have caused the American mythology to evolve in an unfortunate way

235

or, more specifically, to have bred two divergent variants, one conservative, the other liberal, each incomplete and maladaptive. The liberal variant, which has its roots in the unprecedented and irrecoverable domestic prosperity and international preeminence of the earlier postwar decades, and especially the 1960s, is characterized by magnanimity, altruism, an eagerness to conciliate, and to a certain extent, self-reproach. The conservative variant, a response to the disturbing developments at home and abroad that began in the early 1970s, is characterized by defiance, self-assertion, an eagerness to impose discipline, and to a certain extent, aggression.

Both of the current variants were born as responses to new challenges confronting American culture as it sought to come to terms with, in turn, its role as the leading power in a shattered world, its own poor and its long-oppressed minorities, an increasingly strong and enduringly hostile Soviet bloc, and the shock of economic vulnerability. Despite their differences, both versions share one central feature: Each defines "us"—members of the mainstream American community—in large part by reference and opposition to "them": the Soviets; other nations, whether cast as dependents or competitors; slackers among us who fail to pull their own weight; the poor; and corrupt or incompetent elites, whether in business or government. We never have been a particularly introspective people, but this obsession with *the other* that both modern variants of our mythology display has led us, as we seek the source of our troubles, to look outward— with pity, fear, or defiance—to a degree unusual even for America. Thus the most complex questions about our place in a changing world, as they are processed by the conceptual filter of political mythology, are reduced to a blunt and binary choice between toughness or charity toward "them." These are the terms of the stories we tell each other, the level of political discourse that ultimately matters the most.

This narrow spectrum of choice—assertiveness versus accommodation, discipline versus conciliation—bounds our political debates, limits how problems are defined and solutions weighed, and blinds us to a subtler set of options. Appeasement and aggression do not exhaust the potential repertoire of relationships—within productive organizations, with our needy or troublesome compatriots, or with our allies and rivals abroad. Neither variant, accordingly, has been a very reliable guide. Liberal conciliation has often degenerated into an indulgence that invites exploitation. Conservative assertiveness has often hardened the resistance of the intended objects of discipline, sparked resentment, and undermined trust. Much of America's recent history can be understood as a series of reactions, first to the failures of conciliation, then to the failures of assertiveness. The conventional wisdom at any given time—for dealing with the Japanese or the Soviets or the Third World, for managing the economy, for coping with the poor, for bridling inept or unscrupulous elites—is usually rooted in revulsion against the dismal results of the contrary approach, which had been the conventional wisdom just before.

The common error of both variants is the rigid delineation of "us" and "them." Modern liberalism—as distinct from its more balanced New Deal ancestor—is too ready to coddle the other; modern conservatism, to defy him. Both tend to envision human encounters as blunt conflicts of interest in which one party improves its lot and the other, out of weakness or magnanimity, concedes. The conservative morality tales speak of the other's strength and deviousness; the liberal morality tales, of his weakness and need. Neither variant of the basic mythology features stories of mutually rewarding encounters, or common efforts to overcome perils. The tension between a basic stance of accommodation or one of confrontation excludes the middle ground of negotiations and collaborations that both assert "our" interests and comprehend "theirs." It is here, in the premise of generally opposed interests, that the prevailing myths serve worst as guides to reality. For in any of the areas we have discussed there are few encounters in which one side wins and the other loses, apart from sporting events, litigation, and quick wars on small islands. The general case is for interests to overlap, if not completely; for all parties to gain or lose together, if not all to the same extent; for each to depend on the other, if not all to the same degree and in the same encounter. This holds for international commerce as well as for international diplomacy, for dealings between managers and workers as well as dealings between the poor and the prosperous.

2

All human organization depends on reciprocal obligation and mutual trust that others' obligations will be fulfilled. Indeed, civilization may be defined as the state where humans have achieved a richer, more secure and convenient existence through some system of mutual obligation; barbarism, where no such system exists and where confrontation prevails because there are no potential gains from cooperation to be lost. Because most of us are so enmeshed in webs of mutual responsibility—because certain rights and responsibilities are so basic to our culture and so universally enforced—we tend to forget that civilization, so defined, is not natural but an accomplishment of culture. When I leave my office to teach a class I can be confident that my students will not greet my lecture with gunfire, even if they are bored or offended by what I say. Similarly, I do not worry that my colleague next door will profit from my absence to steal my computer. When the university pays me for my labors with a piece of paper, I accept it because I know I can convey the check to the bank and through that institution's agency can acquire things I need by presenting other pieces of paper. My confidence in each of these encounters is rooted in my experience of the culture legitimating and enforcing certain rights and obligations. This allows me to go about my business in the world without the burden of equipping myself with weaponry or my office with booby traps, or carrying around a bundle of goods to trade should I wish to acquire something from someone else. The cultural basis for this kind of confidence is so pervasive that we appreciate it only when we hear of instances where it breaks down, as in Beirut (as of this writing) or the insecurity and organizational chaos of any nation ravaged by war, plague, or thuggery.

Crucially, the want of social devices to bond responsibilities forces individuals not only to be wary, but to be aggressive. Each party, knowing the other may exploit him, is led to preemptive exploitation.[1] The grim state that confronts those who cannot rely on a culture of mutual responsibility is often stylized as the "prisoner's dilemma." The basic version: Two suspects, caught with the loot after a bank robbery, are kept apart and interrogated. If they both remain silent, they will each get off with a one-month sentence. But if one agrees to testify against the other, the betrayer will go free, and the other will get twenty years. And if *both* rat on one another, they will each get five years. Since neither can trust the other not to betray him, they both end up talking, and both receive five-year sentences. Had they had some device for binding trust, their situation would have been far better. Social scientists, nuclear strategists, and game theorists have used the prisoner's dilemma as a model for endless examples of the breakdown of trust and the resulting mutual losses endured and mutual gains foregone.

This classic version of the prisoner's dilemma is deliberately structured (by the police) to be impossible to overcome. The prisoners are forbidden any opportunity to build trust.[2] In most analogous situations, however, some such opportunities exist or can be developed. Suppose, for example, that the two prisoners are not petty criminals who met only this morning to plan the heist, but rather a pair of underground French Resistance fighters suspected by the Gestapo. Each will likely know that the other shares a culture, a set of values, and a sense of commitment to a cause that will deter him from betrayal. Each, in turn, can confidently refuse to betray the other. Or suppose the two robbers are old partners in crime who've been through the interrogation game many times before, and each is secure the other knows how to handle it.[3]

The problem and the approach are quite general. In any circumstance where we require the cooperation of others to achieve what we want or avoid what we fear, we depend on organizational and cultural devices that make trust possible. Where we lack such devices, we fearfully abandon the possibility of joint gains or must accept as inevitable joint losses. Civilization is in large part a blanket term for systems of such devices. Organizations and understandings that let us act together are cultural tools that broaden, enrich, and safeguard our existence.

This is precisely why the *technical* changes that increase the integration of global economies and societies pose so urgent a *cultural* challenge. Global integration ups the stakes. The potential for collaborative gains is greater, as is the threat of losses all around. There are more, and more important, opportunities for profitable collaboration or disastrous betrayal. We have explored several aspects of this global change: National borders are eroding as money, information, goods and services, weapons of destruction, pollution, and immigrants can all slip easily through them. Global corporations are losing connection even with the advanced nations in which they are headquartered. The populations of the Third World are growing rapidly and impatient to find their places in a world system they are ever more intimately aware of. Ongoing technological advances are making it possible to control or liberate the work place, destroy or feed whole continents, bring us immediately closer or terrifyingly apart. The challenge to our capacity to undertake joint endeavors, forge commitments, and cement trust is correspondingly greater.

These social and economic transformations can be difficult and frightening for many people. As change occurs—industries decline, populations shift, technologies are rendered obsolete, older values are challenged—there is a temptation to dump the burden onto others. The pervasive context of fluidity and uncertainty, moreover, makes it more possible to betray without fear of consequence: Exploiters may not again encounter those whom they betray, and the exploited may not be able to identify the origins of the burdens that fall on them. In such circumstances, trust tends to decay, commitment becomes more perilous, and the odds lengthen for joint gains and shorten for joint losses.

The renunciation of cooperation—either through withdrawal or betrayal—has taken many forms: Advanced nations have tried to seal their borders to immigrants and cheaper goods from abroad; poorer countries have been seduced by the romance of leftist revolutions or military dictatorships, or entranced by xenophobic religious movements. Both sets of responses have pushed the burden of change onto other, similarly resistant members of a linked world system. Advanced nations have tried to impose the costs of their inflation or industrial overcapacity on one another; one superpower has tried to gain a strategic advantage over the other. These moves have generated retaliation, ultimately escalating the potential losses for all. Closer to home, managers and financiers have, on occasion, appropriated economic gains to themselves through paper enterpreneurialism and the manipulation of laws and rules; some workers, convinced that they will not share the gains from improved productivity, have sabotaged the work place through rigid work rules, shoddy workmanship, strikes, and slowdowns. These responses have undermined the productive system. Many Americans, rich and poor, have cynically exploited social insurance or welfare and imperiled the system of social benevolence. Some American businesses have sought to circumvent regulations and impose the burdens of pollution and ill health onto others, and have balked at investing in the skills and knowledge of their workers. Public officials have betrayed the trust of office and sought personal power, convenience, or profit at the expense of their compatriots.

Such exploitative maneuvers have undermined trust and stalled progress in many spheres. The result has been a tightening gridlock—with our trading partners, the Soviets, the Third World; within our businesses among workers, managers, shareholders, and other stake holders; within the welfare state, among the poor and the rest of us; in the relationship between government and business. Many of our more visible and immediate problems are symptoms of this basic dilemma. Liberal accommodation has offered no answer. Its foundation of principles and priorities has been too weak to define and guard against betrayal. Its assertion of rights without corresponding mutual obligations has too often served to veil exploitation. Thus it has tempted us to the emotionally satisfying toughness and assertion of modern conservatism, and exposed us to the peril of escalating rounds of retaliation and deepening suspicion. The prisoner's dilemma is played out on a grand scale.

But we are not bound by the grim logic of distrust and preemptive betrayal. Different aspects of the same broad trends can be turned to our mutual advantage. How well we do depends on our culture's capacity to create and sustain the organizations that allow collective action, to define and enforce mutual obligation. For example, a more dynamic and adaptable world economy could allow those who gained in the first instance to fully compensate those on whom the burden of change fell heaviest, and restore a broad upward trend in living standards. Domestically, firms that fostered group learning and collective responsibility could generate greater wealth. Public investments in education, child nutrition and care, job training, and public health could lead to a more prosperous economy and society. And a domestic market whose rules were determined explicitly with social "bads" and "goods" in mind, could avoid many heavy-handed government controls. Yet how can we confidently undertake mutual endeavors that inevitably render us more vulnerable to each other? How can common purposes be pursued when they overlap but do not coincide point by point with individual interests? How can we prevent betrayal and exploitation when there are so many opportunities and incentives to renege on trust?

The only response to the dismal logic of the prisoner's dilemma is the accretion of common interests, patterns of mutual endeavor, traditions of trust—in short, a political culture that engenders an ongoing search for possibilities of joint gain and continued vigilance against the likelihood of mutual loss. And culture is the creature of mythology. Culture is encoded within the tales we tell one another every day. Hence the importance of these tales, and of their evolution.

3

It is not just geographic isolation that inspired the basic American myth of the Mob at the Gates. America's earliest settlers were moral dissidents; our nation's defining documents were expressions of moral theories. The sense of the United States as an ethical exemplar in a deeply flawed world is an abiding aspect of the American mythology. But the current version of this myth has become needlessly exclusive and dangerously insular. We tragically narrow our options when we regard other cultures, until proven otherwise, as parts of a hostile mob that can only be appeased or kept at bay. Our neighbors on the planet vary enormously in the proximity of their values with our values and the consistency of their interests with our interests. Some of them are our natural allies in many spheres, and not even the most extreme manifestations of our mythology have kept us from recognizing and acting on this to some extent. Others will inevitably be opposed to many or even most of our interests, but even with them we share a common concern for avoiding mutual catastrophe. A few groups profess values so repellent that we can only view them as enemies—consider the Nazis of the middle third of the century, or the terrorist groups of the last third, or fascist or Communist butcher regimes. Yet our best response to such true members of the Mob has been and continues to be making common cause with other peoples against them.

Myths cannot be simply edited nor their evolution forced. But I suggest that a successful adaptation of this mythology would engage us in subtler discriminations among other peoples and greater attention to the forging and shoring up of mutually beneficial relationships. It is increasingly apparent, for example, that the world economic system is coming to require new norms and institutions to enforce mutual responsibility among nations for easing the strains of industrial overcapacity, currency misalignments, incompatible national economic policies, and the flow across borders of dangerous drugs, pollutants, and surges of immigrants. Our role in the formation of such institutions is too often warped by the tendency for our internal debates to turn on the question of being either tough or generous toward "them." It is difficult to decide what burdens and responsibilities we should accept, as our part of common agreements, when the choice is cast in these terms.

The proper way to frame the issue is neither as a matter of charity and appeasement nor as a ploy in a competitive struggle, but rather as an expression of a larger and more enlightened self-interest. The new public philosophy would reject the notion—so deeply embedded within both liberal conciliation and conservative pugnacity—that the central competition of our age is over the division of a fixed quantity of global wealth. There are more and less advantageous roles to search for, and some of our perceived rivalries are real. We can do better than we have done in casting such competition not as a struggle for survival, but as a contest in which even the laggards can gain enormously. The faster and less traumatic the transition is for any one group or nation, the smoother and more rewarding it may be for everyone else. Rather than seek to constrain or appease an apparent Mob at the Gates, we would do better to concern ourselves with the ecology of the world economy as it develops and adapts.

International policies, if informed by such vision, would aim to make manifest interdependencies and build new institutions to manage reciprocal obligations. A few possibilities will give the flavor of policies that might follow from this revised tale (but should not be taken as any considered agenda). In order to avoid global recessions, inflation, or extreme currency swings, the Federal Reserve Board and the central banks of other major economies would attempt to adjust their money targets in light of world liquidity conditions and trends. Similarly, the United States would better synchronize its spending and taxing decisions with those of other key nations. When the productive capacities of the world were being underutilized, we would seek a coordinated expansion; when the world economy was in danger of overheating, we would try to negotiate a reduction in global spending.

Our trade policies would welcome the transfer of basic industries to poorer nations, steering around the grim choice between deindustrialization and protection. The goal would be to orchestrate a balanced global expansion of wealth creation and exchange; as "they" progressed, so would we. As part of our contribution to this common purpose, we would work to ease the transition of our firms and workers out of low-skilled, standardized businesses of the sort that Third World nations are entering. Simultaneously, through the International Monetary Fund or another international lending agency, we would offer Third World nations access to the kind of long-term financing they desperately need. We would reverse the flow of capital from poor nations to rich, inviting other advanced nations to join us in investing in the Third World. This is far from utopian; the Marshall Plan, through which America invested in the reconstruction of Europe after World War II, stands as a rousingly successful precedent. The mechanics of such a campaign might involve limiting Third World nations' debt service payments to a fixed percentage of their export earnings, an arrangement that would give them greater confidence that we would fulfill our commitment to open markets.[4]

So far as these and similar measures cushioned the trauma of global change, the Soviets would have fewer opportunities to insinuate themselves into local upheavals. We could feel more secure about reducing our military support to the Third World and would avoid the periodic left-wing reactions that such martial alliances sometimes inspire. At the same time, the world's poor would have somewhat less reason to uproot themselves and surge across our borders in search of jobs, or to turn to the cultivation and transportation of noxious drugs as a means of livelihood.

To the extent we solidified our reputation for pursuing our own interests but respecting those of others, for sincerely seeking to identify and act on opportunities for mutual gains, it would become increasingly difficult for our detractors to plausibly cast the United States as either global patsy or global bully. Our hostility to those groups that deserve the label of Mob—terrorists, aggressors, and tyrants of both left and right—would become more respectable, and our appeals to other peoples to join us in closing the gates around such international pariahs would become more credible. By moderating the moralistic fervor and self-righteousness of our rhetoric, we could reclaim true moral leadership in the world.

4

Our prevailing version of the fable of the Triumphant Individual is similarly out of phase with the challenges our culture faces. The mythology invites us to pose the wrong questions, particularly about individualism in the modern economy, and confounds debate. We wrangle over bids to up the financial reward to lone entrepreneurs and crack down on drone workers on the one hand, or to control enterprise through rigid regulation, constraints on layoffs and factory closings, and union work rules on the other. Neither approach engages the reality that while we may triumph *as* individuals, in the modern economy we must triumph *through* teams.

Personal competence, dedication, and pride in accomplishment—those splendid traditional American virtues—will continue to matter a great deal, but to an increasing extent they are forged and have effect principally in the context of collective endeavor. Interestingly, there is evidence that the stories we tell one another are coming to reflect this understanding. As noted earlier, an ever rising proportion of scientific discoveries are made by groups of researchers, and most Nobel prizes are now shared. When I thought of "science" as a child I would usually envision a wild-eyed genius in a lonely lab; my children are more likely to picture teams of white-coated colleagues arguing, comparing notes, and working together on impressive-looking and no doubt staggeringly expensive devices. Popular culture now depicts groups of people, each with different strengths and temperaments, struggling together to design new computers.[5] Stories about Triumphant Teams—composed, like any assemblage of Americans, not of selfless and subservient drones but of creative, idiosyncratic individuals, yet devoted to common goals and committed to reaching them through common efforts—may well already be working their way into our mythology. Triumphant Individuals are being replaced by collective entrepreneurs.

To the extent our domestic economy is animated by this new version of the tale, the central problem of economic policy becomes less how to discipline drones or tease the last ounce of genius out of lone entrepreneurs, but rather how to create the kinds of organizations in which people can pool their efforts, insights, and enthusiasm without fear of exploitation. As the earlier discussion of economic gridlock suggested, this is far from a simple task. What kinds of economic arrangements can infuse a broadly shared sense of responsibility throughout productive organizations and build mutual confidence and trust? One possible approach to this problem is to encourage some version of worker ownership and participation.[6]

This may be seen as an old answer to a new question. Employee ownership has been widely advocated on largely ideological grounds. It has been just as widely condemned as inefficient. Different groups of employees—like younger and older workers—will often have different interests in immediate wages and dividends versus long-term growth, for example. Potential outside investors may suspect the motives and doubt the accountability of worker-owners and refuse to invest their funds. Talented and diligent workers risk being exploited by the incompetent and lazy. And all worker-owners, if most of their wealth is tied up in the firm, bear more risk than if each owned a diversified portfolio of investments.[7] If there were nothing to the notion of collective entrepreneurialism, if productive organizations were simply the sum of their fungible parts, it may well be that worker ownership would be a bad idea. But if our future prosperity does depend on ongoing learning through collective efforts, then some kind of worker ownership may be an important device for generating shared experience, cementing common aims, and building trust. It may be sufficiently promising as such a device to warrant considerable efforts to overcome its inherent problems. Indeed, when its purpose is framed this way, it may itself help to overcome some of these problems.

A direct ownership stake can go a long way toward creating a sense of collective responsibility. Employees would reap the benefits of effort and innovation. Honing their firm-specific skills instead of basic skills that could be peddled anywhere would be a less risky strategy. Each worker would have a direct interest in training his colleagues, rather than jealously guarding expertise lest his own position become less secure. Workers would monitor one another, and managers, to guard against lapses of judgment or diligence.

The virtues of employee ownership would not be solely motivational. It would also allow the enterprise more flexibility.

When sacrifices were needed to make it through lean times or develop new products or processes, worker-owners would be more ready to accept austerity, knowing they would reap the eventual rewards and not be shouldered aside once they had made their contributions.[8] Secure in their place in the organization, they would not need to fear new technologies or endeavors.

The point is that some form of employee ownership and control could provide a superior context for forging joint commitment and fostering trust. Reciprocal dependencies would be clearer. Relationships would be longer-term, and reputations correspondingly more important; the slacker and exploiter would bear the burden of their actions. Such arrangements could go far to reduce the appeal of opportunism and increase the perceived advantages of collaboration, and thus lessen the dilemmas that give rise to economic gridlock.

5

The American fable of the Benevolent Community is increasingly adrift from the actual American system of social benevolence. Here, what is required is both an adaptation of the stories we tell one another, and a greater appreciation of what is actually occurring with our social insurance and welfare programs. I have suggested that we should stop making "the poor" into the objects of our compassion or suspicion, recognizing instead the pervasiveness of our system of social benevolence and the crucial importance of mutual responsibility for sustaining it. In the revised tale, altruism would be replaced by solidarity.

Social policy, if informed by such a vision, would dispense with the two parallel schemes we now have (one dubbed social insurance; the other, welfare) and institute instead a single, inclusive system of common insurance against misadventure. In broad outline: We would eliminate oddities like the tort liability system, which enriches lawyers predictably but compensates victims only erratically and with whimsical inconsistency, in favor of universal disability insurance.[9] Unemployment insurance and many types of welfare would be merged into a single set of programs for the economically dislocated. Benefits would come in large part in the form of training and retraining services, training stipends, and (for those least ready for regular jobs) temporary wage subsidies. No able citizen would be simply supported in idleness, but at the same time no willing worker would be left stranded.

At the same time, we would strengthen and enforce the reciprocal obligations of beneficiaries as members of the community. No aspect of social insurance would come as an "entitlement," delivered irrespective of individual behavior. The community must stand ready to guarantee each member against misery. But each member, in turn, must be induced to take responsibility for those factors within his control that determine his fate. As earlier sections suggested, this is a difficult balance to strike. But our national community will be better off by applying the principle of reciprocal responsibility more stringently—or, to be more accurate, for the first time—to those programs that benefit all of us. Eligibility for subsidized health insurance would require a preventive program of health maintenance; absent fathers would be required to pay a portion of their paychecks to support their offspring; teenage mothers would receive aid only if they remained in school. One generic device for inducing greater responsibility may be channeling benefits through intermediary groups that have the capacity and can be given the incentive to help monitor and enhance their members' vigilance against mishap. The models for this are the health maintenance organization and, in the area of tax-subsidized indirect social insurance, the corporations that provide such benefits to their workers. The model may be capable of extension to other intermediary groups, perhaps including, in different ways and varying situations, civic organizations, churches, neighborhoods, and even the family.

But there is one daunting problem to using intermediate groups as agents of community benevolence: Many of our most chronically needy compatriots are either isolated from the most promising kinds of intermediaries, or concentrated within enclaves of poverty and despair. They are poor not only in resources but in organization. So long as this condition holds, it will be difficult to develop systems of mutual responsibility; social benevolence for "the poor" will be apt to again degenerate into special programs funded by the charity of the rest of "us"—unaccompanied by either expectations or esteem. Hence, a somewhat radical proposal: In order to universalize our instruments of community, disperse chronically poor Americans more widely among the rest of us. Laws against housing discrimination should be mercilessly enforced. Zoning ordinances that effectively bar the disadvantaged from more prosperous areas should be challenged. Small clusters of low-income housing should be built in high-income neighborhoods. Current patterns of economic segregation make a self-fulfilling prophecy of the claim that the poor are not like the rest of us.

Finally, we should take seriously the bromide that the future depends on our children. The potential public return warrants substantial public investments in prenatal care, preschool learning, basic education, and abundant opportunities for training and retraining thereafter. Here again, the immediate beneficiaries would be made to understand that these expenditures entailed reciprocal responsibilities. Failure to accept the obligations they implied (by, for example, disrupting or vandalizing a schoolroom) would properly result in whole or partial exclusion.

6

This brings us, finally, to the fable of the Rot at the Top. Looking on the powerful with a jaundiced eye is not a uniquely American trait, but the nature and degree of our suspicion distinguish us from other cultures. This aspect of our mythology is, in a broad sense, healthy. Yet its current manifestations, once again, convey lessons inappropriate to the problems we face. It is undeniably important to guard against the perennial tendency toward venality, corruption, and arrogance in our public and private institutions. But I suggest the most threatening danger—most threatening because we are so little vigilant against it—is irresponsibility. America faces a crisis of stewardship. Rapid changes in the world, and in our place in it, have undermined traditional assignments of responsibility. For many of the purposes most important to us, there is nobody clearly, accountably in charge.

The cycles of righteous fulmination—against business and government in turn—distract us from the need to enforce joint responsibility for our collective prosperity. When we succumb to a distrust of business, we neglect the imperative to keep up with the quickening pace of global development. When we indulge in contempt of government, we perilously neglect the public sector's role in ensuring that such economic activity is aligned with the long-term interests of our citizens. There are ever fewer automatic links between technology, capital, and corporations of American origin and the interests of American workers; increasingly, these links must be forged by policy. The current version of our mythology of the Rot at the Top, and the sharp division between business and government it assumes and encourages, undercuts any rational assignment of these responsibilities. Business has no clear mandate of stewardship for the development and employment of our workers; government alone lacks the competence to take on the task.

Stewardship will never be enforced solely by laws and regulations. Consider the miasma of regulation that confounds efforts to achieve far simpler public goals when business feels bound only by the letter and not the spirit of the law. Business executives must attend to the cultural norms and expectations that lie behind the law. Government leaders, in turn, must recognize their limited capacity to dictate specific economic outcomes and tend to their responsibility for designing the market in accordance with social priorities.

Such stewardship can be propelled only by political culture. We will know our mythology of the Rot at the Top is evolving appropriately when we tell fewer stories that sweepingly denounce either the greed of businessmen or the meddlesomeness of government—the chaos of markets or the scourge of planning—and when our scorn falls instead on private power that is willfully unmindful of the public interest and public power that neglects the importance of harnessing private initiative.

7

These suggestions are meant only to illustrate what the new tales might inspire, not to sketch out an agenda for action. They exemplify a common theme. Throughout the areas this book has discussed, the central question is not how or how much to discipline or accommodate some other group, but how to enlarge the sphere of "us." How can we create the conditions for confident engagement in joint endeavor? How can we build patterns of trust that serve the pursuit of mutual gain and cut the risk of mutual loss? The generic predicament stylized as the prisoner's dilemma is especially pernicious in eras like the present, in which old norms and traditions are breaking down under the weight of rapid change, national borders do not hold, the burdens of change seem to fall randomly and unfairly, and notions of membership (within a firm, a nation, a trading or diplomatic system) seems ever more contingent and temporary.

We will never be able to enlarge the sphere of "us" to encompass everyone. The interests of some groups are simply too sharply opposed to our own; some others are simply too anarchic, devious, or even irrational. But if hostility and intransigence were as pervasive in the world as some aspects of our mythology seem to suggest, we would never have been able to achieve the quiet marvels of coordination and mutual confidence that our culture now enjoys. The challenge is to create settings in which obligation and trust can take root, supported by stories that focus our attention on discovering possibilities for joint gain and avoiding the likelihood of mutual loss—stories of the ecology of the world economy, of collective entrepreneurialism, of social solidarity, and of stewardship.

8

A central tenet of this book has been that the most important function of political culture is not the crafting or evaluation of new solutions, but rather the act of defining core problems. This function is generally submerged and implicit, perceptible only indirectly in the debates that fill the editorial pages and the nightly news. The level of public discourse that ultimately determines the shape of our laws and the results of our elections consists of the metaphors that inform our hopes and fears, and the stories we tell one another. Here data, analysis, and theory matter less than political mythology. This volume is no brief against extended metaphor. A greater abundance of fact provides no guarantee of wiser policy; analytic virtuosity, no deeper insight into the values that animate our collective life.

The problem comes when a changing environment outpaces the political culture. When we become so enchanted with our fables that we wall them off from the pressures for adaptation, the stories may begin to mask reality rather than illuminate it. Instead of cultural tools for coming to terms with the challenges we face, they become means of forestalling them. A living political mythology, while retaining its roots in the same core themes, is constantly incorporating new stories that manifest basic values and beliefs in new and more fruitful ways.

If the broad line of reasoning I present is sound, this evolution of our mythologies is urgent and overdue. If my hopes and speculations are sound as well, the evolution may be already underway. In the years ahead the stories Americans tell one another will haltingly, gropingly, continue to change. Current liberal and conservative variants of our core mythologies, both of them accepting the conventional borders between "us" and "them," will gradually give way to new versions oriented to a subtler assumption of interdependence. These new stories will speak less of triumph, conquest, or magnanimity, and more of the intricate tasks of forging mutual responsibility and enforcing mutual obligation. There will be fewer triumphant loners among the heroes, and more talented teammates and dedicated stewards. The villains will be found not in broad categories of malevolent others, but in the cynical betrayers of trust found even close by.

Such tales are by no means foreign to the American mythology. Indeed, it is just possible that Americans already are telling one another these sorts of stories, and are only waiting for a new set of leaders to give them clear voice.

NOTES

1. Carl J. Friedrich et al., *Problems of the American Public Service* (New York: McGraw-Hill, 1935), 12.

2. Scholars of American history and politics disagree about whether these deeper premises have endured, essentially unchanged through time (see, for example, Louis Hartz, *The Liberal Tradition in America* [New York: Harcourt, Brace and World, 1955]; Richard Hofstadter, *The American Political Tradition and the Men Who Made It* [New York: Alfred A. Knopf, 1948]), or have repeatedly cycled back and forth between periods of experimentation and consolidation (Arthur M. Schlesinger, Sr., *Paths to the Present* [Boston: Houghton Mifflin, 1964], 89–103; Arthur M. Schlesinger, Jr., *The Cycle of American History* [Boston: Houghton Mifflin, 1986], chap. 2). There is ample evidence to confirm either view, depending upon whether one regards the extremes of the cycle as representing fundamentally distinct worldviews or merely the ends of a rather truncated and predictable spectrum. As the reader will shortly discover, my own view departs somewhat from both of these positions.

3. In this book I use the terms "myth," "parable," and "morality tale" interchangeably, but they are not exactly the same. Myths are almost unconscious; they are woven into our very language in the metaphors, allusions, and analogies we use to express ourselves. See, for example, Ernst Cassirer, *Language and Myth*, Suzanne Langer, trans. (London: Dover Publications, 1946), 83–97. Parables, or morality tales, are more deliberate attempts to teach lessons through narrative. In between the two categories are found folktales, fairy tales, epic poems, and a broad range of heroic adventures. The entire spectrum can be understood as means through which

cultural values are transmitted and understood. As the philosopher Alistair MacIntyre has written, "man is in his actions and practice . . . essentially a story-telling animal." Our personal narrative histories are embedded in the stories of our time, our people, and our collective strivings. It is through narratives that we come to understand the actions of others. *After Virtue: A Study in Moral Theory* (South Bend, Indiana: Notre Dame University Press, 1981), 197, 201.

4. The best of these tales, illuminating the universal joys and longings of mankind, still resonate in cultures far removed in time and space from those that first took the stories as their own. Consider *The Epic of Gilgamesh;* the tales of Lao-tse, Buddha, Mohammed, and Zoroaster; the *Illiad* and the *Odyssey;* the tragedies of Aeschylus or the novels of Tolstoy.

5. Older fears and disillusionment about the tractability of public opinion (see, for example, Walter Lippman's *Public Opinion*, published in 1922) have given way in recent years to a new understanding of the public's active role in sorting, screening, and criticizing what it hears. See, for example, Wilbur Schramm, "The Nature of Communication Between Humans," in *The Process and Effects of Mass Communications*, W. Schramm and D. Roberts, eds., rev. ed. (Urbana: University of Illinois, 1971), 8; Gerald M. Pomper, "From Confusion to Clarity: Issues and American Voters, 1956–1968," in *American Political Science Review*, lxvi (June 1972): 415–27.

6. Annual message to Congress, December 4, 1917, in Arthur S. Link, ed., *The Papers of Woodrow Wilson*, vol. XLV (Princeton, N.J.: Princeton University Press, 1984), 194.

7. For a more detailed look at this theme in popular American fiction, see John G. Cawelti, *Adventure, Mystery, Romance: Formula Stories as Art and Popular Culture* (Chicago: University of Chicago Press, 1976); E. G. Bormann, "Fantasy Theme Analysis," in J. L. Golden, G. F. Berquist, and W. E. Coleman, eds., *The Rhetoric of Western Thought*, 3rd ed. (Dubuque, Iowa: Kentall/Hunt Publishing, 1969), 433–49; Will Wright, *Sixguns and Society: A Structural Study of the Western* (Berkeley, Cal.: University of California Press, 1975).

8. John Kenneth Galbraith, *American Capitalism* (Boston: Houghton Mifflin, 1952).

9. For an account of American conspiracy theories, see Seymour Martin Lipset and Earl Raab, *The Politics of Unreason: Right-Wing Extremism in America, 1790–1970* (New York: Harper and Row, 1970).

10. On the uniqueness of the American form of satire, see Leon Samson, *The American Mind* (New York: Jonathan Cape and Harrison Smith, 1932), 13.

11. For a cogent and thoughtful analysis of this tendency, see Samuel P. Huntington, *American Politics: The Promise of Disharmony* (Cambridge, Mass.: Harvard University Press, 1981).

12. See Richard Hofstadter, *The Age of Reform* (New York: Knopf, 1956), 228.

13. Samuel I. Rosenman, ed., *The Public Papers and Addresses of Franklin D. Roosevelt*, 13 vols. (New York: Random House, 1938–50), vol. 5, 8–18, 230–36.

14. Ibid. Professor Samuel Beer provides an insightful analysis of Roosevelt's nation-building efforts, and their subsequent relevance, in "In Search of a New Public Philosophy," in *The New American Political System*, Anthony King, ed. (Washington D.C.: American Enterprise Institute, 1978), 5–44.

15. State of the Union Speech, 1984. See Paul D. Erickson, *Reagan Speaks: The Making of an American Myth* (New York: New York University Press, 1985), 98.

2. THE PREVAILING VERSIONS

1. Polling data reveal a striking consistency in conservative or liberal views. Such basic orientations frequently do a better job of predicting a respondent's views than does objective self-interest in the outcome of a particular political choice. See David O. Sears et al., "White's Opposition to Busing: Self-Interest or Symbolic Politics?," in *American Political Science Review* 73 (June 1979): 369–84; Richard Lau et al., "Self-Interest and Civilian's Attitudes Toward the Vietnam War," *Public Opinion Quarterly* 42 (Winter 1978): 464–83.

2. Public opinion polls clearly revealed a shift in political ideology. In 1977, 30 percent of Americans considered themselves "conservative"; by 1986, 40 percent had adopted that appellation, while only 18 percent called themselves "liberal" (about the same as two decades before). Moreover, while 24 percent attested that their views were "more conservative" than they had been five years before, only 16 percent said their thinking had moved in the opposite direction. (Data based on the Harris Poll of March 1986, and the New York Times–CBS Poll of January 1986.)

3. For a theory about why the public seems to waiver in this way, see Albert O. Hirschman, *Shifting Involvements: Private Interest and Public Action* (Princeton, N.J.: Princeton University Press, 1982).

4. See Walter Fisher, "Romantic Democracy, Ronald Reagan, and Presidential Heroes," *Western Journal of Speech Communication* 46 (Summer 1982): 299–310.

5. Thus writes Professor Richard Pipes in *Survival Is Not Enough* (New York: Simon and Schuster, 1984), 280.

6. This from Herbert Stein, *Presidential Economics* (New York: Simon and Schuster, 1984), 315.

7. Ibid., 328.

8. George Gilder, *The Spirit of Enterprise* (New York: Simon and Schuster, 1985), 290.

9. Charles Murray, *Losing Ground: American Social Policy 1950–1980* (New York: Basic Books, 1984).

10. For a discussion of this view, see Diane Ravitch, *The Troubled Crusade: American Education, 1945–1980* (New York: Basic Books, 1983).

11. According to this view, America in the nineteenth and early twentieth centuries managed crime through a massive investment in "impulse control." Self-discipline was inculcated in schools, churches, and other socializing institutions; and this investment apparently paid off, in terms of reversing the upsurge in crime that had marred the early nineteenth century. Gradually, however, this emphasis was replaced by an "ethos of self-expression" that reached its height after World War II. See James Q. Wilson and Richard Hernstein, *Crime and Human Nature* (New York: Simon and Schuster, 1985).

12. See Fred L. Israel, ed., *The State of the Union Messages of the Presidents, 1790–1966*, vol. 3 (New York: Chelsea House, 1967), 2814.

13. From Roosevelt's first inaugural address, cited in Henry Steele Commager, ed., *Documents of American History*, 7th ed., vol. 2 (New York: Meredith, 1963), no. 476.

14. The appellations "liberal" and "conservative" were infrequently used during this era, and when they *were* used they often meant different things than they do today. In the 1928 presidential campaign, for example, when Herbert Hoover identified his cause with "liberalism," he was referring, as do modern European liberals, to the nineteenth-century movements asserting civil and economic independence from the *ancien régime*. Even after the term became associated with the New Deal, the former meaning lingered on; Robert Taft called himself a "liberal" to the end. Nor was the term "conservative," with its connotations of British paternalism and elitism, particularly welcomed by opponents of the New Deal. The first American politician to embrace the term was Barry Goldwater, in 1964.

15. *Goals for Americans* (Englewood Cliffs, N.J.: Prentice-Hall, 1960).

16. After a best-selling book by the social critic, Michael Harrington.

17. See *The Public Papers of Lyndon Baines Johnson*, vol. 1 (1963–64) (Austin, Texas: University of Texas, 1965), 283, 611.

18. Ibid., (1965) vol. 2, 636.

19. Ibid., (1965) vol. 2, 224.

20. Ibid., (1963–64) vol. 1, 597, 704.

21. See, for example, William Kornhauser, *The Politics of Mass Society* (Glencoe, Ill.: Free Press, 1959); Harry Eckstein, *A Theory of Stable Democracy* (Princeton, N.J.: Center of International Studies, Princeton University, 1961).

22. Cited in Richard Hofstadter, *The Progressive Historians* (New York: Vintage, 1970), 438.

23. Quotations from campaign speeches, Nashua, New Hampshire, December 8, 1975, and Cleveland, Ohio, February 7, 1976.

3. THE NEW CONTEXT

1. Data on world population growth and its relationship to economic development can be found, for example, in *U.S. Policy and the Third World: Agenda 83* (Washington, D.C.: Overseas Development Council, 1983); and Ruth Leger Sivard, *World Military and Social Expenditures* (Washington, D.C.: World Priorities, 1985).

2. Although manufacturing's share of America's gross national product has remained fairly constant over the last two decades, the number of workers engaged in manufacturing has steadily declined.

3. It is necessary to be a bit cautious with these figures, in part because the definition of an "American" producer is becoming less clear as time goes by. If the output of American manufacturers operating in other nations is included, the story is more upbeat. See Irving Kravis and Robert Lipsey, "The Competitive Position of U.S. Manufacturing Firms," National Bureau of Economic Research Reprint No. 659, September 1985.

4. This stagnation has been particularly apparent in comparisons between the United States and other nations. From 1973 to 1984, for example, while American productivity improved by an average of .7 percent a year, the Japanese were producing 2.8 percent more each year. Western European nations also raised the productivity of their workers more rapidly than we did (although it must be noted that several of them accomplished this feat with a smaller portion of their work force actually at work). See *United States Department of Commerce, International Economic Indicators* (Washington, D.C.: United States Government Printing Office), various issues.

5. A distinction must be drawn between average family income, which declined between 1973 and 1985, and average per capita income, which, by some measures, increased over the same interval. Even if one is to focus on the more positive calculation, however, there is evidence that for any given age cohort within the population, per capita income declined. For example, a man passing from age forty to age fifty between 1953 and 1963 increased his real earnings 36 percent; one who passed from age forty to fifty in the following decade increased his real earnings 25 percent. But a forty-year-old in 1973 saw his real income drop 14 percent during the subsequent ten years. See Frank Levy and Richard Michel, *The Economic Future of the Baby Boom* (Washington, D.C.: Urban Institute, 1986).

6. In fact, in all of the ten years between 1970 to 1980 annual cash assistance for each nonelderly poor person in the United States rose by just $93. Few would decline a gift of $93, but this is not a sum likely to tempt crowds of Americans away from honest labor, or to lure poor teenage girls

into motherhood. Adjusted for inflation, benefit levels for Aid to Families with Dependent Children, which is the largest cash-assistance program for the poor, actually declined during the decade, and they have continued to decline since 1980.

4. THE BOOMERANG PRINCIPLE

1. Quoted in Samuel Eliot Morison and Henry Steele Commager, *The Growth of the American Republic* (New York: Oxford University Press, 1940), 280.

2. *Life*, vol. 10, February 17, 1941, 63.

3. This is not to discount the moralistic strain of American policy toward the Mob at the Gates. Nineteenth-century missionaries set out to convert "heathens" toward the west and the south. Teddy Roosevelt launched a holy war on the Spanish and Mexicans. Woodrow Wilson sought a "community of nations" that would subscribe to universal laws and principles of human freedom. John F. Kennedy envisioned America as a beacon light, toward which the poorer nations of the world inevitably strove, and could reach with our help. Jimmy Carter sought to promote international human rights. Ronald Reagan echoed all these themes. But these moralistic ideas were never as significant, in practice, as either of the other two. Americans have never had the stomach for prolonged moral crusades in faraway places. At most, these sentiments provided partial justification for assertiveness in protection of our interests, or rationales for tolerance and magnanimity in the service of isolation.

4. The principle applies to any complex, evolving system in which the principal actors are dependent on one another. Examples are easily found in nature—among plants and animals that inhabit a particular watershed, among the members of one species, even among the organs or cells of a single animal. "The whole dear notion of one's own Self—marvelous, old free-willed, free-enterprising, autonomous, independent, isolated island of a Self—is a myth: Yet, we do not have a science strong enough to discipline the myth." Lewis Thomas, *The Lives of a Cell: Notes of a Biology Watcher* (New York: Bantam, 1974), 167.

5. *OECD Economic Outlook* (Paris: Organization for Economic Co-operation and Development, July 1984), p. 21, table 5.

6. More on this in subsequent chapters.

7. International Trade Commission, annual reports (Washington, D.C.: United States Government Printing Office, 1980–85).

8. Robert Z. Lawrence, *Can America Compete?* (Washington, D.C.: Brookings Institution, 1984).

9. Reported in *The New York Times*, December 20, 1984, sec. E, p. 4.

10. *World Development Report* (Washington, D.C.: International Bank

for Reconstruction and Development, 1985). To take but one example, Brazil's exports to the United States, which had increased substantially in 1983 and 1984, thereafter stopped growing; American restrictions on Brazilian steel, shoes, sugar, textiles, ethanol, and other products, had begun to take their toll.

11. See Ruth Leger Savard, *World Military and Social Expenditures 1985* (Washington, D.C.: World Priorities, 1985), p. 35, table II.

12. Robert Pastor, "Our Real Interests in Central America," *Atlantic Monthly*, July 1982, 36.

13. See *The New York Times*, January 11, 1986, sec. A, p. 1.

5. AMERICA'S TWO COMPETITORS

1. On these and other examples, see Reich, "Making Industrial Policy," in *Foreign Affairs* (September 1982), 852–87; and "An Industrial Policy of the Right," *The Public Interest* (Fall 1983): 3–17; Ann Markusen, "Defense Spending as Industrial Policy," in Sharon Zuken, ed., *Industrial Policy* (New York: Praeger, 1985), 76–85; Thomas Egan, "The Case of Semiconductors," in Margaret Dewar, ed., *Industry Vitalization* (New York: Pergamon Press, 1982), 121–44.

2. Whether publicly or privately funded, other industrialized nations spent a much higher percentage of their national products on civilian research than America did. In 1986, America's total research and development spending topped $115 billion, of which $73 billion was financed by the U.S. government, largely for defense purposes. For an excellent summary of U.S. government sponsorship of private-sector research and development, see Harvey Brooks, "Technology as a Factor in U.S. Competitiveness" (Unpublished, Harvard Business School Division of Research, 1984).

3. In addition to these sums, some $95 billion was spent on procuring new weapons, many of which would incorporate the most sophisticated technologies. See *Science Indicators* (Washington, D.C.: National Science Foundation, 1986).

4. See Council on Economic Priorities, *The Strategic Defense Initiative: Costs, Contractors, and Consequences* (New York: Council on Economic Priorities, 1985).

5. *Washington Post* weekly edition, January 6, 1986, p. 21.

6. On competitiveness in the defense industry, see William W. Kaufmann, "The 1986 Defense Budget," in *Studies in Defense Policy* (Washington, D.C.: Brookings Institution, 1985); Robert DeGrasse Jr., *Is This National Security?* (New York: Council on Economic Priorities, 1984).

7. DeGrasse Jr., op. cit.; see also, George F. Brown Jr., *Defense and the Economy: An Analysis of the Reagan Administration's Programs* (Washington, D.C.: Data Resources, April 1982).

8. These data were gleaned from company reports.

9. *The New York Times*, February 27, 1986, sec. A, p. 1.

10. See John Shattuck, "Federal Restrictions on the Free Flow of Government Information and Ideas," *Government Information Quarterly*, 3, no. 1 (1986): 5–29.

11. In a study of technological transfers from the West to the Soviet bloc during the course of fifteen years, the Congressional Office of Technology Assessment concluded that—even in technological areas where significant transfers occurred—the technological gap did not diminish. United States Congress, Office of Technology Assessment, *Technology and East-West Trade* (Washington, D.C.: United States Government Printing Office, 1979), 220.

6. THE RISE OF THE JAPANESE-AMERICAN CORPORATION

1. This account is based on interviews and press reports.

2. Eric Mankin and I analyzed a sample of one hundred joint ventures between American and Japanese companies and discovered the same pattern in almost every one. See Reich and Eric D. Mankin, "Joint Ventures with Japan Give Away Our Future," *Harvard Business Review* (March–April 1986).

3. See Hajime Karatsu, "The Deindustrialization of America: A Tragedy for the World" (Tokyo: KKC Brief, Keizai Koho Center, October 1985).

4. With the opening of the Tokyo stock exchange, it could be expected that more of this money would drift to Japan. See Jill Andresky, "Ready or Not," *Forbes*, February 10, 1986, p. 94.

5. There were some notable exceptions. Canadians, for example, have never been wholly enthusiastic about American subsidiaries in their midst.

6. Japanese computer manufacturers (like Hitashi), meanwhile, were linking up with American semiconductor makers (National Semiconductor)—not to buy chips, but to sell Japanese computers in the United States.

7. For example, a small turning machine that Bendix sold in the United States for $105,000 in 1985 could have been made in Cleveland for $85,000. But when made in Japan by Bendix's partner, Murata Manufacturing, and then shipped to Cleveland, the machine's total cost was just $65,000. Company report, 1986.

7. LOCKING THE GATES

1. In the spring of 1986, the U.S. Commissioner of Customs set off a diplomatic tempest when he blamed America's drug problem on "massive drug-related corruption" in the Mexican government, including the Mexican president's cousin and a state governor.

. 2. Andrew Pasztor, "Meese's Ambitious War Against U.S. Drug Abuse Is Faltering as Cocaine Use Continues to Spread," *Wall Street Journal*, January 9, 1986, p. 48.

3. Estimate of the Drug Enforcement Administration, "Report on Interdiction of Dangerous Drugs" (Washington, D.C.: United States Government Printing Office, 1986). See also *Report of the National Intelligence Consumers' Committee on Cocaine Abuse* (Washington, D.C.: 1986).

4. Funding for interdiction, eradication, and surveillance was increased substantially more than that for education and treatment.

5. Stuart Auerbach, "Non-Producers Ship Steel to U.S.: Industry Sees Trend as Way of Getting Around Import Limits," *Washington Post*, November 12, 1985, sec. E, p. 1.

6. In 1984, Congress strengthened the laws to allow American companies to get relief even before the "dumped" product actually injured them.

7. Estimates based upon 1980 Census. The Bureau counted 2 million illegal immigrants, and estimated that this represented roughly half of the total.

8. When this system was abandoned in 1965, we substituted another, only slightly less restrictive, but without the same biases toward the current population mix. As a result, the legal flow changed from overwhelmingly European to mainly Asian and Latin American.

9. The latest reform effort was passed by Congress and signed into law by President Reagan in the fall of 1986. It granted citizenship to aliens who had remained illegally in the United States for several years, and imposed penalties on employers who hired illegal aliens. But in all likelihood it, too, would fail to resolve the underlying contradictions. Western fruit and vegetable growers claim that they need "guest workers" to help pick perishable crops during the harvest season; not enough American citizens are willing to do this work. Small manufacturers claim that without access to cheaper labor they could not compete against Third World importers; thus, if barred from hiring aliens, they would have to move their operations south, across the border. Meanwhile, American labor unions claim that the immigrants take jobs away from American workers. Hispanic groups fear that efforts to penalize employers for hiring illegal aliens will deter employers from hiring Hispanics. Such is the tenor of our inconclusive debate.

10. The ABM treaty was one of two agreements that resulted from SALT I.

11. The agonizing negotiations over arms control during the 1970s and early 1980s did not involve first principles about whether arms control was good, but second and third principles about how it could be achieved without giving one side a strategic advantage in the process. For detailed histories see Strobe Talbott's two masterly accounts, *Endgame: The Inside Story of*

SALT II (New York: Harper and Row, 1979), and *Deadly Gambits* (New York: Harper and Row, 1985).

9. OF ENTREPRENEURS AND DRONES

1. Andrew Carnegie, *The Empire of Business* (New York: Doubleday, Page, 1902), 192.

2. *Iacocca: An Autobiography* (New York: Bantam Books, 1984), 3.

3. Peter Ueberroth, *Made in America* (New York: William Morrow, 1985).

4. George Gilder, *The Spirit of Enterprise*, op. cit., 213.

5. In one survey of the early ¦980s, only 24 percent of American workers said they were being as effective as they were capable of being; 63 percent of the public asserted that people did not work as hard as they used to; 69 percent said that workmanship was growing worse; and 73 percent agreed that worker motivation was down. See Daniel Yankelovich and John Immerwarn, *Putting the Work Ethic to Work* (New York: Public Agenda Foundation, 1983).

6. George Gilder, op. cit., 147.

7. Several of these empirical issues are addressed in Robert Kuttner's *The Economic Illusion* (Boston: Houghton-Mifflin, 1985).

8. One government-sponsored study found that 40 percent of the 11.5 million workers who lost their jobs because of plant shutdowns or relocations between 1979 and 1984 remained unemployed during that period. A large proportion of them were middle-aged, and had been with their former companies for many years. And the factory jobs they lost were not replaced elsewhere in the economy by similarly high-paying jobs. Instead, the new jobs tended to be lower-wage service jobs, such as bank tellers, hotel clerks, and fast-food workers. The study found that two thirds of the displaced workers who found new jobs were paid less than 80 percent of what they had earned before. See Office of Technology Assessment, United States Congress, "The Displaced Worker" (Washington, D.C.: United States Government Printing Office, February 1986); see also Bureau of Labor Statistics, "Survey of Worker Displacement" (Washington, D.C.: United States Government Printing Office, December 1984).

9. Wessily Leontief, *Essays in Economics: Theories, Theorizing Facts, and Policies* (New Brunswick, N.J.: Transaction Books, 1985), 193–99.

10. Variations on these themes could be found in the pronouncements of labor union leaders and Democratic candidates in the early and mid-1980s. Among the most influential books propounding these views were Barry Bluestone and Bennett Harrison, *The Deindustrialization of America: Plant Closings, Community Abandonment, and the Dismantling of Basic*

Industry (New York: Basic Books, 1982) and Robert Lekachman, *Greed Is Not Enough: Reaganomics* (New York: Pantheon, 1982).

10. COLLECTIVE ENTREPRENEURIALISM

1. For sophisticated versions of the product life cycle theory, see Raymond Vernon, *Metropolis 1985* (Cambridge: Harvard University Press, 1960), and William J. Abernathy, *The Productivity Dilemma* (Baltimore: Johns Hopkins University Press, 1978).

2. This summary only slightly caricatures the model of competitive strategy first popularized by the Boston Consulting Group. For a more rigorous treatment see D. C. Mueller and John E. Tilton, "Research and Development Cost as a Barrier to Entry," *Canadian Journal of Economics*, vol. 2, no. 4 (November 1969), 25.

3. *The Next American Frontier* (New York: Times Books, 1983), 130–39.

4. For ways in which computers have been used to enhance labor value, see Shoshana Zuboff, "New Worlds of Computer-Mediated Work," *Harvard Business Review*, September-October 1982, 142.

5. Dr. Robert K. Merton of Columbia University found that in 1920, single authors accounted for 93 percent of scientific papers; by 1940, the proportion had dropped to 65 percent; by 1960, a mere 26 percent were authored by lone individuals. See William Broad, "Era of Big Science Diminishes Role of Lonely Genius," *New York Times*, January 1, 1985, 15.

6. E. S. Browning, "Sony's Perseverance Helped It Win Market for Mini-CD Players," *Wall Street Journal*, February 27, 1986, p. 1.

11. THE GENERAL THEORY OF GRIDLOCK

1. On contractual difficulties that might arise under these circumstances see, for example, Benjamin Klein, "Transaction Cost Determinants of 'Unfair' Contractual Arrangements," 70 *American Economic Review Papers and Proceedings* 356 (1980).

2. Arthur M. Okun, "The Invisible Handshake and the Inflationary Process," *Challenge*, January–February 1980; see generally, Arthur M. Okun, *Prices and Quantities: A Macroeconomic Analysis* (Washington, D.C.: The Brookings Institution, 1981). For an extension of this concept to high-wage industries, see Jeremy Bulow and Lawrence Summers, "A Theory of Dual Labor Markets with Application to Industrial Policy, Discrimination, and Keynesian Unemployment" (NBER Working Paper no. 1666, October 1985).

3. Data from Eugene Raudsepp, "Reducing Engineering Turnover," *Machine Design*, September 9, 1982, p. 52.

4. In Japan, the term "engineer" is used broadly to denote almost any-

one responsible for complex tasks. In most firms producing complex products, there are more "engineers" than production workers. See Andrew Weiss, "Simple Truths of Japanese Manufacturing," *Harvard Business Review* (July-August 1984): 119.

5. *The New York Times*, November 26, 1985, p. 34.

6. "Information Thieves Are Now Corporate Enemy Number One," *Business Week*, May 5, 1986, p. 120.

7. Empirical support for this proposition is contained in Charles Ferguson, Jr., "American Microelectronics in Decline" (Massachusetts Institute of Technology, VLSI Memo 85–284, December 1985). See also Harley Rogers, "Silicon Valley: People, Values, and Organizations" (unpublished, 1985).

8. When they purchased the firm, the new owners paid some of these expropriated benefits to the former shareholders in the form of a premium over the market price of their shares. Indeed, that may be where the premium came from. If, as is often the case, the new managers do not bring any particularly valuable skill to the acquired company, and there is no reason to suspect additional economies of scale or "synergy," then any new wealth must come from somewhere else. A likely source: employees and other stake holders, who mistakenly assumed that they would receive a return on their implicit investments made in the past. On this point, see Steven Johnson, Richard Zeckhauser, and John D. Donahue, *Contract and Commitment* (forthcoming).

9. See Reich and John D. Donahue, *New Deals: The Chrysler Revival and the American System* (New York: Times Books, 1985).

10. On the plight of Eastern Airlines, see Kenneth B. Noble, "Labor Takes a Chair in the Board Room," *The New York Times*, March 9, 1986, sec. D, p. 5.

11. See Robert McGough, "Are Contracts Obsolete?" *Forbes*, April 29, 1985, p. 101.

12. The average American company lost half of its labor force each year, either because the workers quit or they were fired. See United States Department of Commerce, *Handbook of Labor Statistics* (Washington, D.C.: United States Government Printing Office, 1986), 171.

13. Study by Lamallie Associates, cited in *The New York Times*, November 11, 1985, sec. D, p. 5. See also, Larry Reibstein, "After a Takeover: More Managers Run, or Are Pushed, Out the Door," *Wall Street Journal*, November 15, 1985, p. 33.

14. My colleague Richard Zeckhauser has referred to these phenomena as "reputational externalities." See his "The Muddled Responsibilities of Public and Private America," in Knowlton and Zeckhauser (eds.), *American Society: Public and Private Responsibilities* (Cambridge, Mass.: Ballinger, 1986), pp. 55–57.

15. Robert McGough, op. cit.

16. See, for example, *The American Lawyer*, annual surveys of lawyer compensation and law firm hiring.

13. THE SYSTEM OF SOCIAL BENEVOLENCE

1. Robert Reinhold, "Public Found Against Welfare Idea But in Favor of What Programs Do," *The New York Times*, August 3, 1977, sec. A, p. 1.; Michael Schiltz, "Public Attitudes Toward Social Security, 1935–1965," Research Report #33, United States Department of Health, Education, and Welfare Social Security Administration (1970).

2. Quotation from Frances Perkins, *The Roosevelt I Knew* (New York: Viking, 1946), 282–83.

3. Farmers and agricultural workers were also excluded from the original act, with the result that 90 percent of black males were excluded from its coverage. See Raymond Walters, "The New Deal and the Negro," in John Braeman et al., eds., *The New Deal, The National Level* (Cleveland: Ohio State University Press, 1975).

4. Quotation from Arthur M. Schlesinger, Jr., *The Coming of the New Deal* (Boston: Houghton Mifflin, 1959), 308.

5. These and further data were gleaned from Board of Trustees, *Federal Old Age and Survivors Insurance and Disability Insurance Trust Fund* (Washington, D.C.: United States Government Printing Office), annual reports; Board of Trustees, Federal Hospital Insurance Trust Fund (Washington D.C.: United States Government Printing Office), annual reports. See also Lawrence H. Thompson, "The Social Security Reform Debate," *Journal of Economic Literature* 21 (December 1983): 1425–67.

6. By the 1980s over 85 percent of the total cost of nursing homes was borne by the federal government; 40 percent of all Medicaid funds went to pay for nursing home care. Data are gathered in Victor Fuchs, *How We Live: An Economic Perspective on Americans from Birth to Death* (Cambridge, Mass.: Harvard University Press, 1983), 201.

7. Quotation from an interview with Luther Gulick by Michael McGreary, Institute of Public Administration, New York, Feb. 28, 1980. For a fuller discussion of the metaphors and myths which have grown up around Social Security, see Richard Neustadt and Ernest May, *Thinking in Time* (New York: Free Press, 1986).

8. United States Chamber of Commerce, *Employee Benefits* (Washington, D.C.: United States Chamber of Commerce, 1984).

9. Pensions are not literally tax-free; they are tax-deferred. Taxes on earnings put into pension funds, and on what these funds accumulate, are taxed only when the pensions are withdrawn.

10. Estimates based on data from the U.S. Office of Management and

Budget, *Special Analyses, Budget of the United States Government* (Washington, D.C.: United States Government Printing Office, 1985); Bureau of the Census, U.S. Department of Commerce, *Statistical Abstract of the United States* (Washington, D.C.: United States Government Printing Office, 1985), 357.

11. Welfare is defined to include Medicaid, AFDC cash benefits, food stamps, and low-income housing.

12. Jennifer Hull, "Growing Number in U.S. Lack Health Insurance As Companies, Public Agencies, Seek to Cut Costs," *Wall Street Journal*, June 3, 1986, p. 62.

13. Administrative Office of the United States Courts, Annual Report (Washington, D.C.: United States Government Printing Office), various issues; Survey by Jury Verdict Research Inc., Solon, Ohio, as reported in *The Wall Street Journal*, January 21, 1986, p. 32.

14. By 1986 private insurance companies had grown sufficiently concerned to seek legislative limits on these damage awards, and occasionally deny coverage to their customers. But this was not because the private insurers had suddenly become enamoured of profits. It was because, as the number and magnitude of the awards grew, the insurance companies found it difficult to predict how much they would have to pay out. Nothing upsets private insurers more than the uncertainty of the risk they bear. Were judges and juries to provide more predictable awards—regardless of their magnitude—the insurance companies would again be able to set their premiums at a rate that would cover future losses and yield a profit.

14. THE LIMITS OF BENEVOLENCE

1. Campaign speech, Peoria, Illinois, September 12, 1984.

2. Inaugural speech, January 20, 1981.

3. In 1985 the poorest 20 percent of American families received about 6 percent of the nation's total personal income; this percentage had not substantially changed in twenty years. Of advanced industrial nations, only France came close to matching the United States in inequality of (after-tax) income. See United States Bureau of the Census, *Current Population Reports*, Series P-60 (Washington, D.C.: United States Government Printing Office), 1980–85 issues; see generally, Sidney Verba and Gary Orren, *Equality in America: The View from the Top* (Cambridge, Mass.: Harvard University Press, 1985).

4. For a sampling of poll data, see Michael Schiltz, op. cit.; surveys by CBS–*The New York Times*, January 14–24, 1984.

5. See Richard Coughlin, *Ideology, Public Opinion, and Welfare Policy* (Berkeley, Cal.: Institute for International Studies, 1980).

6. Address to the Annual Concretes and Aggregates Convention, Jan-

uary 31, 1984. See also William A. Schambra, "Progressive Liberalism and the American 'Community,' " *The Public Interest*, 80 (Summer 1985).

7. United States Bureau of the Census, "Current Population Reports," Series P-20; 1980 Census of Population, Supplementary Report, PC 80-S1-9.

8. The 1980 Census revealed a marked trend toward geographic concentration of the poor in many of our largest cities. See *1980 Census of the Population: Poverty Areas in Large Cities* (PC80-2-8D), and *Low-Income Areas of Large Cities* (PC(2)-913), (Washington, D.C.: United States Government Printing Office, 1985).

9. Most Americans continued to oppose laws requiring employers to give special preference to minorities when filling jobs. See *Opinions and Values of Americans Survey (1975–1977)*, cited in Herbert McClosky and John Zaller, *The American Ethos: Public Attitudes Toward Capitalism and Democracy* (Cambridge, Mass.: Harvard University Press, 1984).

10. Michael Harrington, *The Other America: Poverty in the United States*, rev. ed. (New York: Penguin, 1981).

11. The first poverty index was devised by the Social Security Administration in 1964, reflecting the different consumption requirements of families based on their size and composition; the index has been updated every year to reflect changes in the Consumer Price Index, but it only reflects money income and does not include the value of noncash benefits such as food stamps and public housing.

12. For a detailed history of these developments see Hugh Heclo, "The Political Foundations of Antipoverty Policy," in S. Danziger and D. Weinberg, eds., *Fighting Poverty: What Works and What Doesn't* (Cambridge, Mass.: Harvard University Press, 1986).

13. These data were derived from M. Hill, "Some Dynamic Aspects of Poverty," in M. Hill et al., eds., *5000 American Families: Patterns of Economic Progress*, vol. IX (Ann Arbor, Mich.: Institute for Social Research, 1981); and William O'Hare, "The Eight Myths of Poverty," *American Demographics*, vol. 8, no. 5 (May 1986): 22.

14. For a detailed look at these withdrawals, see John Palmer and Isabel Sawhill, *The Reagan Record* (Washington, D.C.: Urban Institute, 1984), 185–86.

15. A MATTER OF RESPONSIBILITY

1. Hearings before the Senate Finance Committe, 74th Cong., 1st sess., 1935, 940.

2. The argument was first advanced by Martin Feldstein. See his "Social Security, Induced Retirement, and Aggregate Capital Accumulation," *Journal of Political Economy* (September–October 1974): 905; and "Social Se-

curity and Private Saving: Reply," *Journal of Political Economy* (June 1982): 630.

3. These data are offered in Christopher J. Zook et al., "Catastrophic Health Insurance—A Misguided Prescription?" *The Public Interest* (Winter 1981): 66.

4. In the parlance of insurers, economists, and others who dwell in gloomy realities, this psychological phenomenon is termed "moral hazard."

5. These and other related data can be found in James T. Patterson, *America's Struggle Against Poverty, 1900–1980* (Cambridge, Mass.: Harvard University Press, 1981), 172.

6. By 1983 over 60 percent of all teenage mothers nationwide required welfare assistance. The *majority* of black children were being brought up in poor families headed by women. See Gregory J. Duncan et al., *Years of Poverty, Years of Plenty: The Changing Fortunes of American Workers and Families* (Ann Arbor, Mich.: Institute for Social Research, University of Michigan, 1984), 18–28; Current Population Reports, series P-70, no. 1, "Economic Characteristics of Households in the United States" (Washington, D.C: United States Government Printing Office, 1983).

7. Charles Murray, *Losing Ground: American Social Policy 1950–1980* (New York: Basic Books, 1984), 228.

8. U.S. Bureau of the Census, "Current Population Reports," series P-60, no. 144 (1983).

9. Zook et al., idem.

10. One model of such a system was New Zealand, which in 1974 replaced personal injury lawsuits with a system of automatic compensation—providing accident victims with medical care, lost wages, and one-time payments no larger than $8,500. See Nicholas Kristof, "Experts Look to Other Countries' Approaches to Problems of Liability Claims," *The New York Times*, April 6, 1986, p. 32.

11. Work requirements imposed under the federal Work Incentives Program, for example, involved little in the way of training. See David L. Kirp, "The California Work/Welfare Scheme," *The Public Interest*, 83 (Spring 1986): 34.

12. For examples of programs like this, see Englander and Englander, "Workfare in New Jersey: A Five-Year Assessment," *Policy Studies Review* (August 1985): 35; Milton Coleman, "When ET Came to Massachusetts, Welfare Dependency Declined," *Washington Post* National Weekly Edition, July 26, 1985, p. 31.

13. In 1950 only one out of four elderly widows was living alone; most of the rest lived with their families. By 1980, two out of three were living alone, largely due to the expansion of Social Security. See United States Bureau of the Census, "Marital Status and Living Arrangements," *Current Population Reports* (Washington, D.C.: United States Government Printing Office, March 1980), series P-2, no. 365, table 6.

14. See Reich and John D. Donahue, op. cit., 249.

15. Johnson & Johnson, Annual Report, 1986; see also, Joseph Califano, Jr., *America's Health Care Revolution* (New York: Random House, 1986).

16. Under a plan adopted in Wisconsin, a fraction of the absent father's earnings, sufficient to support a child under eighteen who lived with the mother, was withheld by employers, and then distributed to the mother as child support. If the father fell into arrears, the state would continue to make minimal payments; if the father's payments dipped below the minimum, the state would also make up the difference.

17. See "Novel War on Teenage Sex," *The New York Times*, November 14, 1985, sec. A, p. 20.

18. This approach was being tried in California, among other places.

16. THE FABLE OF THE FISHERMAN (REVISED)

1. See D. Archer and R. Cartner, *Violence and Crime in Cross-National Perspective* (New Haven: Yale University Press, 1984); E. Doleschal and A. Newton, "International Rates of Imprisonment," National Council on Crime and Delinquency (unpublished, 1979).

2. See *Statistical Abstract of the United States* (Washington, D.C.: United States Government Printing Office, 1985), tables 213–17; United States Bureau of the Census, "English Language Proficiency Survey" (Washington, D.C.: United States Government Printing Office, April 1986); Edward B. Fiske, "American Students Score Average or Below in International Math Exams," *The New York Times*, September 28, 1984, p. 30; University of Texas, "Adult Performance Level Project," cited in *The New York Times*, April 16, 1985, sec. I, p. 1.

3. See data from *A Children's Defense Budget* (Washington, D.C.: Children's Defense Fund, 1985).

4. The Perry Pre-School Project in Ypsilanti, Michigan is recounted, along with several other studies, in Richard Darlington and Irving Lazar, *The Lasting Effects After Preschool*, U.S. Department of Health and Human Services (Washington, D.C.: United States Government Printing Office, 1979).

5. National Academy of Science, Youth Unemployment Training Programs (Washington, D.C.: National Academy Press, 1985).

6. Nathan Glazer, "Education and Training Programs and Poverty: Or Opening the Black Box," in S. Danziger and D. Weinberg, eds., op. cit.

7. The relevant studies are cited in David Blumenthal and David Calkins, "Health Care and the Poor," in M. Carballo and M. Bane, eds., *The State and the Poor in the 1980s* (Boston: Auburn House, 1984).

8. Karen Davis, "Primary Care for the Medically Underserved: Public and Private Financing," in *Changing Roles in Serving the Underserved:*

Public and Private Responsibilities and Interests (Washington, D.C.: American Health Planning Assn., 1981).

9. Gertrude Himmelfarb, *The Idea of Poverty* (New York: Vintage, 1985), 12.

17. THE CYCLES OF RIGHTEOUS FULMINATION

1. More specifically, only 16 percent registered "great confidence" in Congress; 24 percent in the executive; 34 percent for corporate leaders; 28 percent for military leaders; 12 percent for labor leaders; and 16 percent for the press. Data are from Seymour Martin Lipset and William Schneider, *The Confidence Gap: Business, Labor, and Government in the Public's Mind* (New York: Free Press, 1983).

2. Survey data cited in Samuel P. Huntington, "The United States," in Michael J. Crozier et al., eds., *The Crisis of American Democracy* (New York: New York University Press, 1975), 78–85.

3. *Boston Globe*, October 14, 1971, p. 8.

4. By 1983, 2 percent of the nation's households owned half of all family holdings of common stock, 40 percent of all bonds, and over 70 percent of tax-free securities. This distribution was not substantially different from that of twenty-five years before. See study by the United States Federal Reserve Board, October 1984, cited in *The New York Times*, October 9, 1984, sec. A, p. 31.

5. For a detailed discussion of this point, see Samuel Huntington, *American Politics: The Promise of Disharmony*, op. cit., 33–39.

6. Federal expenditures, which had been $18.5 billion in 1919, fell to $4.4 billion in 1929—a far bigger drop than the end of World War I and deflation alone account for. From 1920 until 1932, the number of federal employees steadily dwindled. These and subsequent data from U.S. Bureau of the Census, *Historical Statistics of the United States* (Washington, D.C.: United States Government Printing Office, 1965).

7. Federal Election Commission, 1985.

18. THE MIASMA OF REGULATION

1. Cited by Herbert Kaufman, *Red Tape: Its Origins, Uses, and Abuses* (Washington, D.C.: The Brookings Institution, 1977), 7–8.

2. U.S. Commission on Federal Paperwork, *Final Summary Report* (Washington, D.C.: United States Government Printing Office, 1977), 5; "The Regulation Mess," *Newsweek*, June 12, 1978, p. 86.

3. One estimate blames government regulation for about 25 percent of the productivity slowdown between 1973 and 1983. See Robert Litan and

William Nordhaus, *Reforming Federal Regulation* (New Haven: Yale University Press, 1983), chap. 2.

4. For a sampling of cross-national comparisons, see Joseph L. Badaracco, Jr., *Loading the Dice: A Five-Country Study of Vinyl Chloride Regulation* (Cambridge, Mass.: Harvard Business School Press, 1985); Steven Kelman, *Regulating America, Regulating Sweden: A Comparative Study of Occupational Safety and Health* (Cambridge, Mass.: MIT Press, 1981); David Vogel, *National Styles of Regulation: Environmental Policy in Great Britain and the United States* (Ithaca, N.Y.: Cornell University Press, 1986).

5. Irving Kristol, *Two Cheers for Capitalism* (New York: Basic Books, 1978), chap. 2.

6. Paul H. Weaver, "Regulation, Social Policy, and Class Conflict," *The Public Interest* (Winter 1978): 59–60.

19. THE MYTHOLOGY OF THE MARKET

1. Economists call these negative and positive side effects "externalities" because they fall outside the specific market transactions that give rise to them. That is, the parties to the transactions do not consider these consequences in their decisions, with the result that there are apt to be too many external "bads" and too few "goods" from society's point of view. The notion of an "externality" suggests something inevitable and definitive. It is important to understand, however, that these "bads" and "goods" are external to the transactions only because the prevailing market rules do not include them.

2. See Ackerman and Stewart, "Reforming Environmental Law," *Stanford Law Review,* 37 (1985): 1333.

3. In 1979 the U.S. Environmental Protection Agency initiated a "bubble policy" which allows state and local regulators to offset increases in pollution from one plant by decreases at another. On this and related proposals see Albert Nichols, *Targeting Economic Incentives for Environmental Protection* (Cambridge, Mass.: MIT Press, 1984); see also Richard B. Stewart, "Two Models of Regulation" (unpublished manuscript, Harvard Law School, 1986).

4. In the 1980s, several American cities were experimenting with this approach, with varying degrees of success.

5. For a sampling, see James C. Miller III, "The Case Against 'Industrial Policy,'" *The Cato Journal,* 4 (Fall 1984); Chalmers Johnson, ed., *The Industrial Policy Debate* (San Francisco: ICS Press, 1984); Claude E. Barfield and William Schambra, eds., *The Politics of Industrial Policy* (Washington, D.C.: American Enterprise Institute, 1986).

6. In our rapidly changing competitive environment, the definition of an "industry" becomes problematic (see chapter 10). For present purposes,

let us define an industry as a collection of firms pursuing similar strategies.

7. In 1982 commercial banks paid 2 percent of their income to the government; food processors, 25 percent; auto makers, 48 percent. See Joint Committee on Taxation, "Taxation of Banks and Thrift Institutions," (Washington, D.C.: United States Government Printing Office, March 9, 1983), table 2.

8. This issue arose in Apple Computer, Inc. v. Franklin Computer Corporation, 714 F.2d 1240 (C.A. 3, 1983); Congress grappled with it in enacting the Semiconductor Chip Protection Act of 1984; but in important respects the issue has remained unresolved. While circuit designs may be protected, it remains unclear to what extent the *functions* performed by a design may also be protected.

9. The technical question was whether the government should confer to the pipelines the power of "eminent domain" to take the land, paying the railroads only an appraised market price.

20. NEW VERSIONS, NEW VISIONS

1. For an earlier and pessimistic discussion of this phenomenon, see Thomas Hobbes, *The Leviathan* (Liberal Arts Press edition) (New York: Bobbs Merrill, 1958).

2. The exception is organized crime groups, where members are made to understand that in the event of capture silence will be rewarded and betrayal punished; this device for bonding trust, indeed, is an example of why *organized* crime is so successful.

3. For an appraisal of alternative strategies in repeated rounds of the prisoner's dilemma, see Robert Axelrod, *The Evolution of Cooperation* (New York: Basic Books, 1984).

4. Thus their interest charge would fluctuate from year to year according to their ability to pay; such a swap of debt for equity, familiar to bankruptcy proceedings, would give creditors a stake in their future growth.

5. Tracy Kidder's fine book *The Soul of a New Machine* (Boston: Atlantic, Little, Brown, 1981) was widely read and cited not because it described an unusual occurrence, but because it captured clearly what was increasingly recognized as the norm in important sectors of the economy.

6. The observation that American workers are already major equity owners will come as no surprise to anyone familiar with the central role of pension funds in corporate finance. But the motivating force of this sort of ownership is severely limited, because pension funds are invested in a broad portfolio of stocks over which employees have no direct control, and upon which their job performance thus has no effect.

7. For a representative discussion of these issues see Derek C. Jones and Jan Svejnar, eds., *Participatory and Self-Managed Firms* (Lexington,

Mass.: Lexington Books, 1982). See also Howard Frant, "Is There Any Point to Employee Ownership?" (unpublished, Kennedy School of Government, Harvard University, June 1986).

8. On this point, see Martin Weitzman, *The Share Economy* (Cambridge, Mass.: Harvard University Press, 1984).

9. Negligence could be punished by fines rather than judgments; the current system, which attempts to merge deterrence and compensation in a single transaction, has proven unworkable.

INDEX